LORDS OF PARLIAMENT

Studies, 1714–1914

LORDS OF

PARLIAMENT

Studies, 1714–1914

EDITED BY R. W. DAVIS

STANFORD UNIVERSITY PRESS

Stanford, California   1995

Stanford University Press
Stanford, California

© 1995 by the Board of Trustees of the
Leland Stanford Junior University

Printed in the United States of America

CIP data appear at the end of the book

Stanford University Press publications are
distributed exclusively by Stanford University Press
within the United States, Canada, and Mexico;
they are distributed exclusively by
Cambridge University Press throughout
the rest of the world.

Acknowledgments

The editor wishes to thank Daniel Sargent,
whose efficient research assistance saved him
much time for work on this book.

Contents

Contributors

R. W. DAVIS, Professor of History and Director of the Center for the History of Freedom at Washington University in St. Louis, has written on the House of Lords in the Restoration period, as well as several books on the political history of nineteenth-century England.

G. M. DITCHFIELD is a Senior Lecturer in History at the University of Kent at Canterbury. He has published extensively in scholarly journals on issues of religion and politics in the eighteenth century, and is co-editor of *A Kentish Parson. Selections from the Private Papers of the Revd. Joseph Price, Vicar of Brabourne, 1767–1786* (Stroud, 1991).

ANGUS HAWKINS, Director of International Programs at the University of Oxford, is the author of *Parliament, Party and the Art of Politics in Britain, 1855–59* (Stanford and London, 1987).

CLYVE JONES, assistant librarian at the Institute of Historical Research, is the author of numerous articles, the editor of several highly respected books on the history of the House of Lords, and (since 1986) editor of the journal *Parliamentary History*.

MICHAEL W. MCCAHILL is the author of *Order and Equipoise: The Peerage and the House of Lords, 1783–1806* (London, 1978).

E. A. SMITH recently retired as Reader in History at the University of Reading. Author of a much acclaimed biography of the second Earl Grey, his most recent book is *The House of Lords in British Politics and Society, 1815–1911* (London, 1992).

STEPHEN TAYLOR is a Lecturer in History at the University of Reading. He has published in several scholarly journals on issues of church and state in the eighteenth century and is currently working on a book entitled "The Church and the Whigs: Politics, Religion and Culture in England, 1714–1760," to be published by Cambridge University Press.

ELLIS WASSON is the author of *Whig Renaissance: Lord Althorp and the Whig Party, 1782–1845* (New York and London, 1987).

CORINNE C. WESTON is Professor Emeritus of History at the Herbert H. Lehman College of the City University of New York. She is the author of *English Constitutional Theory and the House of Lords, 1556–1832* (London, 1965), as well as of several articles on aspects of the history of the House of Lords in the late nineteenth and early twentieth centuries. Her latest book, *Lord Salisbury and Conservative Ideology: The Referendal Theory and the House of Lords, 1846–1922*, will be published by the American Philosophical Society.

LORDS OF PARLIAMENT

Studies, 1714–1914

Introduction

R. W. DAVIS

The common perception is of a House of Lords in thralldom to the king's government before 1832, and to the House of Commons and the party governments that came to control the Commons, after 1832. In recent years it has become increasingly evident that such a picture is a serious distortion. Never much studied, and almost entirely neglected for several decades, since the 1980s the history of the House of Lords has benefited from a blossoming of scholarly interest. The resulting reinterpretation has been, and continues to be, broad and extensive. Far from having been a mere pawn of ministers such as Sir Robert Walpole, the Lords in the eighteenth century saw opposition as persistent and sometimes better organized and more dangerous than that in the Commons. Though the Lords as a body were usually inclined to support the king's government, this attitude cannot fully be understood in terms of the once standard explanations: the traditional loyalty of the aristocracy to the Crown; the Lords' community of interest, both as a House and as an order, with the monarchy; government's skillful manipulation of patronage in church and state, which included much that might catch the fancy of any peer or bishop; the large creations of the younger Pitt. Neither by themselves nor taken together are these considerations sufficient to explain the Lords' behavior.

Successful management of the upper House also required taking account of strongly held opinions within that body. The famous pun was inapt: the bishops never forgot, their heavenly Maker, at least; and on matters of religion and morals they were not responsive to government pressure. Peers too were likely to have personal or party principles from which it was difficult to budge them. Loyalty to the Crown was undoubtedly prominent among those principles, but it was a different kind of loyalty than that which could be bought. And the loyalty of few lords, if any, was unquestioning. Independence was a virtue honored in the upper House as well as in the Commons.

Though the nineteenth century has been less thoroughly reexamined than the eighteenth, it is clear that here too the old shibboleths will no longer do. The Great Reform Act, though a decisive confirmation of already existing tendencies, was not the crucial turning point in the history of the House of Lords that it is still commonly believed to have been. On the one hand, concern over conflict between Lords and Commons, especially a House of Commons perceived to be backed by public opinion, preceded the Reform Act, affecting the attitudes both of governments and of the Lords themselves at least as early as the 1820s. On the other hand, for several reasons, even after 1832 that concern did not develop into anything approaching subservience of the Lords to the Commons. Breaking the independence of the House of Lords was no more the aim of Lord Grey and his government than it was of the Tories, and it did not happen. Apart from a lack of desire to emasculate the power of the Lords, it soon became apparent that on certain issues their opinions were more consonant with the opinions of the country than were those of the Commons. The clever exploitation of these issues—mostly Irish or religious—by a remarkably able run of Conservative leaders, combined with their ability to recognize where it was necessary to adjust and concede, kept the Lords a potent force in politics throughout the century and into the dawning of a new democratic age. Indeed, despite two Parliament Acts trimming their veto powers, the Lords still remain an effective force in affairs.[1]

This volume will carry on the work of reinterpretation, by many of the same scholars who initiated it. In this volume, they will concentrate on representative figures who illustrate important tendencies. In most cases, the figures chosen were also important politicians; but in all cases, their careers help to probe and illuminate significant questions.

Studying the careers of individuals serves as a useful corrective to the current tendency toward over-heavy reliance on the social science approach to politics, invaluable though that approach has been in many recent advances in our knowledge. Like other historians, historians of Parliament seek to identify patterns of behavior. Yet, as in other areas of human activity, politics are resistant to the methods of the more exact sciences. The political arts of management and persuasion rely at least as much on a just appreciation of the importance of human frailty and irrationality, as on the ability to appeal to the rational faculties. Sir Lewis Namier rightly reminded us of the powerful incentives provided by fear, greed, and ambition; or on the other side, of affection and benevolence, in shaping political actions. Namier vastly underrated the effect of reason and principle. But none of these qualities is capable of exact measurement, the more so because they almost always occur in combination. Statistical methods can tell us how people behave. Often they can also help us to determine why they behave that way. But, as the most distinguished quantifiers are well aware, statistics can never give us a complete answer. Human beings cannot be reduced to abstractions, and politicians are not automatons. Especially in the intimate and clubby world of parliamentary politics in the eighteenth and nineteenth centuries, personality made a great difference. True of the House of Commons, this has always been even more characteristic of the still more intimate and loosely organized Lords.

As the volumes of *The History of Parliament* illustrate, an excellent way to gain insight into why parliamentary politics work as they do is to study the careers of parliamentary politicians. Because *The History of Parliament* does not treat the House of Lords, our detailed knowledge of its membership is less. We need to know more, and this volume will make a modest contribution to that end. Of course, a concentration on individuals will not provide complete answers any more than the methods of social scientists do. It will, however, provide better questions to put to the statistics, and it will also supplement the answers they provide, especially by probing into areas of human behavior beyond their reach.

In the first essay, focusing his attention on Edmund Gibson, bishop of London, Stephen Taylor examines the role of the bishops in the eighteenth-century House of Lords. When dubbing Gibson "the Whig pope," his contemporaries did not mean to suggest that he possessed final authority on religious matters in Walpole's regime. But, while Gibson did his best to be a good Whig politician (and he was a very effective one), he never conceived that this could prevent him from being a good churchman as well. And, when the two roles came into conflict in the 1730s, he did not hesitate to make his choice for the Church, resulting in a permanent breach with Walpole. Taylor's essay provides a striking refutation of the traditional view that eighteenth-century bishops were mere time-servers, prepared to sacrifice the interests of religion.

In the second essay, Clyve Jones considers the role of the first Earl Cowper in developing the first recognizably modern opposition in the House of Lords. From 1720 to 1723 the former Whig lord chancellor headed a small group of politicians which provided effective leadership and efficient organization to a politically mixed group of Jacobites, Hanoverian Tories, and discontented Whigs. Rallying their followers around a central political philosophy of independence from party, the so-called Cabal was able to make an impression not only in the Lords, but, as was their design, on the wider public as well. In sum, they developed the harrying tactics of "attrition" into an art form, thus leaving their mark upon opposition for the next half century and more. Besides illuminating the history of political organization, Jones's essay will help to clarify the much debated role of Jacobitism in the early eighteenth century.

Cowper and Gibson were politicians of the first rank. The sixth earl of Denbigh, the subject of Michael McCahill's essay, was not. Nonetheless, Denbigh had several characteristics which make his career of interest to historians of the eighteenth century. He was one of the Tories whom George III brought to court at his accession, and Denbigh's political life after 1760 will therefore help to clarify the fate of the Tory party after that date, a subject of debate among historians. As a lord of the bedchamber from 1763–99, Denbigh was also a member of the king's household, like the bishops, usually considered one of those impregnable bastions of support which made the hold of a government possessing the monarch's confidence secure in the House of Lords. Yet Denbigh was at the same time at the center of a coterie of peers who proclaimed their independent attachment to any government supported by the king—and not only did he claim independence, he exercised it in criticizing specific measures with which he disagreed. Denbigh's career, like Gibson's, throws doubt on key aspects of current historical orthodoxy.

Though no one doubts the importance of the first Lord Thurlow, lord chancellor and the leading ministerial spokesman in the House of Lords for two separate periods, 1778–83 and 1783–92, his political career has never been the subject of a serious and careful study. G. M. Ditchfield's essay goes a long way toward filling that gap. As Ditchfield points out, the relatively small number of lawyers in the upper House as compared to the lower, put them at a premium there and often placed them in a leading position. This was true of Thurlow, as it would later be of Lords Lyndhurst and Brougham in the 1830s. And like them Thurlow was also a highly effective speaker. Unlike them, however, he had as his greatest asset the confidence of the king, though that was in part based on his superior talents as well as his fierce loyalty and courage. It was the king's confidence that allowed Thurlow to marshal majorities in the Lords, though in that activity too he was more effective than most. When he lost the king's confidence, as he increasingly did after his maneuvers to safeguard his office during the Regency Crisis, Thurlow's power went with it.

In 1807, the year after Thurlow died, the second Earl Grey succeeded to his father's peerage and reluctantly took his seat in the upper House. No figure is more important (though the first duke of Wellington may be as important) in the transition from the eighteenth to the nineteenth century House of Lords. Traditionally, the Great Reform Act over which Lord Grey would preside in 1832, is seen as ending the eighteenth century system in society and politics; not least, in that the method of its passage is held to have destroyed the effective power of the House of Lords. As his colleagues knew, and as Grey's distinguished biographer, E. A. Smith, demonstrates in his essay, Grey was in fact the Lords' staunchest protector. He did not want to coerce them, and by successfully avoiding peerage creations, he maintained the basis for their continuing authority. As a consequence, the Lords would prove a much more serious check to the Whig governments of the 1830s than to the ministries of the 1820s.

But if it was Grey and the Whigs who were initially responsible for preserving the authority of the House of Lords, it was in the nature of things that it was the Tories, or Conservatives as they came to call themselves, on whom the major burden fell to make the system work; for, as soon became apparent, there were more Conservatives than Whigs in the upper House. In a sense, then, the duke of Wellington, as Conservative leader in the Lords, had his preeminent role in defining the post-reform relationship between the two Houses thrust upon him. It was, however, a happy coincidence. Almost as soon as he became prime minister, in 1828, Wellington had showed in his handling of the repeal of the Test Acts his concern to avoid conflict between the two Houses, especially as he believed that the House of Commons was backed by public opinion. In his own peculiar way, he acted on this concern in the final crisis over the passage of the Reform Act in May 1832, and it continued to guide his actions thereafter. Though neither Wellington nor Sir Robert Peel was quick to grasp the conservative potential in public opinion, when they did they worked together to realize it, for their party and for their conception of the national good. Wellington's contribution was, first, to mold fractious elements in the Lords into a party under his leaderhsip; and then, successfully to restrain it, until its and the Lords' time had clearly come. Richard Davis's essay will examine Wellington's role.

Grey was prepared to tolerate the Lords' obstreperousness after 1832, galling though he often found it. One might expect that Lords Tavistock, Althorp, and Milton, who would all succeed to their fathers' peerages in the 1830s, would have taken a different attitude. As so-called "young" Whigs in the 1820s, they had worked closely together in reinvigorating the party and in pressing for reforms that they hoped would make the political system more open and responsive to public opinion. Yet (as with Grey himself) the desire for such reforms was in no way inconsistent in their minds with a vigorous and effective House of Lords. As Ellis Wasson's essay shows, none was more aristocratic and Whiggish than the duke of Bedford and Earls Spencer and Fitzwilliam. Their careers demonstrate how the Whigs continued to strive to make the political system and the partnership of the two Houses of Parliament work.

Realism and restraint, perhaps the duke of Wellington's two most important qualities, continued to characterize the Conservative leadership of the Lords for the rest of the century. As a party leader, the fourteenth earl of Derby, a much neglected figure, displayed his own distinctive combination of the same qualities. Though three times prime minister, Derby has gone down in history as a haughty aristocrat, rather above politics and distinctly lackadaisical in his exercise of political leadership, whether in office or out. As Angus Hawkins shows, nothing could be further from the truth. Out of office, Hawkins argues, Derby pursued a policy of "masterly inactivity," skillfully playing on the tendency to splinter of a Liberal party composed of several elements, Whig, Radical, Irish, and later Peelite. By refusing seriously to challenge Liberal governments, Derby deprived them of the pressure for unity which determined opposition would have provided. This was restraint, and in 1852, 1858, and 1866 it brought the Conservatives into office. The complement to "masterly inactivity" in opposition was the vigorous pursuit of moderate reform in office. This was realism, and, as Hawkins convincingly argues, realism of a distinctly Whig variety. Like the great Reform ministry of 1830–34 of which he was a member, Derby reformed in order to preserve. And, as Hawkins demonstrates, it was Derby rather than Benjamin Disraeli who made parliamentary reform a Conservative issue. Derby led the Conservative party for 22 years and for all that time from the House of Lords. The success of his policy, too clever for many, is also a measure of the sway he exercised over his fellow peers. From every point of view, Derby has been seriously underestimated and Hawkins's essay shows the necessity for a thoroughgoing reevaluation of his career.

The next great leader of the House of Lords after Derby was the third marquis of Salisbury. True, Disraeli, after being created earl of Beaconsfield, led his government and party from the Lords after 1876. But he went there weakened by bereavement and ill health; and, though he had no difficulty operating effectively in his new arena, it was not one he liked, nor did he leave his mark upon it. Not so Salisbury, who succeeded Beaconsfield as Conservative leader on the former's death in 1881. In her forthcoming book, *The House of Lords and Ideological Politics: Lord Salisbury's Referendal Theory and the Conservative Party, 1846–1922*, Corinne C. Weston traces the impact on the Lords and the Conservative party of Salisbury and his son-in-law and ideological heir, the second earl of Selborne.[2] The referendal theory was based on Salisbury's contention that the Lords were the guardians of democracy, responsible for making sure that governments and their potentially tyrannical majorities in the Commons did not ride roughshod over the popular will, but rather submitted all divisive issues on which the electorate had not had the opportunity to express an opinion, to its judgment. Under Salisbury's skillful leadership, the theory was effectively deployed to give the Conservative majority in the Lords a decisive role in handling major questions such as parliamentary reform and Irish home rule. Like the later 1830s, Salisbury's years as their effective leader marked a high point in the exercise of the Lords' power in the nineteenth century.

Professor Weston's essay in this volume concerns the period after Salisbury's death in 1903, and especially those last few years before the nineteenth-century world ended in the great cataclysm of World War I. History has not dealt kindly with the Lords nor with the Conservative party which dominated their proceedings during this period. Still strongly under the influence of George Dangerfield's well-known book, *The Strange Death of Liberal England*, historians are apt to see the Conservatives as following a suicidal policy, not only insane but criminal because of their willingness to take the country with them to destruction. And it was the Lords who precipitated the crisis by throwing out Lloyd George's budget in 1909, making the situation much worse by almost rejecting the reform of their House embodied in the Parliament Act of 1911. Thereafter, in pursuing the maintenance of union with Ireland, which was literally the defining issue for the party, Conservatives (or Unionists) actively encouraged Irish rebellion and something close to mutiny among British officers; that is, when they were not engaged in endangering the army itself by the threat to throw out the annual Army Bill in the Lords in 1914.

Whatever the wisdom of the Lords' course between 1909 and 1911, Weston argues in an important revisionist essay that thereafter the charge of extremism cannot be made to stick either on the Conservative party as a whole, or on the party in the Lords in particular. Weston shows that the threat to the Army Bill was merely a device to force the Liberal government to put the Irish home rule issue before the electorate. Beyond that, while the new party leader, Andrew Bonar Law, himself with strong Ulster connections, may have been willing to go to extreme lengths, he was effectively restrained by his colleagues in the Conservative leadership, not only by the well-known "hedger" in 1911, Lord Curzon, but also by a leading "ditcher" or "diehard," the earl of Selborne. Though there were extreme elements within the Conservative party, it was moderation and good sense that dominated it in the final years before World War I.

In the sense that even before the Great Reform Act there was a clear recognition among those who dominated the proceedings of the House of Lords that their chamber could not stand against the fixed determination of the House of Commons backed by public opinion, 1911 was a more important turning point in the history of the Lords than 1832. For in 1911, almost until the very end, few if any of the Conservative leaders in the Lords realized that their House was in real danger. Only when it was made clear that they would be swamped by creations if they did so, did it become obvious to some that they could not simply throw out the Parliament Bill. Only then did leading "hedgers" such as Curzon advance the argument that it was better to have an independent House with curtailed powers than to have a House which was a mere creature of the government of the day. This argument proved effective, and as a result an absolute veto was reduced to a two-year (since 1949, a one-year) veto.

This might seem a drastic reduction of the Lords' power, but was it? The duke of Wellington himself never claimed more for the Lords than simply the power to restrain the Commons from precipitate action and to give them and the public they represented time to reconsider. The upper House still continues to fulfill these functions, certainly as efficiently as the Commons fulfill theirs. By the early twentieth century the Lords (as they partly recognized in their careful handling of new social legislation, as opposed to partisan Liberal measures rooted in the past) could have retained an absolute veto only so long as they did not try to exercise it on what the public perceived as vital questions. Under these circumstances losing it was losing nothing at all. Curzon and his allies could perhaps be given more credit if they had recognized this fact before they were hit over the head with it. Even then they did not fully grasp it.[3] But they understood enough to save an institution to which there is still no viable—or at least acceptable—alternative advanced, and which the country would be hard pressed to do without.

"Dr. Codex" and the Whig "Pope": Edmund Gibson, Bishop of Lincoln and London, 1716–1748

STEPHEN TAYLOR

Ever since the dissolution of the monasteries by Henry VIII the bishops have occupied a unique position in the House of Lords. While inroads have been made into the hereditary principle, temporal lords sit in Parliament by virtue of their titles; the bishops alone sit by virtue of their offices. In the eighteenth century the distinctiveness of the bishops was emphasized by the fact that they sat apart from the peers, on the right hand side of the chamber as viewed from the throne, robed in their episcopal habits. Thus they formed a separate and very visible bloc within the House of Lords. As a group, however, their importance was declining. The Reformation had dealt a severe blow to the influence of the clergy in the Lords: the creation of five new sees, bringing the total of English and Welsh bishoprics to 26, was meager compensation for the loss of the abbots. Even so, at the end of Elizabeth's reign the bishops still accounted for almost one third of the membership of a House that numbered only 85 in total. However, while the number of bishops in the Lords remained the same (and still does, despite the creation of further new bishoprics in the nineteenth and twentieth centuries[1]), the size of the peerage has gradually increased. By 1719 there were approximately 194 English, British, and Scottish peers in the Lords. This number remained relatively stable until William Pitt's creations in the 1780s and 1790s which inaugurated a rapid expansion of the peerage: there were some 273 peers in the Lords by 1800 and 559 by 1900.[2] In the nineteenth century the behavior of the bishops could still provoke controversy on occasions, as, for example, did their opposition to Reform in 1830–32. In general, however, they were an increasingly insignificant presence in Parliament. By contrast, their importance during the first half of the period covered by this volume should not be underestimated. Eighteenth-century bishops took their parliamentary duties seriously; on the whole their attendance was rather better than that of their temporal colleagues. As a group they formed a significant proportion of the potential voting strength of the Lords, over 12 percent until the 1780s. Moreover, the profile of the episcopate was raised further because it was one of the two groups in the House (the Scottish representative peers was the other) whose composition could be influenced by the ministry, in this case through its control of the royal prerogative of appointing and translating bishops.

The tone of studies of episcopal behavior in the House of Lords in the eighteenth century has been overwhelmingly hostile; Roy Porter's description of the bishops as "voting fodder" is both vivid and typical.[3] This analysis has its origins in contemporary attacks on the bishops, particularly in the "country" depiction of the bench as the servile dependents of ministers like Walpole, Newcastle, and North. There was, of course, nothing new about such attacks: in 1678–79 the bishops were furiously denounced for their support of the court during the impeachment of the earl of Danby.[4] Hanoverian bishops, however, have been portrayed as peculiarly political creatures by comparison with their predecessors and successors. This fact is best explained by changing circumstances. On the one hand, the annual sessions which became the norm in the aftermath of the Revolution of 1688 meant that Parliament and its members occupied a much more prominent place in the nation's political life than they had done in the seventeenth century. On the other hand, as we have seen, the episcopate was much more influential within Parliament than it was to be in the nineteenth century. To some extent, it is pointless to try to refute the charges of political subservience made against eighteenth-century bishops.[5] There were always dissidents; by the late 1730s five bishops were to be found in regular opposition to the policies of Walpole's ministry. But, in general, they remained remarkably loyal to successive administrations. Given the size of the House of Lords, no ministry was going to overlook the opportunities offered by vacancies on the bench to consolidate its support, and it is hardly surprising that almost all of those raised to the episcopate during the years of the Whig supremacy described themselves as Whigs. It would be much more remarkable if the overwhelming majority of eighteenth-century bishops could not be classified as ministerial supporters. Their political loyalty, however, was the expression of much more than mere subservience. In studying the bishops, and perhaps the House of Lords more generally, historians have been too preoccupied with the issue of party. The divisions on the bench which characterized the reigns of William and Anne were not typical, and they were widely deprecated when they did occur. There were powerful pressures encouraging consensus. Party politics distracted clergymen from the concerns of religion; conflict between them was thought to bring discredit on the Church. Even in Parliament most bishops believed that they had little part to play in the discussion of civil affairs, but should submit to be governed by the judgment of ministers. This attitude was reinforced by a feeling of community of interest with the Crown. Not only was the king the head of the Church, but, as few bishops needed reminding, both episcopacy and monarchy had been destroyed in the 1640s. Many bishops believed that their primary loyalty was to the king, rather than to any particular set of politicians, and they thus had a duty to assist in carrying on the king's business in Parliament.

The bishops were, therefore, reliable ministerial supporters at least in part because they were churchmen. For precisely the same reason, however, they could sometimes be found opposing the ministry in the House of Lords. Bishops were very conscious of the fact that they sat in Parliament as the representatives of both the Church and their clergy, and for both Church and clergy Parliament became a much more important place after 1689 as a result of the dramatic increase in legislative activity. Moreover, the absence of a sitting convocation after 1717 meant that Parliament was the only national forum for the discussion of matters concerning religion and the Church. The eighteenth century may have witnessed little major ecclesiastical legislation, at least by comparison with the nineteenth century, but dozens of bills were introduced affecting the Church in particular parishes or localities. Episcopal attendance was always high for debates which touched on religion or the Church, and predictably it was such debates which highlighted episcopal independence. Even at the height of the Whig supremacy, when the bishops appeared to be the most reliable of ministerial supporters, there were three occasions on which the bench united in opposition to legislation which had the support of the administration—the Quakers' Tithe Bill of 1736, the Spirituous Liquors Bill of 1743, and the Bill for Disarming the Highlands in 1748[6]—and there were other divisions in which a significant number of bishops found themselves opposing the ministry.[7]

It should be apparent from these preliminary comments that bishops were conscious of the potential tension between their temporal and spiritual responsibilities as lords of Parliament. During the period covered by this volume, this tension was probably most sharply focused in the first four decades of the eighteenth century. In those years, more than at any other time, religion lay at the heart of political debate.[8] The division between Tories and Whigs was very much a division between high churchmen on the one hand and low churchmen and Dissenters on the other.

The importance of religious issues in early eighteenth-century politics made it inevitable that the clergy, even the bishops, divided along Whig-Tory lines. As G. V. Bennett has pointed out, in the decades after the Revolution of 1688 all clergy faced a "critical choice . . . Were they ready to accept the place in English society of a basically voluntary body working within the legal conditions of the establishment or were they going to agitate for a return to the past when Church and State had conjoined in a single authoritarian regime?"[9] Some Tory clergy undoubtedly hankered after a return to the repressive Anglican policies pursued in the last years of Charles II's reign; all favored limiting as far as possible, if not actually reversing, the concessions made to Dissent in 1689. Whig clergy, on the other hand, were more inclined to embrace the voluntaristic alternative, believing that persuasion rather than coercion was the solution to the problems facing the Church. They were, therefore, more inclined towards a liberal interpretation of the Toleration Act. There was, however, a sharper edge to the polemic. Many Whigs believed that the Tories were tainted by Jacobitism and that therefore the protestant monarchy and, by implication, the protestant religion were not safe in Tory hands. The Tories, in contrast, thought the Whigs to be tainted by their association with Dissent and that the Church was therefore in danger in Whig hands. These attitudes did not disappear in 1714.[10] Long after the Hanoverian succession Tory clergy remained convinced that the Church could never be safe under a Whig administration, a belief which helps to explain the fact that Tory bishops such as Dawes, Gastrell, and Atterbury were in the forefront of the opposition to the Whig government in the House of Lords until they were removed by death or exile in the mid-1720s.[11] Although these bishops repeatedly found themselves voting against the ministry, the problem of reconciling their spiritual and temporal duties was always posed in a far more active form for Whig churchmen. Tories were able to wrap themselves in the banner of "the Church party"; Whigs, by contrast, constantly had to rebut charges of betraying the Church and of allying with its enemies.

An examination of the parliamentary career of one Whig churchman, Edmund Gibson, bishop successively of Lincoln and London between 1716 and 1748, can thus illuminate the pressures experienced by bishops as lords of Parliament and the attitudes which determined their conduct. Gibson provides an interesting case study. He was not only a Whig churchman, but a particularly prominent one, the architect of the Church-Whig alliance which underpinned the religious policy pursued by the ministries of Townshend and Walpole.[12] He was the Whig "Pope": his advice was sought in the distribution of the Crown's patronage and on all other aspects of ecclesiastical policy; he marshaled the Whig bishops and clergy in support of the administration; in the words of Lord Hervey (who was not an admirer) he obtained "more absolute power from the Government in the direction of all church matters than any single churchman before had ever been vested with."[13] In the eyes of the cynical, his aim in all this was Lambeth.[14] Gibson was also "Dr. Codex," so called because he had written a treatise on ecclesiastical law, entitled the *Codex Juris Ecclesiastici Anglicani,* in which he set out to defend the claims of the Church to a separate and independent spiritual jurisdiction. For his advocacy of this position, one often seen as a characteristic of high churchmen, Gibson was condemned by anti-clericals as the successor to Archbishop Laud, for attempting, like Laud, to usurp "a *Papal and Tyrannical Power.*" For pamphleteers such as these Gibson's clericalism was the more threatening because of the power he exercised within the government.[15] There is a certain irony in the fact that he was attacked from both sides: by Tory clergy for allying with the enemies of the Church and by anti-clericals for asserting its rights and privileges. Gibson's career in Parliament reveals the same paradox. In 1718 he supported the Sunderland-Stanhope ministry over the repeal of the Occasional Conformity and Schism Acts, voting against Archbishop Wake and a majority of his brethren. For this he was condemned by Wake for desertion and betrayal.[16] By contrast, in 1736 Gibson led the episcopate in their opposition to the Quakers' Tithe Bill, which enjoyed ministerial support. On this occasion, he was denounced by Walpole as the "*Ringleader of Sedition*" and his "papacy" was brought to an abrupt end.[17]

Most of the remainder of this essay will be taken up with a discussion of Gibson's behavior on these two occasions. It will examine how he reconciled his obligations to Crown and ministry with his responsibilities to Church and clergy. It will suggest that the apparent contrast between Gibson's behavior in 1718 and in 1736 is not to be explained by the fact that he had changed his mind. As we shall see, Gibson himself was clear that his principles had been consistent. What had changed were the circumstances and the specific issues at stake. First, however, to put the events of 1718 and 1736 in context, it is necessary to look more generally at Gibson's parliamentary career.

I

Edmund Gibson was consecrated as bishop of Lincoln on 12 February 1716 and took his seat in the House of Lords on 18 February. He remained on the bench until his death in 1748, having been translated to the bishopric of London in 1723. His effective parliamentary career, however, was considerably shorter, as he attended the House on only seven occasions after his breach with Walpole in 1736. Between 1716 and 1736, however, the records that have survived of the proceedings in the House of Lords show him to have been a typical bishop. Gibson's attendance record sets him apart from his brethren to some extent. Even in the session of 1735, after almost twenty years on the bench, he was present in the House on 53 days out of a possible 71, a figure more typical of younger, more junior bishops.[18] Inside the chamber, however, there was little to distinguish him from his episcopal colleagues. Like most bishops, he was a reliable ministerial supporter, voting with the government in every division between 1716 and 1736 for which a list has survived, except that on the Quakers' Tithe Bill.[19] Like most bishops too, he rarely spoke. Cobbett's *Parliamentary History*, in fact, only records him intervening in one debate, on the Bill for Strengthening the Protestant Interest in December 1718. Too much significance should not be attached to this. We know that Gibson spoke in support of the Bill of Pains and Penalties against Atterbury in 1723 and twice against the Mortmain Bill in 1736; it is likely that he also delivered a speech against the Quakers' Tithe Bill.[20] Nonetheless, it is clear that Gibson and his colleagues tended to limit their interventions to debates on matters concerning the Church and religion. Very few spoke regularly on more political matters—Francis Atterbury and Thomas Sherlock are the notable exceptions during the Whig supremacy—and their oratory provoked comment, and even criticism, from contemporaries. Among White Kennett's collection of parliamentary speeches is one attacking Atterbury for his intervention in a debate on the navy and the "Debts," matters which Kennett believed were foreign to the concerns of the bench.[21]

Gibson, however, was not a typical bishop. The fact that he occupied the see of London made it easier for him to attend Parliament than many other bishops, but the remarkable regularity with which he was present in the Lords was due primarily to the fact that for thirteen years Gibson had, as he put it, "the chief managing and conducting of Church-affairs under the ministry."[22] The nature of Gibson's relationship with the ministry before 1723 is obscure and it is unclear how he came to occupy this position. There is no doubt that he was both ambitious and politically astute. He was certainly well known to Whig politicians even before 1715, having acted as Archbishop Tenison's chaplain and political secretary during his last years at Lambeth. But there is little evidence that he had close links with any lay politicians in the early years of George I's reign. On the contrary, all the evidence points the other way. William Wake, the new archbishop, obtained the bishopric of Lincoln for Gibson and for the next few years Gibson's closest political allies were two other bishops, John Hough and Lancelot Blackburne.[23] He was suspicious of the Junto and its ecclesiastical advisers, Charles Trimnell (Sunderland's former chaplain) and William Talbot.[24] Yet there is nothing to suggest any links with Townshend and Walpole; indeed, Gibson's support of the repeal of the Occasional Conformity and Schism Acts might suggest the opposite. By 1719 he was becoming more involved in the ecclesiastical policy of the Sunderland-Stanhope administration, and it is probably to these links that we should attribute his appointment as dean of the chapels royal in 1721.[25] But, despite the death of his patron Sunderland in April 1722, Trimnell continued to direct ecclesiastical policy, helped, apparently, by the direct access he had to the king as clerk of the closet.[26] Only with Trimnell's illness and death in 1723, which coincided with the growing dominance of Townshend and Walpole within the ministry, did Gibson's influence become predominant. Townshend had been relying heavily on Gibson for advice for some time, and he was the natural choice to succeed Trimnell.[27] Gibson retained this position until 1736, though not without some difficulties. Not until some months after the accession of George II and Queen Caroline did ecclesiastical affairs begin to "return into ye. old Chanel," and Gibson's relationship with the new court was always far more strained than it had been with the old.[28]

Gibson, of course, occupied no official post, other than those of bishop of London and dean of the chapels royal, and it is difficult to describe his position. Clearly he was not a minister; he himself described his role as "the chief managing and conducting of Church-affairs *under* the ministry." But if "ecclesiastical minister" implies too much,[29] "ecclesiastical adviser" suggests too little. No mere adviser would have been provided with apartments at the Cockpit, the government offices in Whitehall.[30] As Sykes makes clear, Gibson played a very active part in the distribution of patronage and the formulation of policy. Even in 1723 one observer noted that "this Sumer, All has been done by the Bp of London."[31] Much less direct evidence has survived, however, to illustrate how far Gibson's role extended in parliamentary management. Trimnell had certainly been active in organizing the bishops in the House of Lords, and it is likely that Gibson continued, and even extended, Trimnell's practice.[32] He was certainly seen by contemporaries as ministerial whip for the bishops. His greatest triumph came in the debates on the South Sea Company at the height of the excise crisis in 1733. On both 24 May and 1 June 24 bishops were present or voted by proxy, 23 of them for the court.[33] The bishops' votes were crucial—the ministerial majority on 1 June was only five—and one pam-

phleteer depicted Gibson reminding Walpole that he owed the survival of
his administration to the support of a solid phalanx of episcopal votes.

> Consider the Ch[ur]ch is your *Rock of Defence*:
> Your *S[outh] Sea* Escape in your Memory cherish,
> When sinking you cry'd, help L[or]ds, or I perish.[34]

Equally impressive was Gibson's success in orchestrating the opposition of
the bishops to the Quakers' Tithe Bill in 1736, not least because on this
occasion Gibson was working against the pressures of the ministry and the
court. On the second reading of the bill in the House of Lords, fifteen
bishops voted against the bill and six episcopal proxies were available for
use if required.[35] The vote had been preceded by a series of meetings at
which the bishops concerted tactics both within Parliament and without.
To Walpole Gibson emphasized that he had always "acted in pursuance of
a joint and unanimous agreement among the Bench of Bishops." Bishop
Hare, however, was in no doubt that Gibson was the prime mover and
leader of the bench.[36]

Gibson's control over the episcopate in the House of Lords should
not be exaggerated, however. As he himself noted in 1736, he was "well
known not to have . . . ye least influence" over many of the bishops who
had joined in the opposition to the Quakers' Tithe Bill.[37] Gibson was
probably thinking of Blackburne, Potter, Sherlock, and Hare, and possibly also of Butts. Blackburne, the archbishop of York, had originally
been one of Gibson's closest allies, but they had fallen out in 1725 as a result
of Gibson's opposition to making Blackburne's chaplain, John Gilbert,
bishop of Chester.[38] John Potter, bishop of Oxford, had remained loyal to
Wake in the early 1720s and possibly through Wake he became a favorite
of the prince and princess of Wales. Some people expected him to supplant
Gibson when George II came to the throne. He did not; but he remained
a favorite with Queen Caroline, was known in 1733 to have the promise of
the archbishopric of York and, largely through the queen's influence, succeeded Wake at Canterbury in 1737.[39] Hare and Sherlock were also known
to be in great favor at court; their elevation, to the bishoprics of St Asaph
and Bangor in 1727 and 1728 respectively, had taken place at the insistence
of the queen and much against Gibson's wishes.[40] Robert Butts had formerly been a chaplain to the father of Lord Hervey, one of Gibson's most
vocal critics at court. His promotion to the see of Norwich in 1733 was
achieved, according to Hervey, on his recommendation and in the face of
Gibson's opposition.[41] To these four, Wake, Willis, Hoadly, and Reynolds
should be added. By 1736 Wake was a semi-invalid at Lambeth, but he had

never shown any inclination to follow the lead of the bishop who had so publicly supplanted him in political affairs, nor to give any succor to the ministry. He was conspicuously absent from the divisions on the South Sea Company in 1733.[42] Richard Willis, bishop of Winchester until his death in 1734, and Benjamin Hoadly, who succeeded him, were both reliable ministerial supporters, but neither was inclined to follow Gibson's lead. Willis had succeeded Trimnell as clerk of the closet in 1723 and had clearly expected to inherit his political influence. The ministry preferred Gibson, Walpole dismissing Willis as a "Coxcombe," and from that time Willis constantly sniped at Gibson.[43] Hoadly was set apart from the rest of the bench by his extreme latitudinarianism.[44] Reynolds, by contrast, followed Gibson's lead in 1736, but he had been the one bishop who opposed the government in 1733 and was regularly to be found supporting the parliamentary opposition until the fall of Walpole.[45]

It is clear that other bishops were not close to Gibson. Edward Chandler, for example, like Potter, had remained loyal to Wake in the early 1720s, behavior which cost him the offer of the Irish primacy, and he was one of the few bishops to support the Mortmain Bill in 1736.[46] Conversely, there was only a small number of bishops who were closely linked to Gibson. Weston, Clavering, Smalbroke, Peploe, and Tanner can all be included in this group on the grounds that they entrusted their proxies to Gibson on at least two occasions; so too can Nicholas Claggett, who held Gibson's proxy in every session from 1737 to 1746.[47] All, except Tanner, who was dead, and Smalbroke, remained loyal to the Whig ministry after Gibson's fall. But it is hardly surprising that Gibson did not create his own party among the bishops. His influence derived from his relationship to the ministry. For as long as he retained its confidence he was clearly regarded, by bishops and ministers alike, as the leader of the bench in the House of Lords. The observer who claimed in 1733 that Gibson had "nineteen Bishops at command, who do everything he would have them," was probably close to the mark.[48]

II

Gibson's success in mobilizing the bench against the Quakers' Tithe Bill in 1736 provoked one of the major crises of the Walpole era and resulted in a permanent breach between the minister and the bishop. On the surface, at least, the contrast with Gibson's behavior in 1717 and 1718 could hardly be more striking. Then Gibson had not merely supported the repeal of the Occasional Conformity and Schism Acts, but he had played a significant part in the formulation of the policy adopted by the Sunderland-Stanhope administration on the issue. In 1718 Gibson was denounced as a betrayer of the Church; in 1736 he was its hero and received a vote of thanks from the London clergy assembled at Sion College.[49] On both occasions, Gibson was certainly aware of the tensions between his spiritual and secular responsibilities. But, as we shall see, the bills of 1718 and 1736 raised very different issues and, in Gibson's eyes at least, the political circumstances were very different.

The Bill for Strengthening the Protestant Interest, which repealed the Occasional Conformity and Schism Acts,[50] caused serious divisions among the Whigs in Parliament. Townshend, Walpole, Devonshire, Cowper, Orford, and Pulteney all voted against the bill, as did Wake, Potter, and Chandler among the Whig bishops.[51] At first sight Whig opposition to the bill appears surprising. The Schism Act in 1714 had encountered fierce Whig opposition, and Townshend, Devonshire, Cowper, Orford, and Wake all subscribed their names to the protest against it.[52] In 1711 the Occasional Conformity Bill had had a much smoother passage, the Whigs agreeing to abandon their opposition in return for Lord Nottingham's support against Oxford's peace policy. Cowper later admitted that he had "never liked ye Act & joynd in passing it as it is, least it should have passed . . . in a worse maner," and Whig attitudes at the time are probably revealed more accurately by the assurances given to Calamy that the Dissenters would receive "relief as to this and other hardships, whenever the Protestant succession should come to take place."[53]

The opposition of many of the lay Whigs to the bill of 1718 is most easily explained by the Whig schism of the previous year; the bill gave dissident Whigs such as Walpole and Townshend an issue on which they could join with the Tories to put pressure on the ministry.[54] But Whig opposition cannot be explained solely in terms of tactical maneuvering. In particular, it is clear that the Whig bishops who opposed repeal acted out of principle. The position of Archbishop Wake is particularly instructive; Potter and Chandler, the two other Whig bishops who opposed the bill, both took their lead from Wake.[55] In the first place, Wake's speech in the Lords on the bill's second reading on 18 December made no mention of the Schism Act, and there is no evidence that Wake was opposed to the repeal of the measure against which he had entered his protest in 1714.[56] The Occasional Conformity Act was a different matter. It had been "lately, and unanimously, agreed to."[57] By 1718 Wake saw the act as one of the "Outworks" of the Church establishment, reinforcing its essential protection, the Test Act. Moreover, the act appeared to be working, as the Dissenters were "decreasing both in number & Interest." To repeal it and open a door to occasional conformity would be of no advantage to the "truly conscientious" and would be merely encouraging men to sin.[58] These arguments, of course, all applied with equal force in 1711. But little is known about Wake's attitude to the Tory attempts to legislate against occasional conformity in Anne's reign, and therefore it is unclear whether or not he had changed his mind.[59] Any change of mind, however, could be explained by changed circumstances. As Walpole noted, many Whigs had opposed the Occasional Conformity Act because they believed it was "only a Prelude to the abrogating their [the Dissenters'] Toleration."[60] Under a Whig government that threat had vanished. As Wake noted gloomily, the threat was now to the Church; that repeal would be the prelude for further concessions to the Dissenters.[61]

Seen in this context, Gibson's support of the bill in 1718 requires explanation.[62] Wake had secured the bishopric of Lincoln for Gibson late in 1715, and initially Gibson was seen, and saw himself, as one of Wake's allies on the bench. In the session of 1716 he fully supported Wake's opposition to the Vestry Bill.[63] Their intimacy goes a long way to explain Wake's bitterness in 1718; it was against Gibson and Blackburne, rather than Hoadly and Trimnell, that his accusations of betrayal were directed.[64] Significantly, moreover, in March 1717 Bishop Nicolson recorded that Gibson, like Wake, was hostile to a ministerial suggestion that the Occasional Conformity Act should be repealed.[65]

If Nicolson's account is accurate, and we have no reason to doubt it, we need to explain how Gibson came to support repeal. It is clear that Gibson became convinced of the necessity for some concessions to Dissent long before the introduction of the Bill for Strengthening the Protestant Interest into the House of Lords on 13 December 1718, but his speech on the second reading neatly encapsulates his main reasons. On that occasion he noted that there had been a time when the Occasional Conformity Act had not existed and, in a remark clearly directed at Wake and other Whig opponents of repeal, he reminded them that they had not thought the Church to be in danger then. Having established that the security of the Church was not threatened by the repeal of the Occasional Conformity Act, Gibson was able to argue for the bill on the grounds that it promoted unity among the king's protestant subjects and thereby strengthened the "protestant Governm[en]t." "He concluded that whatever contributed to Strengthen his Majesty Government was a real advantage to the Church, which must stand or fall with him . . . He was therefore for the Bill." In other words Gibson agreed with Bishop Kennett that it was not "a *Church Bill*," but "a Bill of Civil Policy and Good Government."[66]

Gibson's position was very different from that of some of the other bishops who supported the bill. He conspicuously failed to use the arguments advanced, for example, by Richard Willis, who denounced the Occasional Conformity Act as an "invasion" of the Toleration Act and condemned "Persecution" in a way which tended to undermine the Test Act.[67] There was a clear spectrum of opinion among the episcopal supporters of the bill. At one extreme was Benjamin Hoadly, who supported the repeal of the Test Act. Close to him stood Willis and Trimnell, who was rumored to have preached some twenty years earlier a sermon advancing the same doctrines as the bishop of Bangor.[68] Gibson was at the other end of the spectrum, along with Blackburne and Hough, who firmly rejected the suggestion that they acted "in Obedience to Bp Hoadly's doctrine."[69] These three, however, were crucial to the ministry's strategy. Despite the enthusiasm of the king for a measure to make some public acknowledgement of the Dissenters' support for the protestant succession, the ministry recognized that it could not proceed "if the greater p[ar]t of the Honest B[ishop]s wer[e] ag[ains]t it."[70] The abandonment of its proposal for a straightforward repeal of the Occasional Conformity Act in 1717 was doubtless due not only to the ministry's weakness in Parliament following the Whig schism, but also to the fact that repeal was opposed by "18 or 19 of the Bishops" out of 25, including both Gibson and Blackburne.[71]

Gibson, however, was soon convinced of the necessity for some concession to the Dissenters. His position, and probably that of Blackburne and Hough also, was that he was content to follow the judgment of his "superiors in the State" about the means of supporting the "protestant Establishment," always provided that nothing was done which could "affect the Safety and wellbeing of the Church."[72] He was soon convinced by the ministers of the political necessity of doing something for the Dissenters "in order to prevent a Tory Parliament, and to keep a good understanding among the friends of the present Establishment."[73] By the beginning of the session of 1717–18 action seemed even more necessary, as the Whig schism had led to a considerable increase in Tory "Strength and Spirits."[74] The crucial argument was an electoral one. The Whig position had to be consolidated, especially in the corporations, and, as Gibson noted, only "the Laity" could "judge of the most proper methods of promoting Elections and securing good Returns."[75] However, as Nicolson noted, Gibson remained concerned about "*the opening of any Gap to Occasional Confor-*

mity."[76] This concern helps to explain the search for expedients that went on through 1717 and 1718. A meeting of bishops[77] on 22 November 1717, for example, suggested the abolition of "the Sacramental Test, soe far as it concerns Corporations" and its replacement by a new *"Declaratory* Test."[78] The Dissenters, however, found the proposal unacceptable.[79] Gibson's reservations on this head may help to explain the nature of the bill which was finally introduced in December 1718. The bill not only repealed the Occasional Conformity and Schism Acts, but it also included a clause which made merely offering to receive the sacrament a qualification for office. This clause provoked a storm of protest and was seen by many as a proposal for "evading entirely the Test Act."[80] Sunderland quickly agreed to abandon this clause, but said later that it had only been included on the insistence of Gibson, Willis, and Hoadly.[81] It may well have appeared to the latter two as a way of undermining the Test Act. For Gibson, however, it is likely that it was a genuine attempt to relieve clergymen of the legal obligations they were under to administer the sacrament to someone who they knew was present merely for the purpose of qualifying for office.[82]

To fully appreciate Gibson's position at this time, however, it is necessary to go beyond the arguments about occasional conformity. Gibson's political conduct was based on a creed which he firmly believed he had inherited from Archbishop Tenison. As he explained it to Nicolson,

all my political reasonings proceed upon these 2 positions; "That there is noe way to preserve the Church, but by preserving the present Establishmt in the State; and That there is far greater probability that the Tories will be able to destroy our present Establishmt in the State, than that the Dissenters will be able to destroy our Establishmt in ye Church."[83]

For Gibson, as for many Whig churchmen, the Revolution had been, above all else, a providential intervention by God, once more rescuing his people from the threat of popery. It was the protestant monarchy, as established at the Revolution, which guaranteed the security of the Church of England and Gibson was convinced that the protestant succession could never be safe in Tory hands. It is easy to see how these beliefs informed his attitude towards the repeal of the Occasional Conformity Act—if repeal, by conciliating the Dissenters, strengthened the position of the Whigs in Parliament, it thereby contributed to the security of both Church and monarchy. It is less obvious why this argument should have driven a wedge between Gibson and Wake. Initially, Gibson had believed that Wake was the ideal successor to Tenison.[84] But admiration turned to horror when he saw Wake abandoning "a clear Whig bottom" and "setting up for a better Churchman than his predecessor had been."[85] Gibson's fears of "*his Metropolitan's turning Tory*" were clearly exaggerated.[86] However, when George I quarrelled with his son at the end of 1717, Wake sided with the prince and princess of Wales. From that point on, Wake became increasingly detached from the ministry; his closest political friend, Cowper, was in opposition; his episcopal visitors were ever more commonly Tories like Atterbury and Trelawney.[87] In Gibson's opinion, Wake's behavior had three ill consequences. First, the archbishop risked being made the tool of the Tories, above all in the matter of the repeal of the Occasional Conformity and Schism Acts.[88] Second, as Gibson lamented, "The Center has quitted us"; "Church Whigs" like him were left leaderless.[89] Third, it created a vacuum at court, into which Trimnell or even, more worryingly, Hoadly could step. To Gibson, Wake's failings were never more apparent than during the Bangorian controversy. He fumed at the favor shown to Hoadly by the court and bombarded Wake with advice to attend more often, repeating again the words of Tenison "'That tho' he could doe noe great good at Court, yet he could hinder mischief'; which he always gave as a reason for keeping fair with those, who were not perfectly in his way of thinking."[90] Gibson undoubtedly saw himself, quite consciously, as Tenison's disciple. It would be going too far to suggest that he was using the controversy over the repeal of the Occasional Conformity Act to set himself up as his heir, but there is no doubt that, with Blackburne and Hough, he saw himself as continuing Tenison's "Church-Whig" policies, which, by 1717–18, had been abandoned by the archbishop.

III

There is little evidence that Gibson's principles had changed much by 1736. He was more hostile towards the Dissenters, who, he believed, were not as "moderate" as they had been in the years after the Revolution but now aimed at "*pulling down*" the Church establishment.[91] Gibson's concern about Dissent, however, merely reinforced his longstanding conviction that the Test Acts were bulwarks necessary for the defense of the constitution in church and state.[92] But he remained committed to upholding the Toleration Act, which had guaranteed the Dissenters "an entire liberty of Conscience," and, in retrospect, he saw the repeal of the Occasional Conformity and Schism Acts as reversing encroachments made into that toleration in the reign of Queen Anne.[93] Gibson's fundamental political creed remained much the same as it had been in the early years of George I's reign, which is hardly surprising as he was already 46 when he became bishop of Lincoln. He still saw himself as pursuing the Tenisonian policy in church and state. For Gibson this meant adhering to what he called "the true Whig interest," which he defined "as a Body made up of Lay-Whigs, Church-Whigs and Protestant Dissenters, united on the terms of maintaining the Protestant Succession, the Church Establishment, and the Toleration; as wisely fix'd and bounded at the Revolution."[94] Why, then, did Gibson abandon the Tenisonian alliance in 1736? Why was he so hostile to the Quakers' Tithe Bill and why did he organize the episcopal opposition to it, provoking his breach with Walpole? In the first place, the Tithe Bill threatened the interests of the Church and clergy in a way the Bill for Strengthening the Protestant Interest had not done. Secondly, the political situation had changed considerably between 1717–18 and the mid-1730s. Thirdly, Gibson's own position in relation to the ministry was very different.

If it was possible to argue that the repeal of the Occasional Conformity and Schism Acts did not affect "the Safety & well being" of the Church because their repeal merely restored to the Dissenters the full enjoyment of the toleration granted in 1689, the same could not be said of the Quakers' Tithe Bill. The bill's proponents portrayed it as a relatively minor measure of relief for Quakers who suffered because of their conscientious refusal to pay tithes. It would have denied the clergy recourse to the exchequer and ecclesiastical courts, compelling them instead to prosecute Quakers for their refusal to pay in a summary fashion before local JPs. To Gibson and his colleagues[95] this was a serious threat to the Church. Firstly, if the bill passed into law, the clergyman's task in collecting his tithes would be made more difficult. Secondly, the bill contained an implicit threat to the clergy's right to tithes. Thirdly, it was an attack on the jurisdiction of the ecclesiastical courts.[96]

Gibson himself said little about the clergy's right to tithes.[97] In his comments on the bill, in fact, he was most concerned with the practical difficulties it would create for the parochial clergy in the collection of tithes. His copy of the bill introduced into the Lords is covered with annotations highlighting details, such as the inability of JPs to compel witnesses to give evidence, which were detrimental to the position of the clergy. More generally, he believed that Quakers, who had hitherto found expedients to reconcile their conscientious refusal to pay tithes with their legal obligations to do so, would start refusing to pay if the bill became law, forcing the clergy to institute many more law suits. But if Gibson's prime concern was the rights of the clergy, he also opposed the bill because it attacked the rights of the Church. An early criticism of the bill was that it only allowed an appeal from the decision of JPs to the Quarter Sessions. In the Commons an amendment was passed allowing a limited right of appeal to "any of his Majesty's courts at Westminster." Against this Gibson scribbled: "Why not ye like power to be given to ye *Eccl[esiasti]cal Court*; according to the tenor of a Statute still in being, viz 27 H. 8. c. 20?" This was not a minor issue. Like Sherlock, Gibson believed that the ecclesiastical court was the "proper Court" for tithe cases.[98] In his opinion the Church was, under the royal supremacy, an independent institution. The jurisdiction of the spiritual and temporal courts was therefore separate, both deriving their authority equally from the Crown, and Gibson was very critical of those lawyers who asserted that the temporal courts were superior to the ecclesiastical.[99] The Tithe Bill, by depriving the church courts of jurisdiction in certain cases, was, therefore, an attack on the ecclesiastical constitution itself.

In the political context of 1736 the Tithe Bill appeared still more threatening. The session was dominated by "church matters" and, as Hervey noted, "Parliament, like bull-dogs, sticking close to any hold on which they have once fastened, the poor Church this winter was as much worried as Sir Robert had been any other."[100] The anti-clericalism of the Commons was first manifested on 16 February when the petition of the dean and chapter of Westminster for financial aid towards the restoration of Henry VII's chapel was rejected.[101] There then followed a series of anti-clerical measures. Two of these, the Mortmain Bill and the Quakers' Tithe Bill, received ministerial support. The Mortmain Bill restricted the ability of charitable corporations to receive benefactions of land and was a significant attack on corporate Anglican philanthropy. Despite fierce opposition from the Tories and many, but not all, bishops, it had enough support to pass into law. Only the motion for the repeal of the Test Act on 12 March was opposed by the ministry. Walpole himself spoke against the motion, though his attitude was hardly one to inspire confidence among churchmen.[102]

The session of 1736 was the first occasion on which Walpole gave explicit ministerial support to anti-clerical legislation.[103] But Whig anti-clericalism was not a new phenomenon; 1736 actually marks the culmination of a series of attacks on the Church in Parliament stretching back to 1727. Gibson was predictably worried by the emergence of "an Antichurch Spirit."[104] In 1728 he complained strongly to both Walpole and Townshend about "ye. evil spirit that I saw working against Church men and Church matters in general," which had been manifested in the defeat of the Stepney and Westminster Church Bills.[105] The attacks on the Church, moreover, were being made not only by opposition Whigs, but also by "those who are well with ye. Court, and have Encouragement from it." These court Whigs, indeed, seemed "to understand, that if they go on uniformly with ye. Court in matters relating to ye. State, they are at liberty to use ye. Church and Clergy as they please."[106] Gibson found it particularly afflicting that this anti-clericalism was manifesting itself "now ye. Tories are subdu'd"; it was, felt Gibson, ill reward for the support given to the "Lay-Whigs" by the "Whig-Bishops and Clergy" ever since the Revolution.[107] Gibson observed that this state of affairs was a cause of "great Complaint and general dissatisfaction . . . upon our Bench" and warned ministers that, if the court would not protect them, "it is time for us to look to ourselves."[108]

If, in the late 1720s, it was "not safe . . . to let any thing come into Parliament relating to either [the Church or religion], lest some peevish or spiteful motion, of one kind or another, should be grafted upon it,"[109] the situation deteriorated further in the early 1730s, as a succession of anti-clerical bills were introduced into Parliament. The Tithe Bill of 1731 was followed by the Church Rates and Repairs Bill of 1733 and by Ecclesiastical Courts Bills in 1733 and 1734; all attacked the jurisdiction of the ecclesiastical courts and implicitly denied the claims of Gibson and others that the Church was an independent society. None of these measures appears to have received any encouragement from the ministry, and only the Ecclesiastical Courts Bill of 1733 reached the Lords, where it disappeared after its first reading. Gibson, however, was clear that the ministry bore at least some of the blame for the prevalence of anti-clericalism. It did nothing to restrain those who attacked the Church.[110] On the contrary, many of the "Writers in ye. pay of ye. Court" were prominent pamphleteers against the Church and clergy, and it was well known that the court's position on the Test Act was, not that it was an essential part of the constitution, but that the time was not right for its repeal.[111] By the mid-1730s Gibson believed that the bishops were in an invidious position. Their commitment to the Church did not satisfy the Tories; but, increasingly, their commitment to the protestant succession and the toleration was not enough for the "Lay-Whigs and Dissenters, unless one will also give up the Constitution of the Church and the Rights of the clergy." He then predicted that, if these circumstances continued, some bishops would find it impossible to remain loyal to the Whig government.[112] In 1717–18 Gibson had been convinced that a Tenisonian policy was possible. By the mid-1730s that conviction had been destroyed, because the "Lay Whigs" had abandoned their alliance with the "Church Whigs" and their commitment to the church establishment.

The provisions of the Quakers' Tithe Bill and the growing conviction of Gibson and his fellow bishops that they had to make a stand against the growth of anti-clericalism provide a more than adequate explanation for their opposition to the Quakers' Tithe Bill. Even so, in Gibson's case there is more to consider. It has already been noted that Gibson's relations with the court were never good after the accession of George II. Queen Caroline, who exercised greater influence over ecclesiastical affairs than her husband, looked for advice to bishops like Sherlock, Hare, and Potter, and her patronage of heterodox clergy was much criticized by Gibson.[113] It is probably more than a coincidence that Gibson's complaints about parliamentary anti-clericalism date from the beginning of the new reign. Some of the more prominent of the Church's critics in Parliament, such as Hervey, were favorites at the new court, and Gibson certainly believed that the king and queen could have done more to discourage the public expression of anti-clerical sentiments. What is less well known is that Gibson became more isolated within the ministry from the time of Townshend's resignation in 1730. The phrase "Walpole's Pope" is misleading.[114] Gibson never felt that there was any particular intimacy between himself and Walpole. In the mid-1720s it was Townshend, as senior secretary of state, rather than Walpole, who was primarily responsible for ecclesiastical policy and patronage; it was Townshend with whom Gibson had worked most closely. In 1728 a serious breach had occurred between Gibson and Walpole, who had resented the bishop's complaints about anti-clericalism. That breach had been repaired by Townshend. In 1729 Gibson wrote to Townshend, dissuading him from resigning and emphasizing how much "publick affairs, and particularly in the Church, will feel ye. want of your Service."[115] Townshend's resignation left Gibson without the support of someone whose own churchmanship was far less questionable than Walpole's. Again, it might not be going too far to link the rise of Whig anti-clericalism in the 1730s with the disappearance of Townshend's restraining hand within the ministry.[116]

Gibson's influence over ecclesiastical affairs also appears to have been declining. The Rundle affair, in which he defeated Lord Chancellor Talbot's nomination of a suspected arian to the see of Gloucester, is often cited as an example of his power. In fact, it highlights the way in which power was slipping away from Gibson. In 1727 he had been able quickly and quietly to put a stop to the suggestion that Samuel Clarke, a noted anti-trinitarian, be offered a bishopric; Rundle was only disappointed of Gloucester after a long and very public controversy. In the course of this episode Gibson was acutely conscious that he himself had become the target of some of Walpole's favorite hack writers, notably William Arnall.[117] Isolated within the ministry and with his influence in decline, it was only natural that he became increasingly sensitive to "the charge of sacrificing the interests of Religion and the Established Church to my own private views."[118] Walpole certainly did not support the Quakers' Tithe Bill in order to provoke the break with Gibson;[119] a major political crisis was an expensive way of getting rid of his "Pope." As Gibson notes, the ministry "had unwarily espous'd" the bill.[120] However, Walpole's actions left Gibson with little choice but to act as he did. Gibson was not consulted by Walpole about the bill; he clearly believed that he did not have the credit to persuade Walpole to abandon it. His only option was "to embark wholly with his Brethren" and, indeed, to set himself at their head.[121]

IV

This essay is no more than a case study of a bishop in the House of Lords and of the principles that governed his actions. But Gibson was not a typical bishop. As the Whig "Pope," he was for thirteen years one of the most powerful bishops of the eighteenth century. Much of the success of the ecclesiastical policy of Townshend and Walpole can be attributed to Gibson; and Gibson's success in reconciling the clergy to a Whig administration was made much easier by the fact that he was "Dr. Codex," a high church advocate of the rights of the Church. The fact that he was a high church adviser to a ministry that drew much of its support from anticlericals and Dissenters made him even less a typical bishop. But it is precisely because Gibson was a powerful and committed high church Whig—as Newcastle observed in 1723, he had "more party zeal than any of them"[122]—that he is such an interesting case study. Not once, but twice, in 1718 and again in 1736, his conduct in Parliament brings into sharp focus the tensions that the bishops experienced between their secular and spiritual roles. Gibson resolved this tension by following the maxim that the bishops were under an obligation to follow the judgment of "our superiors in the State,"[123] unless the measures proposed threatened the security of the Church or the rights of the clergy. In essence, the contrast between Gibson's behavior in 1718 and 1736 can be explained by the fact that, in his opinion, the Bill for Strengthening the Protestant Interest did not undermine the Church whereas the Quakers' Tithe Bill did.

Even after 1736 the same principle informed Gibson's parliamentary conduct. He continued to support the ministry, though not in person, by depositing his proxy with a reliable ministerial supporter in every session from 1737 to 1748.[124] But his "Retirement," as he described it, was strictly conditional. In his last letter to Walpole he wished him "success in your Administration," but warned him

that if, on any future occasion, I see an attack made upon the Rights of the Parochial Clergy in which the Court think fitt to take a part, I shall think my self obliged to concur with such of my Brethren as appear to be in the same sentiments with me, in warning my clergy of their danger, and advising them to petition that they may be heard, before they are condemn'd.[125]

His continued vigilance for the Church and religion extended to his own attendance in Parliament. Gibson only appeared in the Lords on seven occasions after 1736. In 1741 and 1747 he attended on the first day of the session to take the oaths, and he was present twice in 1746 for the trial of the rebel peers. On the other three days he was in the House to join with his brethren in defense of the interests of the Church and clergy, by voting against the Spirituous Liquors Bill in 1743 and the clause relating to episcopal orders in the Bill for Disarming the Highlands in 1748.[126] Within four months of the latter debate Gibson was dead. One of his last public acts had been to vote against the ministry in defense of the rights of the Church. Even so, Newcastle lamented that "his Loss is very great both to the King and Nation; To us It is particularly so; For we had not a more cordial, a more able, or a more usefull Friend any where."[127]

William, First Earl Cowper, Country Whiggery, and the Leadership of the Opposition in the House of Lords, 1720–1723

CLYVE JONES

Contemporaries of the first Earl Cowper were in no doubt that in the early 1720s he was head of a new kind of opposition in the House of Lords: "The Lords go to oppose and protest, Cowper at the head of them, who has gained credit by his management."[1] The first modern historian to recognize Cowper's achievement was C. B. Realey, who, while noting the importance of Cowper's new opposition group, regarded the substance of the issues and debates involved as unimportant, but thought "the method by which this group used the right of protests as a weapon against the government . . . worthy of consideration."[2] Realey's basic interpretation has found its way into the historiography of the period,[3] but useful as his preliminary work was in drawing attention to Cowper's opposition he was profoundly wrong in his opinion that "the issues and debates were unimportant." It is also far from "quite evident that his opposition was not based upon the merits of the issues but rather upon a consistent policy of opposing all measures of government."[4] The issues were very important to many members of the opposition and particularly to Cowper himself. His was not opposition for opposition's sake.

Realey was also wrong in claiming that there was no organized opposition by Cowper in the Lords before late 1721.[5] This view was based on his failure to find any evidence on the Lords before October 1721, but much new material has come to light since Realey's time which shows that "the opposite party headed by Lord Cowper" was being commented on as early as January of that year.[6] This month saw the real birth of Cowper's group, though evidence exists to show that conception took place in April 1720 at the time of the "healing" of the Whig Schism (which had begun in 1717 with the departure of Viscount Townshend and Robert Walpole from the Whig ministry), and of the reconciliation within the royal family of George I and the prince of Wales.

Another misunderstanding of Cowper's true position as head of the new opposition in the House of Lords has been articulated by, amongst others, B. W. Hill. While ignoring Cowper's actual work with the opposition, Hill notes that Cowper joined the Tories (and by implication ditched his Whig principles and party loyalty along with his Whig colleagues), and that he was only one example (the others being Bolingbroke, Carteret, Harcourt, and Sunderland) of a switch of political allegiances at this time indicative of some politicians being ready to abandon party for their own purposes.[7] Surely it is open to question whether or not such a sweeping analysis can hold, based as it is on only five examples, especially when it has been shown that two of them—Cowper and Sunderland[8]—did not abandon their party principles for short-term political gains. There certainly was some fluidity of allegiance to party *leadership* in the early 1720s, much of it based on the inability of some politicians to accept both the reconciliation within the royal family and the Whig ministry (when some former followers of the prince of Wales refused to join the new ministry), and that ministry's subsequent handling of the South Sea crisis. Also the far from monolithic Tory party was riven by dissent when one of its natural leaders—Bishop Francis Atterbury of Rochester—entered into negotiations with the Whig leader, Sunderland.[9]

This essay will show that in this fluid political situation Cowper did not become a Tory (much less a Jacobite as some have suggested),[10] and that he remained loyal to certain Whig principles and consistent to his own political standards while at the same time forming a new opposition with various Tory groups (both Hanoverian and Jacobite) and some dissident Whigs. It will further show that the ideology which underpinned this new opposition grouping was largely a "Country" ideology aimed at establishing incorrupt government, an ideology to which Cowper had long adhered despite his holding high office in various Whig administrations. Finally the essay will look at Cowper's development of new techniques of opposition, notably his vigorous campaign of entering protests in the Lords' Journals against defeats in divisions in the House, and their subsequent publication in order to influence public opinion.

I

Cowper's ideological background was Puritan and Whig, with distinct "Country" sympathies, combined with a strong independence of mind, which may well have owed a great deal to his belief in the supremacy of law over political expediency. Many aspects of this ideology appealed to other members of the coalition which formed the new opposition between 1720 and 1723, Whig and Tory alike. It was this which underpinned Cowper's group and, *pace* Realey, did make the issues and debates of the opposition important. The new opposition did not oppose "all measures of the government," but selected those which breached Cowper's ideals of good administration.

Cowper's ideology was essentially based on respect for the Revolutionary Settlement of 1689, and following from that the protestant succession in the house of Hanover, which makes nonsense of the claim that he became a Jacobite in the 1720s. The main reason he had refused to work with the Tory government of 1710, as the prime minister Robert Harley had hoped, was that he believed, despite assurances to the contrary, that the new Tory ministry would inevitably be drawn into measures which would place the Revolutionary Settlement in jeopardy: measures he defined as "hurtful to the publick, and contrary to the true Interests of my Countrey" and "high with Hereditary Right and Passive Obedience."[11]

Cowper's political career illustrates the duality of Whig ideology as identified by J. G. A. Pocock: the schism between a concern with parliamentary sovereignty and a concern over excessive influence of the executive ministry in parliamentary proceedings, their use of patronage and corruption, and their designs to bring in a standing army.[12] During his periods in government he undoubtedly supported the sovereignty of Parliament, though with the caveat that the government was for the public good; in opposition he would emphasize the duty of the executive towards good government to an even greater extent, often adopting an "Old Whig" or "Country" stance.

During the 1690s Cowper appears to have displayed a typical "Country" attitude to the various ministries of William III. He favored incorrupt administration which governed for the public good, while opposing strong, centralized, and in particular unvirtuous government, which might threaten the preservation of "the liberties of England." He also showed a streak of political independence from the ministry in power which was to surface time and again throughout his political career. In 1701 in a speech to the House of Commons he recalled

While they who are in places under the government are in the true interest of England I have and will join heartily with them: as when they were for [standing] armies ('tis well known) I left them.[13] I will not by any reproaches be induced to be against the Court, yet when I have but suspected them I have gone from them, not valued their displeasure on the other hand: and while I do so I think myself in a better way to contribute towards preserving the liberties of England, than if I shall be always running upon the ministry.[14]

Cowper's acceptance of office in 1705 as lord keeper (and later as lord chancellor) did not mean his abandoning of "Country" ideals. It has been shown that even those most countrified of "Country" Tories—the Jacobites—clamored for office for themselves and patronage for others under the Tory government of 1710 to 1714 (though this might be put down to their hypocrisy).[15] Cowper's holding of office, however, is one illustration of how "civic virtue" ideology and "Country" ideals were changing in the period from the Revolution to the 1720s to encompass office-holding. This is part of what Pocock has termed the move from "virtue" to "politeness" or "manners." Even the earlier strain of "Country" thinking called for a return to traditional constitutional principles, and these were not incompatible with the holding of office.[16] Cowper's ideals, combined with his strong sense of duty—"a duty I cannot dispence with my-self from . . . that possibly a particular suffered injustice, or the publick some detriment for want of my Vote"[17]—did often temper his view of government and he acquired a reputation for honesty and integrity which lasted his whole life.[18] Queen Anne recognized this independence and upon his resignation in 1710 "said He's as hard as Steel, and you'll see, He will speak against my Affairs."[19]

Cowper was, however, loyal to the Crown as an institution and respected its prerogatives so long as the Crown remained within the limits established by the Revolutionary Settlement. He essentially favored a neutral or non-party monarch who stood above the party fray. In June 1713 he told his confidant, Sir David Hamilton, who was also the Queen's doctor:

the Queen should be Neuter, leaving the matter [of the contentious Treaty of Commerce with France] to be battled, and debated in Parliament, without concern, and let right take Place, Else she makes her self Queen of a Party, and Her Ministers who should free Her, lay all the Weight Upon her.[20]

Though Cowper regretted the excesses of "the rage of party" which had developed under William III and Anne (an attitude by no means uncommon), Sir David Hamilton is wrong in believing that "my Lord Cowper would be of no Party."[21] "An Impartial History of Parties" written for the edification of George I upon his accession to the British throne recognized the necessity of party. Having laid down the principles and ideas which divided the two parties, Cowper thought that either party was capable of ruling. He came out against the Tories, however, whom he thought needed to be treated with prudence for, though not all of them were Jacobites, the Pretender's supporters were strong in the party. Cowper, possibly because of his experience in the period 1705 to 1708, also opposed mixed administrations for they "would render the operation of government slow and heavy, if not altogether impracticable." He did, however, recommend to the king that whichever party was not in power should be treated well with "a fair share of such places and employments of trust."[22] It is something of an open question of how impartial Cowper's "History" was. The author a confirmed Whig, though a moderate one, had supported the Whig Junto since about 1701.[23] The piece may have been written to make a case for the Whigs, and he may have been put up to it by the Junto as a persuasive advocate. Whether George I was advised that it was impartial we may never know, but he seemed to heed Cowper's advice, for a number of Tories upon his accession were honored with titles while others were kept in the administration. However, the Tory election campaign in 1715 and the intemperate language used by them in the pamphlet *English Advice to the Freeholders of England* (published anonymously by Bishop Atterbury in 1714), resulted in the king's losing confidence in the loyalty of the party.[24] This situation was worsened by the 1715 Rebellion and thereafter the Tories largely became a proscribed party.

Cowper's whole attitude to the Crown and what he saw as the Whig ministry's encroachment upon it may have led to his resignation in 1718 (though the ostensible reason was ill-health). The growing Whig hegemony and the increasing proscription of the Tory party after 1715 went clearly against the advice he had given to George I. The actions of Lord Townshend[25] before the Whig Schism of April 1717, when he and Walpole split off from their colleagues Sunderland and Stanhope and left the ministry, and the actions of Sunderland after 1717 (particularly over the Peerage Bill in 1719 which Cowper almost single-handedly opposed)[26] smacked of the growth of authoritarian government which Cowper had always fought against.

There was clearly also some personal animosity towards Townshend in the period before the schism when Cowper suspected Townshend of wishing to replace him as lord chancellor with Lord Parker.[27] Similar personal animosity also developed between Cowper and Sunderland, and later may have developed between Cowper and Walpole as the latter was almost inevitably tarred with the same brush as his brother-in-law, Townshend. Certainly the French ambassador in 1721 reported on Cowper's "envenomed" speeches in Parliament.[28] Cowper may well have felt that these politicians were pushing for authoritarian power within the Whig ministry at the expense of the Crown and Parliament.[29] This possible difference in political outlook may well have been the result of a generation gap between Cowper and the younger politicians of the Whig hegemony. Cowper (born c. 1665) had had as his principal patrons Lords Somers and Halifax and the duke of Marlborough (born 1651, 1661, and 1650 respectively).[30] By 1716 these patrons were either dead or out of political life. They had all experienced the Revolution of 1688–89 at first hand while in their twenties or thirties, as had Cowper. The younger generation of Stanhope, Sunderland, Townshend, and Walpole (born between 1673 and 1676) were in their teens at the time of the Revolution. Cowper may have thought that these younger men cared less about the Revolutionary Settlement. This antipathy, coupled with animosity, almost certainly colored his actions between 1720 and 1723.

Deciding not to rejoin the Whig government in April 1720 upon the healing of the Whig Schism and also of the concurrent quarrel in the royal family, despite the wishes of his royal patron—the prince of Wales, Cowper was left out in the political cold along with some other erstwhile supporters of the prince, the duke of Wharton, and the earl of Orrery. It was, however, the staggering level of corruption in the government revealed by the South Sea crisis which drove Cowper into outright opposition to the Whig administration (his opposition had been only fitful since 1718). Gradually during 1720 he came together with dissident Whigs and the various groups within the Tory party to form a coalition of the new opposition.[31] Though the ideology of these groups was not identical (not all members were to support every move by the new opposition), there was sufficient common ground to make the opposition under Cowper coherent and effective. They all agreed on the need for an incorrupt government. In the words of Lord Coningsby, a dissident Court Whig and scarcely a model of incorruptibility in his earlier political career, but who had joined the opposition:

After thinking seriously one half hour of the present hous of commons and its Governours consider if it is possible for you [Stanhope] to support the Good king your self as his faithfull minister and to restore The Trade, The Creditt, and the honor of the British nation, with a parliament compossed off and 3 to one influenced by the director of the South Sea [Company], the Bank [of England] and the East india company or by a whigg hous. Noe my Lord its impossible since [?] that once noble Vertuous party which consisted formerly of all patriots are now degenerated into the corruptest sett of men in all the earth.[32]

Coningsby's solution was for Stanhope to set himself at the head of a new administration of moderate Tories and to dissolve the present corrupt Par-

liament. Similar views were expressed by other supporters of the new opposition. In the 1722 election campaign, Archibald Hutcheson, Tory MP
and lawyer wrote to Cowper, "My chief View therein is to persuade honest
Whiggs and Tories to Unite against the Common Enemys of the Liberties
of the Kingdome."[33] "Country" ideology was the basis of this new coalition, and though some members of this opposition walked a fine line between being against the current administration and generally anti-Court,[34]
Cowper himself was not anti-Court as such. He was, however, pushed by
events in the early 1720s into a more countrified position than the one he
had held since the 1690s. He probably did not wish to change the Whig
administration for a mixed one as some of his colleagues did, but to
change the leadership (presumably with himself in high office) and the
political thrust of the ministry.[35]

Throughout his political life Cowper seems to have retained a basically
consistent approach to honest government. Even holding high political
office did not significantly alter his vision. His commitment to incorrupt
public administration was an extension of his own honesty in office—upon his appointment as lord keeper in 1705 he refused to accept
gifts commonly tendered on New Year's day, and in 1715 he refused to
appoint his brother as solicitor-general because he wanted to make it clear
that he had "no designs of interest" in making appointments to legal offices.[36] It was also an extension of his early commitment to moral reform.[37]
In this he was not unlike Robert Harley in his self-conscious parading of
"virtue." Though not above the party fray—Cowper was attacked by the
Tories for putting Whig party advantage before legal impartiality over the
new charter for Bewdley in 1708, an imputation he strongly rejected[38]—
his integrity was widely known and respected. However, he was not liked
by all his colleagues, particularly those with whom he disagreed: "peevish
and difficult" was one assessment.[39] Like all who bend little with the prevailing wind, he may have struck more malleable politicians as a prig.
Despite being satirized in the 1690s for hypocrisy, for being both a moral
reformer and a rake,[40] there was little of the hypocrite about him in the
1720s. He seems to have followed the maxim, "Principle [is] the surest
Ground to rely on."[41] And although personal characteristics undoubtedly
played a role in his relations with the Whig administrations after April
1720, it would be a mistake to deny the strong political convictions he held
in the 1720s in the face of a seemingly invulnerable ministry.

One historian has postulated the highly contentious argument that
the departure of Bishop Atterbury into exile after the Jacobite plot and
the arrival of Lord Bolingbroke on the political scene, both in 1723,

marked the real end of Whig and Tory as the most important dividing line between politicians, and that thereafter Court and Country took over.[42] Was Cowper's coming together with the Tories a precursor of the anti-ministerial, anti-Walpole coalition known as the "Patriot" party, which emerged in the late 1720s and lasted well into the 1730s? Could a disintegration of old party allegiances be, at least for the House of Lords, pushed back to the aftermath of the South Sea Bubble? While such a view of the relative importance of the terms Whig and Tory, and Court and Country in parliamentary politics has been rightly disputed,[43] the whole basis of Cowper's opposition campaign can be seen to rest on some, if not all, of the ideological elements which, since the 1690s, went into the formation of Country attitudes: suspicion of central government, the need for virtue in administration, being against an increase in the standing army, against corruption, and against the growth of government expenditure. The new opposition's protests between 1721 and 1723 over public credit, the mutiny bills, naval debt, the election bill, national debt, the suspension of the Habeas Corpus Act, the detention of the duke of Norfolk on suspicion of involvement in the Jacobite plot, Layer's trial for complicity in the plot, and the bills of pains and penalties against Plunkett and Atterbury for their part in the plot, all betray traces of Country ideology.

In times of great political fluidity, such as the 1690s, Country attitudes often over-rode loyalty to Whig and Tory ideals. The early 1720s were again a time of political fluidity and they saw the revival of a similar ideology. This, however, does not mean that Cowper's opposition group was a revival of the "Country party."[44] To view the new opposition in terms of a party in the modern sense of the word (or even in the much looser sense used in the early eighteenth century) is a misconception.[45] One anonymous contemporary, recently identified as Atterbury, described the opposition in 1722 as "four different Sets of Men."[46] Even the Tories were not a homogenous group, there being at least two major divisions between those who supported the Hanoverian succession and those who followed the Pretender. The Jacobites themselves were riddled with faction and were unable to work together over the proposed invasion of 1722.[47] Added to all this there were undoubted tensions between some of the Whig dissidents—Cowper, for example, held Lechmere in low esteem[48]—while few could have regarded the largely unbalanced Coningsby with more than amused disdain. Yet this motley crowd were able to work together for most of the time between 1721 and 1723 with sufficient cohesion to form a major irritant to the ministry in the Lords. Not all members of the opposition were prepared by any means unquestioningly to follow the group's actions over every issue. Even Cowper, their acknowledged leader, did not support all the protests entered.[49] It was, however, undoubtedly his political stature and organizational abilities which held this disparate group together. It was above all Cowper who attempted to articulate and to make concrete the frustrated opposition that many felt towards the Whig ministry that had survived the South Sea crisis.

II

By the organizational standards of the day, Cowper's direction of the opposition was remarkable, particularly when it was obvious to contemporaries that the opposition would never overcome the ministerial majority which was described in December 1721 as "ordinarily of 60 or thereabouts to 22, but the last of 48 to 22."[50] Though on occasions the ministry's majority could sink to single figures, the average over the period January 1721 to May 1723 was 31, and it could be as high as 62 (on 26 April 1723 on Plunkett's bill of pains and penalties).[51] The average attendance at divisions by the opposition was 30, but voting figures fluctuated between 12 and 47. With such a dispiriting prospect facing the opposition it is remarkable that they continued to return to the fray with renewed vigor. Cowper "asked why he persisted every day in standing out so vainly against the Court, had replied that he was well aware that he would not gain anything, but that when one could not capture an enemy fort, one had to bombard it at least." The French ambassador commented: "Every day he makes such eloquent and at the same time envenomed speeches, that they may be regarded in fact as bombs which he is hurling from afar at the Court."[52] The opposition accepted they would never defeat the ministry, but "consoles itself with the thought that what the court gains in parliament it loses in the minds of the nation."[53] This policy of attrition was also wearing on the opposition itself and problems of attendance at Parliament occurred, particularly towards the close of a session. Even Cowper himself would depart early for the waters at Bath or Bristol leaving the opposition in the hands of Bathurst or Strafford.[54] During his absences a member of the opposition, or sometimes his wife, would keep Cowper informed of events.[55]

The major new development in political organization for which Cowper's opposition group was responsible was the extensive use of the protest; the right of every member of the Lords to enter into the Journals of the House his dissent from a vote and, if he wished, his reasons for his dissent. This privilege had not been used systematically before the opposition took it up in 1721. The highest number of protests previously re-corded in one session was 19 in 1701, while the average was only 6.6 per session. In the two sessions of 1721–22 and 1722–23 the opposition entered 27 and 33 protests respectively.[56]

It is clear that the campaign of protests was independent of any desire to force the ministry into a vote in order to register a dissent merely for the internal consumption of the House. The protests were published to alert the public outside Westminster to the opposition's actions and ide-ology, and it was this that moved the opposition organized by Cowper on to a new level of political sophistication. This exercise in political propa-ganda had been unequalled before by any group, party or faction within the Lords. It is true that the publishing of protests was not new, but it was rare and never before had publication been part of a sustained campaign. In 1712 27 lords (mainly Whig, and including Cowper) had signed a protest over the "restraining orders" sent to the duke of Ormonde, commander of the British forces in Flanders, orders which in effect signalled to the French that the British government was prepared to ditch the allies and make peace. That protest had been printed and had achieved a wide cir-culation at home and abroad, which led to the Tory ministry expunging it from the Journals.[57] This example may well have been Cowper's inspira-tion. His group, however, refined the publication of their protests far be-yond the simple issuing of a broadsheet. Single printed sheets containing individual protests were published, while larger protests ran to several pages in a pamphlet. These appeared very quickly, often within days of the protest being entered into the Journal. The end of the sessions of 1721–22 and 1722–23, however, saw the publication of collected editions with, in 1723, the addition of Atterbury's final speech at his trial. Much of this publishing activity was advertised widely in the press. Newspapers, how-ever, unlike later in the century,[58] never appear to have carried the texts of the protests. The only periodical to have published the opposition's pro-tests seems to have been Abel Boyer's *The Political State of Great Britain*, which appeared monthly and frequently contained the major protests of the preceding month.

Another form for circulation of the opposition's propaganda was the hand-written newsletter. This offered a more limited distribution than printed protests, being targeted at the rich upper sections of society—precisely those members of the politically literate nation that the opposi-tion wished to influence. The newsletters carried the text of the protests alongside news of the opposition's parliamentary activities and appeared a couple of days after the event, sometimes even the very next day.[59]

This level of sustained propaganda required a highly developed political organization, not only for publication of protests but also for organizing and encouraging attendance at Parliament, particularly when it is remembered that the opposition did not have access to the financial resources of the government.

Not only did the early eighteenth century witness the "rage of party" and the development of more sophisticated party organization, it also was an era in which the administration sought tighter control over Parliament through better management. This was as true of the House of Lords as it was of the Commons.[60] One of the management techniques developed was the pre-sessional meeting of pro-ministerial peers at which the government unveiled the monarch's speech and sought the support of those present. Similar meetings also appear to have taken place during the sitting of the House. Though we cannot be sure that Cowper's group adopted the technique of the pre-sessional meeting, evidence does survive of a campaign of summoning sympathetic peers and bishops (or at least those it was hoped would be sympathetic) to the 1721–22 session.[61]

Once supporters had arrived at Westminster, the maintenance of a momentum of activity and attendance, plus the necessity to react quickly to events, led to regular meetings of the leadership of the opposition. There is clear evidence that Cowper's group developed a tactical meeting prior to the sitting of the House—a sort of "shadow cabinet." The French ambassador reported in December 1721 that it was "customary for the opposition peers to hold a meeting each morning before going to parliament, where it is probable that they planned their debates, issues and protests"; a fact confirmed by an English newsletter, which announced that the previous day the duke of Wharton, who had just deserted the opposition for the ministry, "did not come to the meeting as usual, before they went to the house."[62]

The organizing of protests was not an easy matter. By the standing orders of the Lords, the text of a protest and the signatures had to be entered into the Journals by the end of the next sitting of the House.[63] This did not always mean the following day, particularly if a protest was made on a Saturday. Nevertheless, the composition of a protest in such a short time, which was agreeable to the majority of those who voted with the opposition, required a good organization and an agreement in principle on policy between the main leaders. The high percentage of supporters of the opposition who regularly signed the protests testifies to this, and unavoidable absence may probably account for some failures to sign protests.

The organizational ability to deliver protests quickly was put to a further test when on 3 March 1722 the standing orders were altered so that protests had to be entered before prayers on the next sitting and signed before the House rose on the same day. If the next sitting was on the following day (as it was in the majority of cases), this meant that the protests had to be entered into the Journal by 2 p.m.[64] This change was a direct result of the opposition's protests of 17 January, 13, 19, and 20 February 1722 on the London clergy's petition over the Quakers' Bill, the Election Bill, and the votes on the navy and the national debts, which had enraged the ministry, particularly the earl of Sunderland.[65] He accused the opposition of an abuse of the right of protest, an abuse the opposition denied in a further protest of 3 March.[66] The four offending protests were ordered to be expunged from the Journal, an echo of the actions of the ministry in 1712.[67]

This restriction placed on protests was intended by Sunderland to diminish, if not cut off, the flow of protests. He had been particularly angered at their publication, claiming "it was grown customary to protest even against bills that were passed into law, and to get them printed, and handed about in coffee-houses, and sent over the kingdom, to inflame the minds of the people against the administration."[68] The record number of 33 protests in the following session of 1722–23 is eloquent testimony to the failure of Sunderland's plan and to the organization of the opposition. Clearly Cowper was helped by the revelation, investigation, and subsequent trial of the Jacobite plotters (particularly Bishop Atterbury a prominent member of the House) which aroused interest perhaps unprecedented since the trial of Dr. Sacheverell in 1710. All but 3 of the 33 protests of this session were directly connected to the plot and its ramifications. The higher level of turnout for the opposition reflected in the voting and protesting figures was boosted by extra Tory support appalled at the ministry's attempt to destroy Atterbury and the other leaders of the opposition (including Cowper)[69] in the face of no strong legal case.[70]

Can this organization of the opposition be credited mainly to Cowper, or were others closely involved? There were several men of talent in the opposition with extensive political, administrative, diplomatic and legal experience, not least Atterbury and Strafford. No doubt the former's literary and propaganda talents were used, and there is evidence that Strafford was involved in organizing support for the opposition within the City of London.[71] The evidence for the pre-sessional campaign to summon peers and bishops referred to above, does show that a small core of peers was responsible for organizing attendance at Westminster as well as tactics during Cowper's absence.[72] This identifiable group of leaders also bore the brunt of the debates in the Lords. Prominent amongst them was the duke of Wharton who had, like Cowper, been a follower of the prince of Wales and who felt himself to have been deserted as a result of the royal family's and the ministry's reconciliation in April 1720. One observer regarded the relationship of Cowper and Wharton as one of teacher and pupil.[73] Wharton was young, energetic, enthusiastic, and a talented speaker and propagandist, who undoubtedly made an impact within the opposition. He was, however, also erratic, switching from one party or faction to another as temperament or circumstances suited. On 6 December 1721 he deserted the opposition for the ministry, reputedly for money,[74] only to rejoin them in May 1723. Such a mercurial character was not the stuff of sustained and effective leadership. Nor did Atterbury's impatience, irascibility, and unpopularity with many of his Tory colleagues, not least for his negotiations with the Whig ministry in 1720–21,[75] fit him for the role of leader of the opposition. Furthermore during the opposition's most active session he was imprisoned in the Tower awaiting trial. Cowper's reputation for integrity, on the other hand, fitted him for the leadership. It enabled him to arbitrate between the various factions and groups which constituted the opposition. The regrets at his absence from Parliament expressed by colleagues point to his central importance: "we have no spirit left since your Lordship has been absent."[76] Contemporary observers were in no doubt that the management of the opposition was Cowper's, and his major participation in debates underlines this evaluation. The French ambassador even referred to the new opposition as "Cowper's cabal."[77]

In Cowper's papers at the Hertfordshire Record Office, there are a number of manuscript drafts of protests in his handwriting, often with corrections and additions inserted. These drafts cover 12 of the 64 protests for the years 1721–23.[78] For some protests there are more than one draft. Clearly these are the work of Cowper. His legal mind was well suited for the task. There is some highly questionable evidence from a Jacobite plotter that Atterbury "drew most of the Protests, and Earl Cowper revised some of them, but that his Alterations were principally [e]rasures, when the Bishop had writ too warmly."[79] There is also a statement by the bishop himself recorded in exile that:[80]

it was I . . . that made them all [the protests], and the only fault found with them, was that they was Commonly too Long, tho always to the Purpose, and I Remember one I made in objection to a project When the Plague Rag'd in france that the Citty of London should be Surround'd with Souldjers and Barracks.[81]

Both these claims are essentially given the lie by the fact that Atterbury joined the opposition after the protesting campaign had begun, that many of Cowper's drafts cover the years 1721–22 when Atterbury was a major figure in the opposition, and that the most extensive protesting took place in 1723 in Atterbury's enforced absence. The bishop may have been involved to some extent—it would be strange if he had not been—but he was not the major force behind the campaign; a fact that even Walpole recognized.[82] The survival of drafts in such numbers in Cowper's papers, when the papers belonging to other members of the opposition—notably Atterbury, Bathurst and Strafford—have produced no drafts for this period,[83] underlines Cowper's pre-eminence. There were of course the odd protests that Cowper did not sign, though this does not necessarily prove that he was not involved in their composition. Significantly no protests were entered by the opposition during Cowper's absences from London, while after his death in October 1723 the protesting campaign virtually ceased: only 1 in 1724, and only 31 in the seven years up to 1730.

III

What was the legacy of Cowper's leadership of the opposition after 1723? The immediate result of his death in October 1723 was to deprive the opposition of its powerhouse. Not only did the steam go out of the protesting campaign, but the opposition showed signs of breaking up. In the wake of Atterbury's trial the Whig Lord Lechmere, and the Tory Lords Bathurst and Gower (together with the Tory Sir William Wyndham from the Commons) made overtures to the government in July 1723. The latter three

declared themselves weary of the situation they were in, and ready to enter into any measure with your Lordship [Townshend], and your humble servant [Walpole]; . . . and were desirous to rid Themselves of this disagreeable Situation they were in by renouncing Jacobitism, etc.

Walpole, however, having found out that they had been in correspondence with Lord Carteret, his chief enemy within the ministry, responded that "it was both impossible, and unadvisable for me to enter into any such negotiation."[84] Lechmere, however, as a dissident Whig, was to be cultivated.[85]

After the death of Cowper there were reports that the ministry were "the absolute power in both Houses of Parliament," and that the Tories showed indolence, inactivity, and "almost despair" so that "they have indeed great reason to appear quiet and to act with the utmost caution."[86]

The gloom that quickly settled over the opposition persisted for some years, Orrery reporting in 1724 that "many of the Tories thinking it better to lye still, and to give no provocation where there is no prospect of success," and in 1725 that the parliamentary campaign was "indolent and careless."[87] None the less protests continued to be entered into the Journal, though in fewer numbers, and they continued to be published and appear in newsletters.[88]

Tory, and particularly Jacobite pessimism in these years was probably more a product of the close shave the party had experienced with the Atterbury plot and the ministerial witch-hunt which followed than of their loss of Cowper, though no leader of the opposition was to emerge who commanded the respect Cowper had done and who had his powers of leadership. Eventually Strafford appears to have been the man who stepped into Cowper's shoes.

The mid-1720s were relatively quiet in parliamentary terms, and the opposition did not really revive until the late 1720s when a new group of Whig dissidents joined with the Tories to form what became known as the "Patriot party." This phenomenon, which lasted throughout the 1730s, shared much of its ideology with Cowper's group. They also carried on many of Cowper's techniques of opposition: there is evidence of sessional meetings designed to organize tactical responses to the ministry, and a growth of protesting intended to probe and exploit ministerial weaknesses.[89] Though protests in the 1730s and 1740s never reached the level of the early 1720s, they continued to be published in significant numbers, and this carried on throughout the eighteenth century. It has been shown that a reasonable level of protesting coupled with extensive publishing (this time in newspapers) proved effective for such opposition groups as the Rockinghamites.[90] All this clearly owed its origins to Cowper and the opposition of the early 1720s. Cowper proved there was a place for propaganda emanating from the upper House in opposition to the ministry. His example influenced succeeding generations of oppositions. Bolingbroke may well be seen as the heir to this tradition. Cowper, by showing that opposition despite being heavily outnumbered could mount an effective campaign both in and out of the Lords' chamber, may well have been partly responsible for keeping alive the Tory party as an effective rump of opposition. He certainly helped generate a climate of opinion whereby opposition to the king's government became an accepted part of the British constitution.

CHAPTER 3

The Bedchamber Lord: Basil, Sixth Earl of Denbigh

MICHAEL W. MCCAHILL

In one of his recent books Jonathan Clark asserts that the court was a major power center in the political life of eighteenth-century England. It was a self-contained world, in which the voice of the people was more a rhetorical than an actual reality, in which grand political designs usually gave way to considerations that were personal and petty. Moved as well by a sense that the nobility's role was to serve the sovereign, courtiers often found themselves trapped within the charmed circle. Most could only find the interest, power, and profit they sought within its confines, for they tended to lack the talent or the individual power base that might enable them to make a mark on their own. Yet, even at court, the greatest rewards went to those who possessed sufficient subtlety and dexterity to adjust their sails to the fluctuations of the prevailing winds.[1]

Dr. Clark's work, the most recent assessment of the place of the court in the eighteenth-century structure of power, provides a starting point for a study of Basil, sixth earl of Denbigh (1719–1800), the subject of this essay. Denbigh spent much of his childhood on the continent. His first public act, in seeming defiance of his father's Jacobite sympathies, was to raise and command a company of foot in the wake of the 1745 invasion.[2] Subsequently, he was an active commander of the Warwickshire militia as well as a justice of the peace for many years. In February 1760 he received a pension of £1,000 from George II, becoming at the same time a privy councillor, a position to which he was reappointed by George III. Through the influence of Lords Bute and Temple he was made Master of the Royal Harriers in 1761, retaining the office till its abolition in 1782; from 1763 until 1800 Denbigh also served as a lord of the Bedchamber. He was an active member of the House of Lords from his accession to the earldom in 1755 until the mid-1780s.

Though he held only minor offices, Denbigh was a controversial figure in his own time. Whigs such as Horace Walpole or the third duke of
Richmond dismissed him as a "creature" of Lord Bute. Walpole obviously
despised this "lowest and most officious of the Court tools" and remarked
that his intended second wife, the widow of Sir Charles Halford, "certainly
can never have a more disagreeable suitor."[3] Yet the Chathamite Lords
Camden and Temple remained friends even after Denbigh went over to
Bute: Temple, who dubbed him "your Eagleship" in celebration of the
earl's enormous nose, met periodically with Denbigh to try to settle business between the opposing groups they represented in the House of
Lords.[4] Likewise, successive government leaders of the House reiterated
their appreciation of his services there. Like his contemporaries historians
have regarded Denbigh variously, classifying him as a "snarling courtier,"
a high Tory grandee or an "independent in the House of Lords." Nor is
this lack of consensus surprising, for, as Governor Thomas Hutchinson
noted after their first meeting, "Lord Denbigh is a singular character, full
of words, &c."[5]

His financial status provides one clue to understanding Denbigh.
During his adult life he received several large infusions of funds. As a
young man he won enough gambling to rebuild the family seat, Newnham
Paddox. Each of his two wives brought with her a substantial fortune, and
he inherited 17,000 Dutch florins from a maternal aunt as well as £20,000
from Lady Blandford, an English aunt. He was also an active landlord who
took pride in his reputation as an agricultural improver.[6]

Still, Denbigh never achieved lasting financial ease. At the end of his
gout-ridden life he complained he had "neither Legs or Money"; thirty
years earlier he had pleaded with Northington, the lord president, to in-
tervene to secure him some additional office to bolster his situation.[7] His
difficulties had several sources. Denbigh's was not a rich family: his mother
and sisters received royal pensions before him. Poverty led to the loss of
an estate after his accession, and the earl compounded his problems by
spending large sums unsuccessfully at the Leicester election of 1768. Even
more burdensome were expenses arising from his military career and that
of Lord Feilding, his son. As late as 1767 he was complaining of debts
incurred as a result of raising his company in 1745, and he laid out large
sums to launch Feilding's career, only to find the latter reduced to half pay
at the same time reformers abolished the more lucrative of Denbigh's own
court offices.[8]

To relieve his situation Denbigh turned to the government. After
overcoming the king's objections, Newcastle secured him a £1,000 pension
in 1760. The next year, probably through Bute's influence, he received the

lucrative mastership of the Harriers, and in 1763 he became a lord of the bedchamber at Bute's request.[9] Though these two offices increased his income by at least £2,400, they did not eliminate his need. Thus, in 1762 and again in 1764 he applied for the Post Office under the mistaken notion that it would enlarge his income; in 1767 he once more appealed for assistance. While nothing came of these requests, Denbigh did receive the legacies from his aunts. Possibly as a result, there is no record of further applications until 1784 following the abolition of the mastership of the Harriers and the launching of Feilding's military career. Soon after his accession both the father and the son pressed Pitt to make the latter vice-chamberlain of the king's household, hinting at diminished future support if the post was not forthcoming.[10]

Denbigh was only one of a number of lords who turned to the court out of financial necessity. To maintain their dignity the fourth earl of Essex and the fourth Lord Onslow had to receive secret service pensions in addition to their salaries as lords of the bedchamber, the latter because of huge debts which led his creditors to attach his house. In 1779 the second Viscount Wentworth lamented that his affairs were in so bad a state that "I despair of ever setting them to rights." Eventually he was persuaded by his friends to become a place hunter: "my poverty not my will consents, & perhaps I may soon have the Superlative Honour of putting on the King's Shirt."[11]

Though Denbigh was one of a group of peers drawn to the court out of financial necessity, he was not a typical courtier. Many of the latter lacked interest in politics or national affairs. Wentworth, for example, confessed in 1782 that he knew little about politics and, since he was unlikely to gain by them, cared even less. The fourth earl of Jersey, who served as a lord of the bedchamber from 1769 to 1777, reminded his correspondents that he took little part in politics, and the historian of their family concluded that the three Brudenell peers of the late eighteenth century chose the court of George III as the focus for their activity because they were insufficiently talented to make a mark in Parliament.[12] What distinction these noblemen achieved came as a result of their participation in the ritual of the court, not because of their behind the scenes political maneuvers.

Denbigh attended to his undemanding court duties. The Harriers took care of themselves; there is no reference in his correspondence to duties attached to a job which did not, in any case, involve proximity to majesty. However, the twelve or thirteen bechamber lords divided among themselves weekly waitings on George III according to a roster prepared by the Groom of the Stole in consultation with the king. When in waiting, a lord escorted his monarch on the round of formal duties, to church services, the theater and concerts. They danced at royal balls, attended the king as he received addresses from Parliament and other bodies and accompanied him on the English tours he launched in the 1770s. Royal birthdays were a command occasion to which lords came even in the most difficult circumstances, and they participated in special court ceremonies such as weddings and funerals. Proximity to the monarch enabled a few including Lord Onslow or the duke of Roxburghe to become close friends of George III. Others such as Jersey or the second Earl Harcourt counted the queen, the prince of Wales or one or more of the princesses as friends or correspondents.[13]

Denbigh's rustic manners and bombastic nature precluded such intimacies. He enjoyed bawdy stories, and his conversation was peppered with oaths: Sophia Curzon could hardly "sit at Dinner, & indeed was oblig'd to leave the room immediately afterwards, as Ld D forced all to go by his *shocking* conversation." The earl's flow of talk was as endless as it was colorful; even his friends found him tiresome. After one of his visits to Kirkby, Wentworth reported that Denbigh was as "ridiculous as ever"; in 1784 he was reluctant to visit Newnham because its owner had "grown so captious, deaf & covetous, that he is a great Boar."[14] Nor did George III care for Denbigh. The king had a low opinion of his abilities and recognized that his tendency to exaggerate made him an unreliable source of political intelligence. During the 1790s, when illness prevented his appearance at court, Wentworth occasionally reported to Denbigh that the king asked for news of him. But aside from the report that the queen was pleased by a Stilton cheese he sent her, these casual inquiries are the only testaments of royal favor or interest in the earl's letterbooks.[15]

However, it was Denbigh's sense of his political role and responsibilities more than his deficient manners that prevented him from joining the inner circle of courtiers. A self-proclaimed "country peer," the earl was less concerned to serve the person of the king than to uphold his service. This he did by taking an active part in the affairs of Warwickshire and Leicestershire and by devoting substantial time and energy to the business of the House of Lords.

Periodically Denbigh reported to his correspondents his satisfaction at being a "plane Country Squire." In fact, he was a prominent local leader who was an attentive, active commander of the Warwickshire militia. During the Seven Years War, for example, the earl browbeat the War Office into relieving his force of inappropriate duties and improving its barracks at Salisbury and Portsmouth.[16] In an era when few peers performed the duties of justice of the peace, Denbigh took on those responsibilities both in Leicestershire and Warwickshire where the dearth of other justices in his vicinity or their constant drunkenness added substantially to his burden.[17]

Denbigh also participated in local electoral politics. The fact that his interest in Warwickshire was modest did not prevent his trying unsuccessfully to influence the return of a county member. However, he devoted most of his energies to enlarging the Corporation interest at Leicester. In this role he lobbied ministers for military commissions and ecclesiastical livings as well as for such posts as window keeper or collector of stamps. Indeed, he told North in 1771 that previous ministers had "generally favoured me by taking my recommendations for the little offices under Govt that have become vacant in that Country."[18] In addition he was assiduous in attending town ceremonies, subscribed to the Leicester Infirmary of which he was a vice-president and helped promote the canal and paving bills that transformed Leicester as well as other towns at the end of the eighteenth century. His endeavors did not obtain the electoral successes he anticipated, but they did earn the gratitude of his allies for the "many Signal favours you have from time to time confer'd upon this Corporation."[19]

However, for much of the year the House of Lords was the focus of Denbigh's energy and interest. David Large has established that the court peers were especially active in attending the House of Lords during the 1780s. Likewise, about a quarter of the 75 peers Professor Lowe identifies as regularly attending twenty or more times a session between 1760 and 1775 held court office.[20] Between 1756 and 1790 Lord Denbigh's average attendance was 40.2 meetings per session, even though during the early years militia duties kept him away from London just as ill health increasingly prevented his attendance after 1782. During his active period, 1762–84, his average attendance was 47.8 days per session. In the 1760s and 1770s only half a dozen other court peers compiled a record of participation that began to compare with Denbigh's: none of these peers was as assiduous in leaving his proxy, nor did any attend as actively over the entire twenty-year period.[21]

Clearly attendance at the House was a priority for Denbigh. Like all government supporters he received a ministerial summons from successive leaders of the House for meetings at the opening of a session and for important debates. However, his unusual level of activity entitled the earl to special treatment. In 1772 he reminded Lord Rochford, the leader, that "we agreed I should not mind an office summons, but that you wou'd write to me yourself if my attendance was necessary." Sometimes these summonses were unwelcome. Denbigh disliked fall meetings; that in November 1767 was all the more unpleasant because opposition politicians "thought proper to deal forth more Billingsgate than I ever remember to have heard in Parlt." Its only effect, the earl complained, was to keep him longer in "this filthy house." Yet, so long as the special notes were forthcoming, Denbigh's sense of duty compelled him to attend. In June 1767 he left Newnham where he was enjoying fine weather and his family after receiving an urgent note from Grafton's secretary. In 1770 his physician ordered Denbigh to Bath to seek a cure for his gout, yet he scheduled his trip only after learning when Parliament would assemble. Likewise, in the 1780s and 1790s an elderly, deaf, and semi-crippled Denbigh regularly assured Lords Sydney and Grenville that in addition to leaving his proxy in friendly hands, he would attend in person if there was a special need.[22]

In addition to attending important divisions and debates, many lords came to the House to support or oppose bills that touched on their own interests and those of friends. Denbigh was a careful guardian of his personal needs who also received applications of assistance from neighbors and political allies. These testify both to his skill as a parliamentary maneuverer and to his willingness to advance the interests of his locality.[23] When a measure in which he was interested ran into trouble, Lord Bute called upon the earl, who had continued to visit him regularly after his departure from office. Denbigh assured Bute "we would not have been *run so near on the commitment* of the Bill had I the least idea of an opposition"; he took charge of the measure, which passed without further incident. Samuel Garbett, the Birmingham manufacturer, especially admired Denbigh's legislative prowess. In 1769 he thanked the earl for the

cleverness with which you saved our Lamp Bill at a critical moment, for which my Neighbours have a very high sense of gratitude as well of your acuteness as Influence to effect it whilst the Petitioners against it were at the door of the house of Lords with their Petition. I don't ever expect so much pleasure from the lamps, as I have from the manner in which you picked the proper time for passing the bill and confirming to this Town what I have always said of your alertness & Precision whenever you patronize anything.[24]

As well as tending his own legislative interests and those of his friends or neighbors, Lord Denbigh also helped to manage the flow of legislative business through the House. During the 1771–72 session he and Lord Boston stood in as chairman of the committees while the first Viscount Wentworth retired to the continent on doctors' orders. Boston, who immersed himself in the details of legislative business and filled in for Wentworth again in 1773 before becoming acting chairman for the 1774 session, performed much of the business. In contrast, Denbigh, who chaired a dozen committees in 1771–72, took on the job out of friendship: in 1770 he had recommended to Weymouth, the new leader of the House, that the chairmanship be bestowed on Wentworth, a fellow "country lord." However, he never shared Boston's passion for managing details of legislative business and used his wife's poor health as an excuse for not taking on the role again in 1773.[25]

In fact, Denbigh devoted most of his attention to the Lords' political rather than its procedural management. Shortly before he resigned the Treasury in 1762, the duke of Newcastle sniffed that he would do what he could "to prevent the House of Lords from being govern'd either by My Lord Denbigh or My Lord Marchmont."[26] Nor was this merely another expression of the duke's notorious peevishness. During the first two decades of George III's reign Denbigh took a lead in sustaining the government's hold over the House of Lords.

In this role he performed a variety of tasks. Between 1758 and 1778 Denbigh acted as teller for the government's position at 26 divisions, a job that required some expertise as well as good eyesight. After 1775 the earl's activity as a teller fell off sharply, partly because he lacked close ties to Suffolk and Stormont, the Lords' leaders from 1775 to 1782, but primarily because his sight deterioriated. Lord Jersey wrote of Denbigh in 1776: "Bishops & Peers he can fish out when they are to vote in the H. of Lords, but I do not know that he can see any other living Creature." In fact, he told only three divisions after 1776.[27] However, he continued to act as unofficial whip, especially to other court peers. Thus, the bishop of Lichfield complained to Lord Pelham, master of the wardrobe, that he "was so attacked by that active minister Ld Denbigh, & so uncertain about the thoughts of Ld Rochford" that he had to recommend that Pelham come up from Sussex to attend the House as Denbigh demanded. The earl advised a number of the king's friends on their parliamentary attendance, emphasizing that they should appear at the opening of the session and at other major contests between government and its opponents. He also saw to it that those who did not attend dispatched proxies either to him or to others of the administration's friends. Even Lord Hillsborough, a substantial political figure, turned to Denbigh for information as to when he should attend because "as You know I consider you our Leader in the House of Lords."[28]

Denbigh assisted political leaders as well as other peers with various aspects of the Lords' management. He took credit for the appointment of Wentworth to chair the committees.[29] While at the Treasury, Grafton entrusted him with the management of his divorce bill in the upper House, just as the eighth duke of Hamilton looked to Denbigh to take a lead in overturning the 1711 order that barred Scottish peers from taking their seats by right of a British peerage. Periodically he also communicated with the opposition, especially through his friend Temple, to try to arrange a satisfactory schedule of business in the Lords.[30]

It was while the fourth earl of Rochford served as its rather hesitant leader (1770–75) that Denbigh enjoyed his greatest prominence in the House of Lords. The two were friends and frequent correspondents, and because of his diplomatic postings, Rochford had limited experience in the House or knowledge of its members.[31] Thus, he called upon Denbigh to edit lists of peers to be invited to the leader's meeting at the opening of the session. Denbigh also helped identify and enlist lords to move and second addresses. Beyond these chores, he advised Rochford on procedural and tactical matters and was usually one of a small group summoned to meetings to prepare strategies and polish arguments for upcoming debates.[32]

These last sessions were of special importance to him because Lord Denbigh was an eager speaker who made a mark in the House by his distinctive contributions to its debates. At his best he was a forceful, witty participant. Richard Rigby reported after the Lords' final debate on the Cider Bill in 1763 that the earl made "a speech of more wit and good sense mixed together with it than almost I ever heard: such a one as if Lord Chesterfield had made it, would have been immortalized. He silenced Lord Temple completely." Bute, who found himself unsupported even by cabinet colleagues on this occasion, so appreciated Denbigh's performance that he got George III to make his advocate a lord of the bedchamber.[33]

What leaders valued in Denbigh was his combativeness. Walpole claimed Newcastle had bestowed the Harriers on Denbigh in 1761 because he feared his "brutality in the House of Lords." The earl had no qualms about abusing his adversaries, and so the Duke's successors in the Lords also curried his favor while they pressed for his attendance at debates. Thus, Rochford appealed for him to attend deliberations on the Dissenters' Bill in 1772, "for we have no match for Lord Chathams Billingsgates amongst us when you are absent." Hillsborough wrote on another occasion expressing the hope that the earl's voice would be "in good order to thunder in the Senate."[34]

Denbigh relished his role in debates as much as his leaders relied on his services. In 1774 he apologized to Rochford for his absence while the House considered American legislation:

Could I have conceived that Lord Chatham would have attended nothing should have prevented my being present for tho' there are many parts of the Bill which I highly disapprove of, yet I shall always think it my duty as far as in me lies to check the vehemance [sic] of that noble Lord's career, especially when it is directed as in the present instance to drive millions into faction and rebellion.[35]

Beginning in 1770 the two engaged in ongoing skirmishes. In December Chatham intervened to protest Denbigh's dismissal of monied men in the House of Commons as "muckworms." Though Chatham claimed "that as an old friend he only meant to set Lord Denbigh right," the latter refused to be bullied and went on to finish his remarks. Several years later, when Chatham condemned the use of native Americans against rebellious colonists, Lord Denbigh first reminded his adversary that he had recruited similar allies against the French during the Seven Years War and then dismissed him as "the great oracle with the short memory."[36]

In fact, Denbigh took on the whole range of government's critics. In 1765 he ridiculed Newcastle for opposing the Regency Bill, a measure that largely duplicated one the duke had authored earlier, and suggested that age had made the duke "forget one of his favorite children." Likewise, he attacked the formidable Lord Mansfield for venturing to support the Chatham administration's opponents in 1767 and, fourteen years later, rejected as ignorant and absurd the earl of Shelburne's contention that Rodney's capture of St. Eustatius "was an instance of perfidy."[37] However, his favorite opponent was the third duke of Richmond, who himself disliked Denbigh. Richmond's onslaught against Chatham in December 1766 provoked Denbigh to comment "that his Grace was as usual absurdly in the wrong." For his part Richmond attacked Denbigh as a bully and a tool of Lord Bute. Given their mutual antipathy, contests between the two were frequent and lively. When the duke in 1775 attacked a bill prohibiting commerce with rebellious Americans as "cruel, oppressive, tyrannic," Denbigh criticized him for "reprehensible and disorderly expression." No act of the king, Lords and Commons, he proclaimed, could be tyrannical, and he ended by announcing that "those who defend rebellion are themselves little better than rebels; and that there is very little difference between the traitor, and he who openly abets treason." Richmond refused "to be intimidated or deterred from my duty by loud words" and, in an allusion to Denbigh's Jacobite connections, remarked that "there are no traitors in this House now a days."[38]

However, the earl did not reserve his attacks exclusively for opposition luminaries. Early in his career he challenged the earl of Hardwicke on Pitt's bill to extend Habeas Corpus and taunted Lord Marchmont for his

Jacobite associations when the two differed on the Seaman's Wages Bill in 1758.[39] His opposition to the claims of the Church in Chaplin v. Bree, a tithe case, provoked a determined riposte from the archbishop of Canterbury, and he battled so fiercely with his friend Lord Sandwich over the Speaker's Warrant Bill that Lord Sandys, who was in the chair, moved for a conference with the Commons in order to halt their wrangle. Denbigh triumphed in this contest, for the House soon passed the bill Sandwich opposed. However, he was less successful in his challenge to the earl of Mansfield's legal eminence. The prose of Debrett's *Parliamentary Register* reflects what must have been general astonishment at Denbigh when he "very unexpectedly ventured into competition with the learned Lord who spoke last [Mansfield], concerning the regularity and necessary form of their Lordships' proceedings." This rare, if misguided protest was unavailing. "Not a syllable was offered in reply" to Denbigh, and Mansfield's motion quickly passed.[40] Still, this and other incidents reveal that Walpole's craven courtier was something of a terror in the House of Lords where he was prepared to give emphatic expression to his political beliefs and attachments.

Through his activities in Parliament Denbigh hoped to contribute to the establishment of firm government under the aegis of the monarch. To him the central political contest of the 1760s was "whether Lord Rockingham the Newcastles & their friends, should storm the Closet door, & again assume their weak reins of Government; or whether the K. should be able to choose his own Ministers: Nay Servants." Fifteen years later the issue had hardly changed: he lamented in 1782 that the opposition was about to dictate a ministry to the king and refused a year later to have any communication with a coalition he condemned as "unnatural."[41] Denbigh looked in the 1760s for the establishment of "firm Government" and so was delighted in 1767 that "the D. of Grafton's Affability gains him new friends every day." But he was not prepared blindly to support any minister to whom the king entrusted his business. He abhorred ministerial hesitancy almost as much as factious opposition: "In my opinion the greatest Solecism that can happen in Politicks are half measures & protracting measures."[42]

The need for firm government was all the greater because of the prevalence of popular agitation and sedition at home and in America. Denbigh complained that Wilkes' resistance to law and the will of the House of Commons "Is call'd Liberty." The size and scope of the petitioning movement in 1769 alarmed him; he wanted government to take action against members of the Commons who signed petitions; he also attacked the Remonstrance of the City of London in 1770 as "a false, lying, scandalous & seditious Paper" whose authors should be punished.[43] Infuriated by a press that took up Wilkes's cause, he became the scourge of reporters who dared, in violation of the Lords' standing orders, to report on its proceedings or malign its members. Thus, he invariably moved for the arrest of journalists who authored such reports; "lenity mis-applied always does more harm than good," he informed Lord Beauchamp. Denbigh was also one of the authors of the remarkable scene which transpired in the House of Lords on 10 December 1770. As the duke of Manchester introduced a motion regarding the garrisoning of Gibraltar, he was interrupted by Lord Gower, the lord president, who moved that the House be cleared of strangers, including members of the Commons, on the grounds that a Spanish agent might be lurking in the gallery. A mob scene ensued with Lords Marchmont and Denbigh at the head of the pack. According to Isaac Barré, a Chathamite,

it seemed as if the mob had broken in, and they certainly behaved in a very extraordinary manner. One of the heads of this mob for there were two, was a Scotchman [Marchmont]. I heard him call out several times Clear the Hoose! Clear the Hoose! The face of the other [Denbigh] was hardly human; for he contrived to put on a nose of enormous size that disfigured him completely.

Not surprisingly, the earl was disappointed when the House, in his absence, agreed to readmit strangers in December 1774 thereby opening the way for regular reporting of the Lords' proceedings.[44]

Denbigh also opposed the Americans' pretensions. Deploring what he saw as the tendency of men ambitious for power to incite the Americans to rebellion, he urged his colleagues in the House to show the colonists that no subject could be "safe under any species of protection whatever, but such as the laws and constitution afford."[45] Because he rejected the legitimacy of American claims and was ever the opponent of half measures, he was proud that North's peace proposals in 1778 "had not the Sanction of my Vote." If conciliation in his eyes was pusillanimous, the more extreme possibility—independence—was unthinkable: "whatever minister advises the *King* to that idea I must as an Englishman, whenever the opportunity offers, Vote him to be hanged."[46]

Despite his uncompromising views Denbigh was uneasy about the ministry's war strategies. He questioned the wisdom of a major military action in America, believing it was better to withdraw the troops and impose a naval blockade. To impress Americans and Englishmen with the Crown's determination to quell rebellion, he advocated "sending a Duke or any peer or two to the Tower, if they continue to hold the same language in Parliament." Such a tactic would "go farther towards settling matters in America than winning a battle."[47] Unfortunately, ministers adopted the military strategy half-heartedly and ineffectually. Even before news of Saratoga Lord Denbigh dismissed the 1777 campaign as "very bad and disgracefull" and predicted that the government would face an invigorated opposition when Parliament reassembled. Increasingly it seemed beyond the capacity of ministers or their military and naval advisors to devise and execute an effective strategy. In the face of deepening crisis the politicians were at best irresolute, at worst consumed by quarrels among themselves. Thus, by the summer of 1778 he wrote despondently to Thomas De Grey, under secretary for the colonies, expressing his wish for peace: "(excepting your Lord [George Germain]) we have not a Minister able to plan, or an Admiral or General to execute any military operations that can do credit to this country." Yet, because the Americans would accept nothing less than independence, Denbigh had to stand behind ineffectual ministers who were at least prepared to resist those claims.[48]

After the end of the American War and the grant of colonial independence Denbigh became an observer rather than a participant in parliamentary affairs. He only attended two parliamentary sessions more than twenty times after the accession of Pitt, and only one report of a speech by him survives from these years. Instead, he expressed himself indirectly through the proxies he bestowed on Lords Thurlow, Amherst, and Boston and through the letters he addressed his friends. Though age left Denbigh nearly blind, quite deaf, and intermittently crippled by gout, his infirmities did not diminish his interest in political affairs or soften his views.

From its outset Denbigh was uneasy about Pitt's administration. In 1784 he fretted that "our Bottom is but very narrow, and our Cabinet somewhat flimsey." Nor did success at elections eliminate the need to refurbish the ministry. "For the good of our Master, I most sincerely wish the downy chins of our juvenile Ministers may be strengthened." He worried about Pitt's tendency to compromise and complained that minister adopted half measures to combat radicalism in the 1790s. Like many country gentlemen, Denbigh was skeptical about the wisdom of committing British troops on the continent. His doubts regarding this strategy and a yearning for peace increased as Britain experienced defeats abroad and economic hardship at home.[49] However, what most disturbed him was Pitt's attraction to reform. Denbigh dismissed Pitt's plan for parliamentary reform in 1785 as foolish and cast one of his last votes by proxy against a bill to prohibit the slave trade on portions of the African coast. Having offered tactical advice to that measure's opponents, he rejoiced at their victory, a victory, he claimed, that did him more good than any physician's tonic, especially as it was secured by the solid resistance of the lords of the bedchamber. Only the king's support for the measure could have induced him not to give his proxy against it.[50]

Despite his occasional willingness to consult the king's views, throughout the 1760s and early 1770s Denbigh described himself and his friends as "country lords." At Newnham the earl entertained neighbors who, he claimed, looked to him to explain public events at Westminster. In return he gained insights into their sentiments which he regularly conveyed to politicians between 1760 and 1782. Professor Brewer claims he had as good a sense of the country gentlemen's views as any peer.[51] The elder Pitt was careful to give country gentlemen such as Denbigh a sense that they had a part to play in the conduct of the Seven Years War though the two disagreed in 1760 about how those gentlemen felt about sending British troops to Germany; even George III turned to the earl when he wanted to learn of their attitude to the government in 1772.[52] For his part, Denbigh never hesitated to educate politicians on "country" attitudes. He warned Bute that independents would not take kindly to his alliance with Henry Fox, and, according to Grenville, later worked to induce country gentlemen to desert him and support the Chatham administration. During the 1770s he urged, on their behalf, that the duke of Beaufort be named lord lieutenant of Monmouthshire in 1771 and warned the leader of the House that country gentlemen would ignore calls to attend the opening of Parliament as early as November. By 1777 Denbigh recognized that their patience with the lack of military progress was wearing thin; shortly before the news of Yorktown arrived, he informed John Robinson that "you will not find the country Gentlemen so Steedy [sic] in the Support of the American War as they have hitherto been."[53]

Yet, during his early years in the House this self-proclaimed country lord attached himself to politicians to whom he looked for place and patronage. At first he allied himself to a childhood friend, Earl Temple, and through him to Pitt who was beginning to attract independent and Tory support. Denbigh's correspondence reveals the degree to which he relied on the Pittites to procure him a place in 1760. The fact that Bute probably obtained the Harriers for him and was expeditious in handling other patronage requests made it all the easier to switch allegiances to him after Pitt's resignation.[54] Lack of similar consideration weakened his ties to Grenville just as Grafton's failure to bestow a cathedral stall on a cousin diminished Denbigh's enthusiasm for that minister. His annoyance at

Pitt's refusal to find a place for his son as much as his poor health kept him away from the House of Lords for much of the 1785 session.[55]

Though Denbigh expected successive ministers to bestow favors on him and his friends, he only attached himself personally to one of them—Lord Bute. During the debates on the Cider Tax in the Lords Bute's cabinet colleagues sat quietly while the opposition lambasted their leader; only Denbigh and Lord Pomfret came to his defense. The earl made regular visits to Bute after the latter's retirement, and in 1765 Grenville correctly interpreted Denbigh's absence at the pre-sessional meeting as a sign of the favorite's hostility to his government. Denbigh joined several of Bute's followers to oppose the Poor Bill, a privately sponsored measure strongly supported by the duke of Bedford.[56]

However, Denbigh and Bute made their most energetic foray into opposition against the repeal of the Stamp Act in 1766. Bute, with many of his followers, opposed retreat in the face of American agitation, and their opposition was made all the easier by the king's open toleration of it. In January 1766 Denbigh and another of Bute's followers went to George III, told him they would oppose repeal and offered to resign their places, but the king said "that they *were at liberty to vote against him and keep their places*." Denbigh agreed not to speak against the measure. Otherwise, he did all he could to insure its defeat. In addition to voting against repeal in February and March, he was one of the friends of Bute to spread the rumor in the Commons that the king disapproved of the bill, a rumor whose repetition complicated the measure's passage and permanently soured relations between the monarch and the Rockinghams. Moreover, at the height of the crisis he and Temple tried to patch up relations between Bute and Grenville and Bedford as a means of driving Rockingham from office.[57]

This effort failed, and Denbigh never again bound himself so closely to a political leader. He liked Grafton but was critical of the half-measures he adopted against Wilkite opposition. Though he supported North on the American War, he confessed he had "no particular connections" with that minister, and he detested the Coalition. "For as long as this unnatural Coalition lasts," he wrote, "I neither can as an honest man, or a good subject, have the least concern with them."[58] If he developed a tie to any politician, it was with Lord Chancellor Thurlow, another crony of George III's, whose relations with Pitt were even more ambivalent than Denbigh's. In 1788 the earl announced he would pledge himself in politics until he knew the chancellor's views, and in 1790 he professed to want no "Conection with any other of his Majesty's Ministers but such as concur

with me in Your Integrity, Honor, and Ability." Unfortunately, this association ended by embarrassing Denbigh. Ever more hostile to Pitt and his
associates, Thurlow not only voted against a measure the king favored in
1792; he cast Denbigh's proxy against it as well, though without the earl's
permission. In consequence the latter had to dispatch several letters to
assure Lord Grenville of his attachment.[59]

Courtiers, who were never as submissive to the Crown as Whigs
claimed, sometimes opposed ministerial policies over a sustained period.
George III complained during the 1760s of court peers who voted in opposition but was slow to take action against these mavericks. Lords Buckinghamshire and Eglintoun followed Grenville and the duke of Bedford in
opposing first Rockingham's, then Lord Chatham's administrations but
only lost their posts in November 1767; Lord Coventry, an independent
follower of Grenville, and the duke of Manchester, a Rockinghamite, continued at once to vote in opposition and retain posts in the bedchamber
until their resignations in 1770. Likewise the fourth earl of Jersey kept his
bedchamber post for two years after joining the opposition to the American War in 1775, just as Lord Carmarthen and the tenth earl of Pembroke
retained theirs after they joined that opposition during the 1779–80 session.[60] Some who avoided sustained resistance managed to retain their
posts indefinitely even though they spoke or voted against the government. George III condemned the first Earl Talbot in 1763 for "conduct the
whole winter [that] has been unaccountable, either silent in the house or
attacking friends and commending foes." North later dismissed Talbot
as "pernicious," for, as Denbigh explained in 1772, "excepting in matters
where the King's wishes are to be gratified I am convinced he will be glad
of any opportunity to oppose Ld North."[61] Nevertheless, Talbot remained
lord steward from 1761 to 1782.

However, the king's friends usually refrained from skirmishes with
ministers. Even Talbot acknowledged that he never considered the possibility of joining the opposition. Instead, courtiers, including Denbigh,
advertised their dislike of ministers and their policies more by their absence than by public criticism. The two instances of Denbigh's open opposition, against the repeal of the Stamp Act and the Coalition's India Bill,
occurred in extraordinary circumstances; in both cases the politicians who
led the oppositions claimed to be acting on the king's wishes against his
own ministers. Far more characteristic of Denbigh's approach was a letter
telling Lord Loudon "if government will support itself, I will most certainly come up & give it all the Assistance I can: but if not, and the Ministers continue to quarrell amongst themselves, I shall think myself better

where I am."[62] Friends of the king commonly acted in this manner. For example, the fourth duke of Queensberry, who opposed continuation of the war by 1797, told Lady Holland that he refused to attend the House because he had made "a resolution never to vote against Government," a position Archbishop Drummond of York took more than thirty years earlier.[63]

Despite his strong views and his frequent, if private criticisms of ministers, Denbigh's conduct was more that of the king's friend than the classic country gentleman. The latter, according to Dr. Kemp, devoted his energies to insuring that the Crown did not dominate Parliament; he looked not so much for smooth government as for an independent Commons and was suspicious of the influence of all administrations.[64] In contrast, Denbigh devoted his energies to strengthening the government position in Parliament. He defended administration policies in debates, served as an unofficial whip and adviser to leaders of the House and was diligent in his personal attendance. In all these ways he fulfilled an obligation that he believed bound peers to the king, and he encouraged friends to equal diligence. Thus, he told Lord Loudon, who was absent at the opening of the 1779–80 session, that "I therefore do most sincerely wish that you will be in town as soon as you possibly can. . . . If our Friends do not attend God knows what may happen."[65] The fruit of assiduous attendance and support was strong government and the smooth functioning of the king's business.

Moreover, Denbigh's political attitudes and instincts made him a natural ally of the Crown in an age in which the operation of government was disrupted by Wilkite agitation, American rebellion and Rockinghamite faction. Financial need dictated that he hunt for a place, and the evidence of his letters demonstrates that ministers' failures to accede to his requests dampened his enthusiasm and, in a few instances, reduced his activity. But pursuit of place never drove him openly to oppose, and his position at court only reinforced strongly held political convictions that bound him to all ministers who enjoyed firm royal sanction. Denbigh's massive letterbooks reveal only one instance of his willingness to accommodate his own position on a controversial issue to that of the king—the Slave Bill of 1799. Where other peers hastened to apologize to their sovereign when a recalcitrant son voted against an administration, the earl made no attempt to justify Lord Feilding when he joined the opposition during the Regency Crisis.[66]

Though the Whigs dismissed the earl and his colleagues as tools of the Crown, many besides Denbigh had a natural political affinity for the court. The Earl Fauconberg, a lord of the bedchamber, repeatedly asserted "his independency of fortune and independency of principle" in the House of Lords during the early 1780s and repudiated the Whigs' constant denigration of the courtiers' honor and integrity. He also thought it the duty of

every loyal subject and friend to the country to stand forth at this alarming time against both our foreign and domestic enemies; against all new-fangled opinions relative to ideal schemes of political reformation, which tended merely to create and nourish discontents, innovations which, if permitted, or encouraged, would end, he feared, in national distraction and public confusion.[67]

Even those such as the second Viscount Wentworth, who claimed to be disinterested in politics, attributed many of the nation's problems to oppositions that "by thwarting every good design, & by depreciating the wealth, the power, ye legal government (in all its branches) of this country, have given encouragement to our enemies, & made them spring up like mushrooms." He also shared Denbigh's suspicion of reform. Thus, he worried that Rockingham's second administration would try to introduce "all the utopian vagaries of the late opposition"; Pitt's proposals for parliamentary reform in 1785 were "the most absurd in my opinion possible"; by 1790 he bleakly concluded that "the whole world I think is gone Mad, & the Cursed new Political Doctrines are spreading about in all parts of the Kingdom. I can perceive but little pains to stop this gaining ground."[68]

There can be no doubt, as Dr. Clark argues, that George III's court endowed many of the nobility who served him with a status and a degree of pre-eminence they might not otherwise have attained. Proximity to a monarch who still acted as a king could not help but make them significant personages. By insuring the smooth operation of the household, by befriending their overburdened sovereign and his family, by providing him with congenial society, these men performed important public functions according to their own standards.

However, the careers of Denbigh and his court colleagues provide little evidence to sustain the assertion that the court, as distinct from the monarch, was a locus of political power. Recent scholars agree that that most maligned of courtiers, the third earl of Bute, exercised little influence over the king after his resignation in 1763.[69] As George III came more and more to deal directly with politicians or to rely on his lord chancellors as emissaries to them, there was less scope for courtiers such as Lord Waldegrave to make a political mark. Thus, aspiring politicians, even at the outset of his reign, regarded the court office as something to avoid. Lord Shelburne told Henry Fox in 1762 that:

I could not help differing from Ld Talbot, who is desirous to remain where he is, & never to be of a Cabinet, nor consulted upon business but always ready to act for the personal service of the King or Lord Bute. Men of Independent Fortune should be Trustees between King and People, & continue, I think, in whatever they do to be occupied in actions of Service to both—without being Slaves to either.[70]

Weymouth, Richmond, and Rockingham launched their careers as lords of George III's bedchamber, but they were among the last politicians of note to do so. Indeed, no peer who filled the offices at court that remained at the king's disposal went on after 1765 to enjoy more than the most modest political prominence. Nor is there evidence to show that courtiers exerted much political influence. They may have helped to shape George III's views on a few important issues including Catholic Emancipation, but such occasions were rare.[71] Instead they lent successive ministers their support in the House of Lords, usually as passive adherents. Courtiers played a negligible role in the formulation of policy or, with a few exceptions, in the passage of legislation.

Rather than make a political mark, most noble courtiers immersed themselves in the daily life of the royal family. As the court evolved from a political center into the monarch's home, the courtier's task increasingly was to accompany the king on his formal duties and insure for him and his family a comfortable, amusing and well-ordered private life; political matters were left to ministers. Perhaps nothing better reflects the developing divorce between the public business of the monarch and the private life of the royal family than the changing nature of the court chronicle. Hervey and Waldegrave, who were at least secondary political actors, achieved lasting distinction on account of their record of the court's political intrigues. The fact that the principal chroniclers of George III's court—Fanny Burney, Mrs. Delany, and Mrs. Howe—were women and, therefore, excluded from the inner political circle did not diminish the value of accounts that focused primarily on personalities and interpersonal relations. George III's court ceased early in his reign to be a platform from which to launch a political career.

If most courtiers were insignificant politically, a study of Denbigh and his associates demonstrates that these men were neither indifferent to nor insulated from public opinion. Like other peers court noblemen took a lead in local government as lords lieutenant or commanders of the militia, fencible or volunteer companies. A few were permanent habitués of London, but most spent as much time as possible on their estates where they opened their doors to neighbors and friends. In the country Denbigh saw himself as a spokesman whose task it was to explain public events and ministerial policies to his neighbors. He delighted in informing successive ministers of the attitudes of country gentlemen; even the king, who was suspicious of the earl's judgment, consulted him on this topic. Finally, he was an active proponent of the needs of his region in the House. But above all, it was public agitation by Wilkes, the Americans or radicals in the 1790s that alarmed Denbigh and his colleagues and reinforced their ties to the Crown. To no small degree the earl's political conduct and attitudes were shaped in reaction to popular sentiments and public agitation.

Of course, Denbigh, in spite of his extended court service, was never a typical member of George III's court coterie. Neither his personality nor his political interests suited the earl for the developing functions of the courtier. His interests remained political and, in a modest way, he fulfilled Shelburne's expectations for a public figure, even though he lacked a large independent fortune. Denbigh never achieved cabinet rank, nor did he aspire to political heights beyond the reach of his talents and fortune. Yet, during the 1760s and 1770s he achieved a political prominence or at least notoriety that was very different from the influence that Clark attributes to Lord Waldegrave. Independent of factional connection after Bute's retreat into obscurity, Denbigh served his monarch at court, advanced the parliamentary interests of neighbors and allies and acted as a conduit between country gentlemen and politicians in Westminster. Above all, he upheld his king's ministers and their policies in the House of Lords and was the only non-politician to play an important part in its political management during the 1760s and 1770s. In this respect Denbigh anticipates the nineteenth- and twentieth-century noble whips in the upper House who in return for their parliamentary labors became masters of the buckhounds or captains of the gentlemen at arms.[72]

Denbigh remained a minor political actor but always a controversial one. An examination of his career demonstrates that Clark overestimates both the court's importance as a power center and its insularity from public opinion. It also shows that Whig critics erred in attributing Denbigh's behavior or that of many of his colleagues to their subjection to the Crown. Denbigh achieved prominence not as a result of his maneuverings at court but in consequence of hard work on behalf of his countrymen and his own estates, attention to parliamentary business, and an ability to lambaste opponents in the House of Lords. That body remained the focus of his political interest and his energies. In his own way Denbigh was a public-spirited nobleman. His impulse to serve did not spring from any religious motive; indeed his first wife worried that her spouse was without religious feeling.[73] Instead, the earl's local endeavors sprang from a patriarchal sense of responsibility and a delight at finding himself a figure of local prominence because of his acts. The need for money propelled him to seek office but cannot account for his conduct in the House of Lords; occasional attendance at divisions there to support the positions of successive governments would have sufficed to gain him the offices he achieved. Nor did Denbigh assume qualities which provoked Walpole or the duke of Richmond to gratify ministers or please the king. His blunt political views and his aggressive behavior in the upper House were natural outgrowths of his character and political principles. He retained the instincts of a Tory and a country gentleman.

CHAPTER 4

Lord Thurlow

G. M. DITCHFIELD

Of the great lawyers who so powerfully influenced the House of Lords in the eighteenth and early nineteenth centuries—Somers, Hardwicke, Mansfield, Eldon—Thurlow has probably received the least scholarly attention. He is, perhaps, less easily labeled than his fellows; Somers was a Junto Whig, Hardwicke a Court Whig of the Newcastle years, Mansfield a Scottish (and, according to some, Jacobite) *éminence grise* of the Bute era, Eldon an ultra Tory. Thurlow can be classified neither as a Tory (he served in four professedly Whig ministries), nor as Whig in a Rockinghamite or Foxite sense. He seems to stand out as an individual, whose first loyalty was to the king, but whose restless, critical and notoriously undeferential manner precluded any possibility of his playing the role of courtier. Nonetheless, Thurlow's proximity to George III has undoubtedly caused his reputation to suffer from that monarch's bad press. "His principles leaned to high Prerogative," wrote Grafton in his memoirs, and his late-Victorian editor added "He is an evil figure in the history of the time, coarse and dishonest."[1] The first (and until 1953 the only) serious biographical treatment of Thurlow was a hostile one by the Whiggish Lord John Campbell.[2] Even in Thurlow's lifetime, the *Rolliad*, with the felicitous if unoriginal rhyme of "scowl" with "growl," had created a facial image of him more enduring than that of any portraitist. It was perpetuated by Macaulay in his famous word-picture of the final act of the impeachment of Warren Hastings on 23 April 1795, when he described Thurlow, deprived of his high place in the order of precedence by his dismissal as Lord Chancellor three years earlier, as "scowling among the junior barons."[3] He remains in caricature an uncouth, aggressive and unattractive figure, Burke's "Iron Pluto" and "Priapus,"[4] partially redeemed only by his genuine interest in classical scholarship and his friendship with Cowper, his kindness to the aging Johnson and the approbation of Gibbon.[5] One reason why this impression has not been challenged by a major revisionist biography is Thurlow's apparent irrelevance to a theme which has long obsessed eighteenth-century specialists, namely the "rise of party." Another reason is to be found in a lack of primary material. Although there are transcripts of some important items among the Egerton Manuscripts in the British Library, and letters from Thurlow in the archives of virtually all the significant politicians of the period, there is no great deposit of Thurlow's papers.[6] Of course, there is scope for a study of Thurlow as a judge, particularly from Chancery records, and that no doubt explains why Thurlow's second biographer, Robert Gore-Browne, was also a lawyer.[7] But for the political historian of the later eighteenth century, and especially for the historian of the House of Lords, there is a received opinion two centuries old from which escape is difficult.

In some ways, Thurlow helped to sketch his own image. For all his prickly consciousness of status, he was fond of casting himself in the role of outsider in an aristocratic world—whether in complaining that, under North, he was "at a distance from that sacred circle, in which the measures of government are formed" or in ironically informing Pitt in 1791 that he had learned of Grenville's appointment as foreign secretary from "the answers of the foreign Missions to the Circular letter."[8] He deliberately emphasized that he lacked the well-traveled cosmopolitan polish of the sophisticated veteran of the Grand Tour when describing his interview with the Russian ambassador Worontzov in 1785 in such terms as "As far as I could understand his Jabber" and "How unable I am to explain myself in French."[9] He was not a landed magnate, possessed no electoral interests or role in local politics, and was content with a less than imposing rustic retreat at Dulwich. He did not forget, conceal or repudiate his origins. "I have many friends still left in Norfolk, with whom I spent the younger part of my Life, upon terms of the most perfect regard, and Intimacy," he wrote in 1775. "If any accident should ever put it in my power to make a better demonstration of my friendship to them, than by meer words, They should certainly hear of me."[10] Nor was the habitué of Nando's Coffee House, unabashed as he was about his liaison with Polly Humphries and his illegitimate children, at all sensitive to what Dr. Langford calls "the new censoriousness" and "a new spirit of prurience" to which politicians and aristocrats were exposed under George III and to which Bute, Grafton, and Sandwich all allegedly succumbed.[11] His reputation did not suffer—even in the eyes of George III—from the scandals (such as the stories

about his supposed marriage to Kitty Lynch, daughter of the dean of
Canterbury) reported in *Town and Country Magazine*. Of course, unlike
Bute, Grafton and Sandwich, Thurlow was not a hereditary peer and he
knew well that the legal profession provided one of the best opportunities
for upward social mobility in eighteenth-century Britain. He emphasized
the point with brutal effectiveness at several stages of his career in the
Lords. In 1779 he dismissed Grafton's sneers at his obscure origins with a
lively assertion of meritocracy, boasting "The peerage solicited me, not I
the peerage," upholding his equality with the duke and deriding him, in a
phrase perhaps consciously echoing Savage, as "The accident of an accident."[12] In 1799 he repeated the rebuke, claiming an "equality with every
Prince of the Blood," when Grenville declined to take issue with the duke
of Clarence over the slave trade because of his inferiority to the duke in
the peerage.[13]

But for two factors, Thurlow would have remained a real, and not
merely a self-proclaimed, outsider. The first was his forensic ability, demonstrated particularly in equity cases, and the second was his association
in Parliament with the Bedford group. It was through one of its leading
members, Lord Weymouth, that he first became an MP (for Tamworth in
1765) and the group's participation in the ministry of Lord North brought
Thurlow to high office.[14] This Bedfordite background contributed to his
firmly authoritarian approach to the dispute with the American colonies.
Like his fellow-Bedfordites he viewed the conflict in broadly imperial
terms, regarded the colonists as ungrateful rebels, deplored the repeal of
the Stamp Act, and took a much more serious view of the burning of the
Gaspée than did North himself.[15] With the legislation of 1774 and the proc-
lamation of a state of rebellion the following year, he quickly became one
of the ministry's most prominent Commons spokesmen in defense of the
policy of coercion. Many years later, when discussing the Canada Act with
Grenville in 1791 he gave his own explanation for the colonists' revolt, "You
seem to refer it to the want of more resemblance in their constitution with
that of Great Britain. I have been used to think it more referable to the
want of connection and dependance in the form of their government upon
the mother country."[16] He repeatedly insisted that ministerial policy was
designed to uphold the authority of Parliament and was therefore a defense of the principles of 1688 and not a departure from them.[17] In so
doing, far from "leaning to prerogative," he was articulating a view very
widely held within the political elite.[18]

No doubt these views helped to commend him to the king, despite

his apparent personal and moral shortcomings. But there might have remained a further obstacle to his attainment of the royal favor. George III
was a convinced as well as a nominal Anglican; Lord North was chancellor
of one of the Church's greatest strongholds, Oxford University, and his
step-brother, Lord Dartmouth, secretary of state for the colonies 1772–75,
had evangelical sympathies and was widely regarded as a Methodist.[19]
How, it might be asked, did Thurlow, whose irregularity of religious ob-
servance, frequent resort to profanity and apparent indifference to theo-
logical orthodoxy were all well publicized, fit into a ministry which was
becoming increasingly identified with Anglican political theology as well
as with the defense of the Church's temporal status?[20] One answer, of
course, is that Thurlow gave no encouragement to the Church's rivals; he
brushed aside applications from protestant Dissenters for relaxation of the
subscription laws and, although he had no sympathy with popular protestantism (his brother, the bishop of Lincoln, was almost lynched by the
Gordon rioters) he was only prepared to accept Catholic relief on very
restricted terms.[21] Secondly, unlike Grafton and Shelburne, he did not
patronize those who were theologically heterodox; indeed in 1777–78 he
helped to prosecute the vicar of Tewkesbury, Rev. Edward Evanson,
whose trinitarian heresy provoked an action in the Church courts.[22] The
engaging whimsicality with which he dispensed the extensive ecclesiastical
patronage of the lord chancellor renders generalization difficult.[23] There is
no evidence to suggest that he used that patronage to pursue a consistent
policy of promoting high churchmen, although the *Morning Herald* of
27 May 1784 described him as "under the right wing of the Right Reverend
Church Militants."[24] But his direct involvement in the elevation of Samuel
Horsley to a prebendal stall and to a bishopric was of the highest significance in view of that cleric's defense of trinitarian orthodoxy against
Joseph Priestley.[25] When the Church's temporalities in Ireland were
threatened, Thomas Orde described Thurlow as "a great champion of the
Church" who "declaims most wrathfully against any attack upon that sacred order and their fullest rights."[26] Above all, the authority which Thurlow championed in the American war was Anglican as well as imperial; he
represented order and security at a time of challenge from colonial sectar-
ians and English Dissenters. He endeared himself to the king by his uncompromising attitude to American independence. By early 1778 the king
himself insisted to North that the attacks of opposition required Thurlow's
presence in the House of Lords to repel them: "I want an able Chancellor
and therefore have pitched on Mr Thurlow," he wrote on 3 April, adding

five days later "I cannot begin to form any plan untill Mr Thurlow is in possession of the Great Seal."[27]

Thurlow's contribution to the House of Lords as lord chancellor did not involve the day-to-day management of the ministerial interest in the upper chamber. That task fell to the leader of the Lords, who was usually the senior secretary of state. On occasions Thurlow deputized for him; he corrected the king's speech for Weymouth just before the latter's resignation in November 1779 and during Shelburne's absence through illness in May 1782 he reported to the king on proceedings in the upper chamber.[28] At times he took a direct interest in the detail of management; in August 1780 he asked John Robinson for lists of "those who voted for and against the great questions of last session" in order to learn "more of the political characters of each House than I have any other chance of doing."[29] In November 1788, as Parliament met to face the Regency Crisis, he issued a circular letter for attendance in the Lords[30] and he regularly held the proxies of peers who were loyal government supporters.[31] He played a considerable part behind the scenes in preparing for the defeat in the Lords of the Fox-North coalition's India Bill in December 1783; Portland, its prime minister, thought it ominous that Thurlow (albeit temporarily out of office) held the proxy of Viscount Wentworth.[32] But the profound impression which Thurlow made upon the House of Lords was not based on organizational skill.[33] An essential pre-requisite for his predominance was the consistently high level of his attendance, whereby he developed a deep understanding of mood as well as of procedure. As lord chancellor he occupied the woolsack on each day of the session unless illness kept him away, when Mansfield or Bathurst would serve as his substitute. As is indicated in the appendix to this essay, there were five sessions during his period of office when he was present at every sitting of the Lords. It was only in 1795–96, three years after his dismissal and seventeen years after his elevation to the peerage, that Thurlow's attendance fell significantly below 50 percent of the days in the session. His presence, moreover, impressed itself upon the minds of his fellow-peers as well as upon the pages of the *Lords Journals*. To some extent this reflected the deference paid to the law lords, the prestige of their offices and their "proximity to majesty." Dr. McCahill has shown how the legal expertise of the holders of the great law offices gave them an ascendancy over many of their lay colleagues.[34] But not all peers who held great legal offices enjoyed the respect granted to Mansfield and Thurlow; Lord Bathurst, for instance, though lord chancellor from 1771–78, made relatively little impression and Loughborough could never match Thurlow's authority. What mattered was force of personality and—as with Chatham—the sheer ability to speak. In these respects Thurlow was pre-eminent. Many contemporaries testified to his eloquence and his ability not only to dominate a debate but to inspire something akin to physical fear in his opponents.[35] According to James Bland Burges, Thurlow had "for so many years carried the House of Lords with a high hand . . . and his known talents as a lawyer, and particularly his singular expertness in all points of Scotch law, had taken from Administration a considerable part of the weight of affairs in that House."[36] Even after 1792 he could still dominate, as he showed in the Committee of the Whole House over the impeachment of Warren Hastings in March 1795, when he guided the Lords towards a series of resolutions to the effect that the Commons had not made good their charges.[37] On 20 May 1801 John (the future Lord) Campbell, a hostile witness, heard Thurlow speak powerfully on a divorce bill and described him as "This great imitator of Gargantua."[38] The most perceptive explanation for Thurlow's success in debate, however, was provided by Lord Chedworth, an opposition peer in the 1780s who was forced into a grudging admiration for him: "The Chancellor has always been singularly happy in dextrously representing as ridiculous arguments which he would find it difficult seriously to answer."[39] Significantly, Chedworth was referring to an exchange between Thurlow and Bishop Porteus over the slave trade; Thurlow's opposition to abolition was so vehement that it was the kind of issue which might have led him into mere bluster.[40] But for most of the time, he could sustain a consistent line of policy, reinforce it where necessary with technical arguments and pour sardonic scorn upon his critics.

It was under North that Thurlow came not only to dominate the Lords but to become a close confidant of the king. The paralysis of the ministry in the crisis of 1779–80 chronicled by Professor Butterfield, the semi-abdication of North himself and the resignation of Thurlow's fellow Bedfordites gave the lord chancellor his opportunity. He at least showed resolution and energy and was entrusted with secret negotiations with opposition groups.[41] It is true that he was widely suspected of remaining within the ministry in order to subvert it and replace North with a Bedfordite leadership;[42] Lord Denbigh thought "he will never be quiet till some Arrangement be made for his two friends, Ld. Gower & Ld. Weymouth."[43] His jealousy over Loughborough's peerage, and his ill-concealed impatience with "the stout and all conquering supineness" of the ministry irritated even his fellow Bedfordite Richard Rigby, as well as the ministry's main props, Robinson and Charles Jenkinson: "The unpleasantness of the Chancellor's conversation is owing solely to his want of manners," complained the latter.[44] Whether or not his motive was the promotion of a Bedfordite coup, there was certainly no doubt as to Thurlow's dissidence in the later part of North's ministry. In 1781 he opposed local measures (the Kingston Enclosure and Coventry bills) which enjoyed some ministerial support. Viscount Wentworth, a supporter of the court, reported that Thurlow was "troublesome" to his own side and that it was "now allmost his constant practice" to vote in the minority.[45] He tormented Lord Sandwich by opposing the Philips Powder Bill in July 1781, provoking the first lord of the admiralty to exclaim "The Chancellor has made a Point of opposing most Bills that have lately been brought up to the House of Lords, and has usually been backed by the whole Opposition."[46]

Thurlow's conduct towards his cabinet colleagues in these years points towards two important conclusions. Firstly, his presence, by helping to preserve the identity of the Bedfordite group, ensured that North's ministry, far from being a Tory administration, was perceived by contemporaries as a patchwork of jostling personalized factions.[47] A year after Thurlow's elevation, Viscount Wentworth thought "there are full as two violent Parties among Ministry as between Majority & Minority, & wd. lay my Money that it will soon be proved," and George Selwyn was not far wrong when, including Henry Dundas in his calculations, he commented in November 1781, "There are now three parties on the Court side of the House, the king's, Lord North's and [the] Lord Advocate's, on which is Rigby and the Chancellor."[48] Secondly, Thurlow's restiveness under North bears direct comparison with his demeanour during his later years—1787-92— as Pitt's lord chancellor. North's much-quoted complaint about Thurlow in cabinet ("he opposed everything—proposed nothing—and decided nothing") was echoed in Pitt's time by Anthony Storer ("he will find fault and scold in all cases, but afterwards support the worst").[49] These were hostile opinions, and many of the best-known stories about Thurlow's contempt for some cabinet proceedings, manifested in real or feigned somnolence, come from his fellow cabinet dissident the duke of Leeds in the early 1790s.[50] But such comments are perhaps placed in context by a private observation on collegiality which Thurlow addressed to Warren Hastings:

It is generally true, that Bodies of Men cannot dispatch Business. The view of India affairs, for instance, sufficient to give efficient directions, is probably seized by very few of the Directors. If more than one assumes the Direction, it is probable the rest, tho' equally informed, intangle the Business. One Hand, well chosen, seems preferable, for Dispach; and Permanency would be an additional advantage. But Power is liable to abuse, or suspicion. Bodies are useful for controul, or sanction; attended alway with impediment, often with the multiplication of abuse.[51]

Burdened with his Chancery work and impatient with colleagues whom he regarded either as his intellectual inferiors (such as North) or as his juniors (such as Pitt), Thurlow oscillated between anger at not being adequately consulted and boredom at the minutiae of administrative detail. It is a tribute to his near-indispensability in the House of Lords that in November 1779 North regarded his presence as essential to the ministry's survival[52] and that when North fell in March 1782 the king turned to Thurlow (in vain) for salvation from the clutches of the Rockinghamites.[53] A year later, at the time of the negotiations for the Fox-North coalition, North tried (unsuccessfully) to keep Thurlow in office.[54]

Thurlow also endeared himself to the king by his loyalty under the brief ministry of Shelburne, whose peace preliminaries he defended effectively on 17 February 1783.[55] There can be little doubt but that during the ministerial instability of 1782–83, Thurlow was George III's most trusted adviser, the one confidant who—unlike Grafton, North and Shelburne—had not deserted his royal master. He co-operated with Lord Temple in preparing for the overthrow of the Fox-North coalition and his powerful speech on the India Bill, appealing as it did to fears of an over-mighty executive, was all the more influential because of his known friendship with the king.[56] His return to the woolsack in December 1783 provided Pitt's new ministry with its most substantial and experienced political figure and the lord chancellor's resolution helped to preserve that ministry in its first uncertain days, when the enforced resignation of Temple brought its future into question. Thurlow's re-appointment provided the clinching evidence that the new ministry possessed that royal approval, the lack of which had been fatal to its predecessor. He used it to the full in his attempts to rally waverers.[57] In the House of Lords his loyalty at this time was impeccable; early in 1784, in the words of Debrett's *Parliamentary Register*, he "panegyrised" Pitt, praising his disinterestedness in declining the clerkship of the pells.[58]

Indeed these early years of Pitt's ministry, before Pitt had fully established his independence of king and lord chancellor, were the most harmonious of all Thurlow's several periods in office. Thomas Orde described him as "perfectly complaisant as well as steady" in November 1784.[59] The following year he spoke with particular effectiveness in favor of the Irish commercial proposals; Charles Jenkinson observed "In carrying the business through the House of Lords, the chancellor is the most firm and able person that government has, and I can assure you he is very zealous and steady."[60] The marquis of Lothian thought his speech on this occasion "one of the very ablest I ever heard."[61] His relations with most of his cabinet colleagues were friendly; with Sydney he shared a distrust of parliamentary reform; he was on good terms with Jenkinson (from 1786 Lord Hawkesbury), whose requests for ecclesiastical patronage he frequently granted;[62] and he enjoyed the confidence of Rutland, the lord lieutenant of Ireland. Expressing concern at Thurlow's serious illness in May 1786, Rutland told Pitt "His loss would be severely felt, and I fear would be attended with some political embarrassment. No one occurs to me competent to fill the office, unless you resort to the purchase of a Loughborough."[63] The translation of his brother from Lincoln to the see of Durham early in 1787 appeared to set the seal on this ministerial harmony: "the Bishoprick of Durham puts the Tyger in good humour" was the comment of one well-informed observer.[64]

But well before the Regency Crisis of 1788–89, Thurlow became increasingly disenchanted with Pitt's ministry. The first major issue of policy which separated them was the impeachment of Warren Hastings, a procedure which Thurlow deplored as an abuse of law and which he tried to undermine. He worked unremittingly for the acquittal of Hastings, who became a close personal friend. Hastings's diary displays a deep suspicion of Pitt alongside much social contact and dining with the chancellor and his daughters.[65] Differences over political appointments arose from Thurlow's annoyance at the removal of his friend Francis Hargrave from the Treasury, his resistance to Pepper Arden's promotion to the mastership of the rolls and his obstruction of George Rose's sinecure. "I believe there were high words in private, and asperity enough appeared in public," noted John Moore, archbishop of Canterbury, but, recognizing Thurlow's political value, Moore also observed "With all these ill-humours he must be borne with; for without him the House of Lords would be a wretched, insupportable place."[66]

Thurlow shared this view and in the Regency Crisis displayed a belief in his own indispensability. There can be little doubt but that the king's illness, the prospect of a regency and the strong possibility of a change of administration led Thurlow to seek to re-insure his own position. Stories of his disloyalty abounded, both in ministerial and opposition circles.[67] Most of them arose from the fact that Thurlow, uniquely among his contemporaries, enjoyed the confidence, simultaneously, of the king, the queen and the prince of Wales. The latter found him far more approachable and sympathetic to his claims than Pitt and used him as a channel of communication to the prime minister.[68] This was a process which continued throughout the next decade, when Thurlow was called in to advise over the prince's debts and the Princess Caroline affair.[69] But the Regency Crisis also brought Thurlow into contact with Fox, inducing the latter to consider the possibility of buying his support by leaving the Great Seal in his hands in a new administration.[70] Again, the inescapable conclusion is that each side would have found Thurlow's presence as lord chancellor essential. Opposition supporters were quick to recognize that this was so. "I find that Mr Fox has had a long conference with the Chancellor," wrote Lord Chedworth on 29 November 1788, "If there should be a change, I should like to bet the Chancellor's continuing in against Mr Pitt's."[71] Sir Gilbert Elliot reluctantly acknowledged "the strength of the Chancellor's interest in the House of Lords," and Loughborough conceded that his rival had "taken a position that puts the command of the House of Lords in his hands."[72] But although Thurlow's negotiations with Carlton House were broken off by late December 1788, the legacy of mistrust was never dissipated. Pitt placed Camden, the lord president of the council, and not Thurlow, in charge of the regency legislation in the House of Lords. When on 15 December Thurlow inflicted on the upper chamber his emotional and embarrassing declaration of loyalty to George III, the reaction of many auditors was one of disbelief. Many years later, William Wilberforce confided to his son:

Do Robert let me tell you this while I remain alive, because history will go down transmitting a perfectly incorrect impression of an important fact. Lord Thurlow when he made that memorable speech, if I forget my King, may my God forget me, was at that very time coquetting with the opposition, & with the prince, & I know from my own knowledge that half an hour before he went to the house of Lords to make that speech, Pitt did not know whether Thurlow meant to oppose him or not. Nay, the first time he went down to Windsor he sat up with some of the opposition till four in the morning.[73]

An important reason for Thurlow's survival after the king's recovery saw Pitt's ministry confirmed in office was the allegiance which he commanded among traditional supporters of government in the Lords. Placemen, courtiers, and bishops looked to him for a lead. Denbigh, a lord of the bedchamber who regularly entrusted his proxy to Thurlow, confided in 1790 "The Divisions in the Cabinet grow serious and . . . if they do not soon subside it would be next to impossible for the Chancellor and Mr

Pitt to continue in Government together. Should this be the case my mind is compleatly made up which side I shall take."[74] It was anxiety on this score that led Pitt to elevate Grenville to the Lords, "in a situation to attend constantly to the conduct of all domestick business," for "while the Chancellor's disposition is such as is represented, it can hardly be expected that the public business can long proceed without leading to some disagreeable incident."[75] Grenville himself acknowledged Thurlow's powerful position by cultivating him assiduously and taking care to consult him about important matters of policy, professing himself willing to act "in the fullest concert with your Lordship."[76] But, partly from resentment at the elevation of a man 28 years his junior (Grenville was born in 1759, the same year as Pitt), partly from a sense that he was no longer quite so close to royalty as before (which explains his splenetic outbursts over the duke of York's marriage in 1791), partly from genuine disagreement with Grenville over the Hastings impeachment (they spoke in the Lords on opposite sides on this subject on several occasions) and over the slave trade and partly perhaps in reaction to his physical ailments and family distresses, Thurlow behaved towards Grenville in a manner which was at once contemptuous, discourteous, and patronising.[77] By the end of 1791 relations between them were icy and their correspondence faded away.[78] Grenville was soon complaining to Pitt and to the king about Thurlow's conduct and their clash in the House of Lords over the National Debt Bill was the immediate cause of Thurlow's dismissal.

Before then, however, Pitt and Thurlow had differed over foreign policy. Dr. Black argues that the lord chancellor's influence in this sphere has been seriously underestimated by historians.[79] Certainly there were occasions on which he defended Pitt's foreign policy in the Lords as powerfully as he had spoken on other issues, effectively countering Lansdowne, for instance, over the commercial treaty with France.[80] In May 1787 he played an important role in the British response to the Dutch crisis, precipitated by the threat posed by the "Patriots," aided by the French, to the Stadtholder, William V of Orange. At a cabinet meeting at his London house on 23 May he has been quoted as urging a policy of intervention, with no half-measures, and full military preparations, and including the subsidizing of German allies. This argument credits Thurlow with the perception of the importance to British security of Dutch independence from France and with pushing a reluctant Pitt into a policy which ended in success.[81] Others have claimed that Thurlow raised the stakes in this way merely to expose the potential costs of a policy of intervention in order to discredit such a policy and so to reduce the likelihood of its adoption.[82]

This seems a sophistical interpretation of Thurlow's case and Dr. Black duly questions it.[83] But Thurlow's reservations about intervention in Holland were genuine. The following September, as Pitt became more willing to contemplate war, Thurlow expressed the most serious doubts about such a course of action. He insisted that every measure should be taken to avoid war: if it could not be avoided, Britain must explain its participation to foreign courts and, more importantly, give it "an acceptable colour here." His advice to Pitt was of a highly cautionary nature and reflects the experience of a cabinet minister who had endured the final disasters of the American conflict, "This Country dreads a War, and nothing will be so difficult, as to persuade Them, They are well served, in that situation, or by Those, who shall have brought Them into it."[84] He was absent from the cabinet meeting of 19 September 1787 which decided upon immediate military and naval preparations.[85] But for Prussian intervention, which brought about a solution acceptable to the British government, the rift between Thurlow and Pitt, already widely reported in the press, might have taken a more decisive turn. Similarly, with the strong possibility of war with Russia over Ochakov in 1791, Thurlow defended Pitt's policy in the Lords (29 March) but in a lukewarm way.[86] He had been ill at ease about the prospect of an open breach with Russia—hence his refusal to resign alongside the foreign secretary, Leeds, when that policy was abandoned—but was reluctant to support Pitt's climbdown either.[87] Foreign policy was not the reason for Pitt's famous insistence to George III in May 1792 that he and the chancellor could no longer serve together,[88] but it did nothing to avert that disruption within the ministry.

Although Gore-Browne exaggerates greatly in stating that Thurlow was trying to "oust" Pitt and Grenville in 1792,[89] it is a measure of his influence in the Lords that as long as he remained lord chancellor, his opposition to any measure could convey the impression that it had incurred royal disapproval as well. This tended to create uncertainty among back-bench peers whose first loyalty was to the Crown. Hence Thurlow could reduce the ministry's majority to a mere six votes over the National Debt Bill on 14 May 1792 and subject Pitt's ministry to its most uncomfortable experience in the Lords.[90] He was dismissed precisely because of his authority, not for want of it. But the more elevated claims that his removal represented a triumph over prerogative or an important step in the evolution of prime ministerial authority over the cabinet may be treated with skepticism.[91] The king's ability to dismiss a ministry (as in 1807 and 1834), to veto the appointment of a politician deemed unsuitable (as with Canning) or to sustain a controversial minister in office (as with

Eldon) was far from extinguished. The events of May-June 1792 are best interpreted in personal terms; a constitutional issue would only have arisen had George III seriously tried to retain Thurlow's services as lord chancellor. As it was, much to the latter's apparent surprise, the king released him with regrets which were only privately expressed;[92] the Regency Crisis had taken its toll.

Some believed that Thurlow's removal would threaten the ministry's control of the Lords especially if, as for a time seemed likely, he made common cause in opposition with Leeds.[93] According to one source, it precipitated a fall in the stocks.[94] The delay between the king's acceptance of his dismissal in mid-May 1792 and his formal resignation a month later, widely attributed to the needs of the court of chancery, led to a belief that there would be a reconciliation. *The Oracle*, a newspaper which received a government subsidy, reported on 30 May that "The general opinion in the Upper Circles appears to be that the Lord Chancellor will remain in office. The good Offices of Mr Dundas are said to have produced certain satisfactory explanations."[95] Despite earlier rumors as to his retirement on health grounds,[96] there seemed a massive permanence about his presence as lord chancellor which made the reality of his departure hard to accept. "Lord Thurlow, whatever faults he may have, must make a considerable blank in the Cabinet," wrote Leeds.[97] James Bland Burges went further, fearing that, unless conciliated, Thurlow would adopt "a hostile line in Parliament," and that in his absence, all the best speakers in the House of Lords, except Grenville, would be on the side of opposition. He believed that the most sensible tactic for the ministry would be "to make up matters in a proper way with Lord Thurlow."[98] Lord Carlisle commented on the weakness of the ministry in the Lords, "not only in debate, but also in the first law department."[99]

Out of office, however, Thurlow proved less threatening to his former colleagues than when in office with a fit of recalcitrance. Indeed, he told Kenyon "I do not wish to spend my breath in a vain opposition."[100] The number of occasions on which he spoke or voted against the ministry was small.[101] He co-operated with the duke of Leeds and was repeatedly mentioned as a figure of influence in any new ministry which the duke—in potential combination with Fox—might join.[102] His objections to the Seditious Meetings Bill in December 1795, based on legalistic complaints rather than a libertarian ideology, were widely reported and won him the unlikely approbation of the radical Unitarian minister Theophilus Lindsey.[103] There remains an irony, perhaps, that one of his few widely quoted sayings was "Cruel laws never conduced to the safety of a Prince or the preservation of an established government,"[104] and his maverick quality is seen in the story that he urged a Middlesex voter to support Sir Francis Burdett in 1804.[105] More typical was his opposition to Fox's Libel Bill in 1792, which occasioned his only Lords' protest.[106] It was characteristic of Thurlow that he combined a vehement public critique of the "licentiousness" of the press with a private friendship with such exponents of it as John Horne Tooke.

For his apparent challenges to convention were entirely personal and could not conceal a profound attachment to the institutions of monarchy, peerage and confessional state. Leaving no ideological legacy (he published virtually nothing) he expressed himself through his legal judgments and through his political career. The two were closely linked. For Thurlow's career symbolizes above all the interaction between the political and the judicial functions of the House of Lords. Throughout his lifetime, all members of the House, irrespective of their legal knowledge and qualifications, were entitled to vote on appeal cases, impeachments and the trial of peers. But increasingly lay lords were disposed to accept the guidance of their legal counterparts in such cases. The authority of Thurlow, together with the advice of the judges, proved decisive in the acquittal of Warren Hastings.[107] Not all lay peers welcomed this development; as Lord Fortescue complained in 1782:

What he had long dreaded had actually come to pass, namely, that the dignity of that House would be lowered and tarnished by the profusion of lawyers which time might occasionally introduce into it. It was no longer a House of Lords or Peers; it was converted into a mere court of law, where all the solid and honourable principles of truth and justice were shamefully sacrificed to the low, pettifogging chicanery and quibbles used in Westminster-hall. That once venerable, dignified and august assembly resembled more a meeting of attornies than a House of Parliament. . . . The learned lord on the woolsack seemed to be fraught with nothing but contradictions and law subtleties, and distinctions.[108]

It was only in the early nineteenth century that the participation of lay peers in the judicial work of the Lords faded away.[109] Probably Thurlow would not have demurred at Fortescue's backhanded tribute. But he saw himself as much more than a lawyer. First and foremost he was the king's servant in a system which was still emphatically monarchical. He wielded the formidable authority of his office to decisive effect in the service of that system. The House of Lords provided him with the perfect arena in which to do so.

APPENDIX

Lord Thurlow's Attendances in the House of Lords, 1778–1806

Dates of Session	No. of Days in Session	No. of Days when Thurlow was present
26 Nov. 1778—3 June 1779	121	121 (100%)
25 Nov. 1779—8 July 1780	95	74 (77.89%)
31 Oct. 1780—18 July 1781	98	98 (100%)
27 Nov. 1781—11 July 1782	99	91 (91.92%)
5 Dec. 1782—16 July 1783	93	76 (81.72%)
11 Nov. 1783—24 Mar. 1784	54	32 (59.26%)
18 May 1784—20 Aug. 1784	56	56 (100%)
25 Jan. 1785—27 Oct. 1785	108	108 (100%)
24 Jan. 1786—11 July 1786	96	48 (50%)
23 Jan. 1787—30 May 1787	78	78 (100%)
27 Nov. 1787—11 July 1788	111	102 (91.89%)
20 Nov. 1788—11 Aug. 1789	127	124 (97.63%)
21 Jan. 1790—10 June 1790	79	75 (94.94%)
25 Nov. 1790—10 June 1791	102	92 (90.19%)
31 Jan. 1792—15 June 1792	87	84 (96.55%)
13 Dec. 1792—21 June 1793	115	58 (50.43%)
21 Jan. 1794—11 July 1794	99	62 (62.63%)
30 Dec. 1794—27 June 1795	110	54 (49.09%)
29 Oct. 1795—19 May 1796	105	44 (41.90%)
27 Sept. 1796—20 July 1797	146	13 (8.90%)
2 Nov. 1797—29 June 1798	127	21 (16.54%)
20 Nov. 1798—12 July 1799	112	18 (16.07%)
24 Sept. 1799—29 July 1800	122	13 (10.66%)
11 Nov. 1800—31 Dec. 1800	37	0 (0%)
22 Jan. 1801—2 July 1801	101	32 (31.68%)
29 Oct. 1801—28 June 1802	131	70 (53.44%)
16 Nov. 1802—12 Aug. 1803	160	0 (0%)
22 Nov. 1803—31 July 1804	138	1 (0.72%)
15 Jan. 1805—12 July 1805	117	4 (3.42%)
21 Jan. 1806—23 July 1806	127	0 (0%)

NOTE: This table was compiled from the presence lists in *Journals of the House of Lords*, vols. 35–45. The session of 1777–8 is excluded, since Thurlow took his seat in the Lords (on 14 July 1778) only in time to preside over its prorogation.

CHAPTER 5

Charles, Second Earl Grey and the House of Lords

E. A. SMITH

Charles, second Earl Grey has gone down in history as the champion of parliamentary reform.[1] Yet he was the most aristocratic of men, by temperament and by conviction, and a firm believer in the aristocratic principle of government. When he formed his cabinet in 1830, with a commitment to bring in a Reform Bill, he made sure that it was one of the most aristocratic of the age. He wrote to Princess Lieven:[2]

In the composition of my Ministry I have had two essential objects in view: the first, to show that in these times of democracy and Jacobinism it is possible to find real capacity in the high Aristocracy—not that I wish to exclude merit if I should meet with it in the commonalty, but, given an equal merit, I admit that I should select the aristocrat, for that class is a guarantee for the safety of the state and of the throne.

His cabinet of thirteen included nine members of the House of Lords, one Irish peer, one heir to a peerage and a baronet. Even in the Commons, the government's leading speakers were Lord Althorp, heir to Earl Spencer, E. G. Stanley, later fourteenth earl of Derby, Lord John Russell, the son of a duke, and Palmerston, an Irish peer. Even allowing for the fact that ministers like Goderich, Holland, Richmond, and Carlisle were neither brilliant orators nor outstanding departmental heads, the House of Lords rather than the Commons was in many ways the real seat of government until the Great Reform Act decisively changed the balance between the two Houses of Parliament.

Grey's background was aristocratic, in the sense that he came from an old-established territorial family of moderate means and estate in Northumberland, but the head of the family acquired a baronetcy only in 1746, and Charles was only the second of his family to hold a peerage. His father, a younger son, was a professional soldier, who made an eminent reputation in the American War of Independence and in the West Indies in the early years of the French Revolutionary War. He asked for, and was given a barony by Henry Addington in 1801 in return for his military and political services: Grenville and Fox promoted him to an earldom when they came into office in 1806 in order to give that rank to his son when he inherited the peerage, which he did towards the end of 1807. Charles, however, was the most unwilling of entrants to the House of Lords. He resented the fact that his father had neither consulted nor even told him about his intention to seek a peerage, and there can be no doubt that, had the law at the time allowed the renunciation of peerages he would have done so. His reputation had been made as an orator in the House of Commons: making a great speech to a crowded audience there was always a tonic to his often depressed spirits, but in the Lords his powers were muffled by the dull atmosphere of the chamber: "with just light enough to make darkness visible," he wrote to his wife after his debut in 1808, "it was like speaking in a vault by the glimmering of a sepuchral lamp to the dead. It is impossible I should ever do anything there worth thinking of." Matters did not improve over the next half-century: Robert Lowe, another new arrival in the House fifty years later, likened it to "addressing dead men by torchlight."[3]

Thus Grey, though an aristocrat by temperament and inclination, found the House of Lords uncongenial as a political home. He came increasingly to see his political life as existing in the past, lacking in positive achievements, and the future as a bleak and frustrating prospect of continued failure. His reputation in the twenty years after his election to the House of Commons in 1786 had been made as a vigorous opponent of Pitt and his government, an enemy of George III, and an advocate of moderate but thorough reform of the political system. In 1806–7 he had served for the first time, and the only time until 1830, in the cabinet, and had shown energy and talent at the admiralty and as foreign secretary, but after the death of Fox, the collapse of the "Talents" Ministry had put an end to his official career and, it seemed, to his prospects of ever resuming it. His mood for the next twenty years and more was one of despondency. Lacking the stimulus of the House of Commons, he found it difficult to sustain any enthusiasm for politics. He tended more and more to retreat to Northumberland and his family life, to avoid having to deal with the quarrelsome factions in the opposition or to speak in Parliament, restricting himself to matters of broad, general principle rather than the detail of administrative questions. In these respects his membership of the Lords both confirmed and reflected his disinclination for political engagement.

Grey's despondency in these middle years of his career also illustrated the practical difficulties of leading an opposition from the upper House. The Commons was the chamber in which the major debates took place, and one of the most important attributes of a leader of opposition was the ability to sway votes and influence the public by oratorical brilliance which was only remotely possible in the House of Lords. Wellington on one occasion even remarked that "Nobody cares a damn for the House of Lords: the House of Commons is everything in England and the House of Lords nothing."[4] This was an exaggeration, but contemporaries recognized that an effective opposition needed to be led from the Commons. Lord Holland remarked in 1815 "no party can be well led that is not in a great measure really governed as well as nominally led by a member of the House of Commons."[5] Governments could still be led successfully from the Lords, and indeed they continued to be so until the end of the nineteenth century. After Pitt's death in 1806 and until the retirement in 1902 of Salisbury, the last peer to serve as prime minister while in the Lords, Commoners occupied the premiership only for a total of just over thirty-six out of ninety-six years. Oppositions, however, were essentially led from the House of Commons even before 1832: Grey was the last recognized leader of the whole opposition to operate from the upper House, but even he kept the leadership after becoming a peer for personal rather than political reasons: partly because of his own political stature and partly because the Whigs could not agree to follow any of their members in the Commons. Brougham and Whitbread, the only two commoners who would have been serious contenders for the post, were distrusted by some influential leading members of the party as being too radical in their views or unreliable in personality. The leadership in the Commons was therefore given to George Ponsonby, who was expected to be Grey's subordinate rather than leader of the party as a whole.

Grey himself tried to push the overall leadership on to other shoulders—Grenville in 1807, Holland in 1815, Lansdowne in the 1820s—but they were unwilling to displace him. His friend Rosslyn told him bluntly in 1815 that it was not possible to transfer the responsibility to any other person; "No other man of the present day can undertake it—no other will carry with him the same share of public confidence, or the same respect from all persons of whatever party; no other person can keep your own friends together."[6] In truth, Grey never wanted to be superseded as leader of the Whig party and certainly not by Whitbread, Brougham, or any other commoner. When Landsdowne acted on the assumption in 1827 that Grey had handed the post over to him, Grey quickly made his displeasure known. As soon as the prospect of winning power for the Whigs seriously arose, in 1830, Grey quickly returned to reassume their leadership and to become prime minister when Wellington was defeated.

Grey's refusal to give up the leadership of his party in opposition had only delayed, however, the inevitable development: already leadership of the opposition could only be effectively conducted from the Commons and it was Grey's reluctance to serve under anyone else and the lack of a suitable candidate amongst his followers that delayed the recognition of the fact. The ineffectiveness of the Whigs in opposition between 1807 and 1830 arose in some considerable degree from their failure to find an adequate replacement for Grey in the House of Commons.

The House of Lords was not yet a political cipher, however, nor was Grey always ineffective as leader of the opposition there. Despite his dislike of speaking in it, the Lords' chamber did not stifle Grey's oratorical powers. James Grant, the parliamentary reporter of the 1830s, remarked on the quality both of his set speeches and his speeches in reply to debate.[7] The former, he declared, were distinguished by clarity, elegance of style and expression, and close reasoning, the fruit of careful study and preparation. The latter were equally brilliant, the fruit of long experience and of a natural ability to analyze and penetrate the arguments of his opponents. Grey's manner, Grant wrote, was dignified, grave, and thoughtful, "his voice . . . soft and pleasant, and his articulation clear," his language "beautifully correct, without being what is called elegant." In an age of great orators, from Pitt, Sheridan, Burke, and Fox in Grey's youth to men like Brougham and Canning in his later years, Grey shone as a leading light in parliamentary speaking. He provided a link between the occasionally over-embellished and emotional oratory of the late eighteenth century and the more measured, informative style of Peel and Gladstone. Lord Holland said of him in 1832 that "Lord Grey's judgement and execution exceed those of the greatest orators or statesmen I have known. He is more perspicuous, clear and methodical than Mr. Fox, more conciliatory and just than Mr. Pitt, more circumspect and cautious than Mr. Canning, yet as full of spirit, life, and energy as any of them." Princess Lieven wrote in 1820 that "Lord Grey has the noblest, the most admirable delivery possible. I do not know if you have heard him speak in the House of Lords. If not, you cannot boast of knowing either Lord Grey or a great orator. . . . [His] attitude is magnificent; his voice has the resonance of bronze; his gestures are always noble; it is impossible not to respect him when he speaks."[8]

Grey's major set speeches were carefully prepared, though delivered without notes, and several of them were remembered as landmarks in parliamentary oratory. Especially notable was his speech summing up the evidence against Queen Caroline on the Bill of Pains and Penalties in 1820. He reviewed the evidence presented to the House in a tone of judicious impartiality, leading his hearers to his conclusion that the case against the queen had not been sufficiently proved, and that although her conduct had been reprehensible it did not warrant the full condemnation and drastic penalties proposed.[9] He concluded with an impressive declaration of his political principles:

My lords, a great part of my political life has been spent in storms and convulsions. As far as human infirmity would permit me, I have endeavoured to pursue a direct and steady course. I have never courted power. In the course of my life I have also been the object of much popular reproach. These, I trust, are proofs of the determination which I have invariably evinced to resist the undue encroachments of the Crown, and at the same time to defend from the attacks of the people those rights and prerogatives which are not more necessary for the dignity and splendor of the monarch, than they are for the protection and the happiness of the people. In the case before your lordships, I have not made up my opinion without much anxiety and much consideration . . . but, such a case has been made out . . . first on the ground of justice and secondly on the ground of expediency, I feel, that if I were to vote for this bill, I should never again lay my head down upon my pillow in peace.

The speech was acclaimed by his colleagues. It was, wrote Thomas Creevey, "beautiful—magnificent—all honour and right feeling, with the most powerful argument into the bargain. There is nothing approaching this damned fellow in the kingdom, when he mounts his best horse." Holland too thought it "the most perfect speech I ever heard in Parliament."[10] Of his other speeches in the Lords, that against Canning in 1827, those in support of Catholic Emancipation in 1829 and the Reform Bill in 1831–2, and his retirement speech in 1834 were particularly praised.

The speech attacking Canning's appointment and policy in 1827 again took the form of a review, in this case of his opponent's conduct throughout his public career, and like his speech on Queen Caroline it was based on a view of moral principles rather than political expediency.[11] He particularly censured Canning for what he considered his inconsistency on the Catholic question, saying that he had never done anything practical for the Catholics although he had always professed support for their cause. Similarly, his reputation as a friend to civil liberty was fraudulent and his foreign policy, on which his major reputation was built, was likewise meant for show and lacked a true appreciation of principles and national interests. The speech was so powerful that it was said that Canning intended to take a peerage in order to answer Grey in the Lords himself, and even that his early death, which prevented his doing so, was hastened by his distress at Grey's attack upon him. There was certainly no shortage of praise for the speech, even among Grey's political opponents. Greville called it a "brilliant success" and Wellington said that "he never heard him speak so well and quite unanswerable." On Grey's own side, Lord John Russell wrote that it touched "every sympathy of my heart" with an effect "more touching than the tenderest scene of any novel."[12]

More impressive still were Grey's speeches on the Catholic Relief Bill in 1829. Here he was able to present himself as a national statesman acting on a principle to which he had always been committed, and in furtherance of the traditional Foxite Whig slogan of "civil and religious liberty all over the world." That Grey as leader of the opposition should support Wellington's government was significant: it also enabled him to appear as the spokesman of liberal public opinion, citing the numerous petitions in support of the measure which had flooded into both Houses. His speeches sustained a statesmanlike tone, and lifted the debate on to high moral grounds. He ranged over the history of the anti-Catholic laws since the sixteenth century, pointed out that their purpose had always been political and not religious, and asserted that the English and Scottish Catholic subjects of the Crown were now as true and loyal subjects as any others and that the loyalty of the Irish would be won by the concession of full civil rights. He concluded with a tribute to Peel's honesty and bravery in sacrificing his career to principle which drew applause from Wellington himself, and one to Wellington's distinguished services to his country in this as in other fields. Grey's statesmanship was never better demonstrated, and tributes came from all sides: his friend Sir Robert Adair wrote that he was "a statesman standing on your own individual character."[13]

It could of course be said that, since Catholic Emancipation had long been a party commitment by the Whigs, Grey's speech in its support owed something to his desire to promote his party's interests, though on this occasion George IV's personal hostility towards him and towards emancipation meant that the speech could not promote Grey's chances of office. It was typical, however, of Grey's effectiveness as an orator, which lay to a considerable extent in his ability to present what were essentially party political interests in a framework of moral principles. The attack on Canning certainly owed its origin and character to Grey's personal resentment of Canning, who had supplanted him as foreign secretary in 1807 and whose support of Toryism thereafter had robbed the opposition of one of its most effective potential speakers. It also reflected Grey's objection to the highest office being in the hands of "the son of an actress" rather than a member of the aristocracy. Similarly, his judicious tone against Queen Caroline might be thought to have been tinged by the Whig party's desire to embarrass and discredit George IV, also their former potential political ally, who they believed had betrayed them in 1811 and 1812. Grey's politics were based on a belief in the importance of the Whig party as the only vehicle for constitutional government against the autocracy of the Crown, and his speeches were always designed to promote the party's interests. It was so with his speeches on parliamentary reform, starting with his attack on Wellington in 1830 which did much to bring the duke's government down, and those on the principles and purpose of reform which punctuated the struggle.

The finest of Grey's reform speeches was that on the second reading of the English Reform Bill on 14 April 1832.[14] As on the Catholic question, he summed up the course of the movement since its early years, asserted the Whig case for reform as a means of reconciling the middle classes to the existing constitution, and answered the arguments of its opponents in the preceding debate. His speech was instrumental in winning a majority of nine votes for the second reading and, Holland declared, it "restored [him] entirely to the confidence of the whole party." He described the speech as "almost miraculous." The struggle in the Lords was only beginning, however, and it was not until the king had attempted to replace Grey by Wellington and had been forced to take back his former ministers and agree to the creation of enough peerages to force the passage of the bill that the crisis was surmounted.

The experience of the near-revolution, or so it had seemed in the autumn of 1831 and the spring of 1832, that popular pressure for reform had threatened, completed Grey's determination to resist further constitutional change. It was as a conservative statesman that he ended his political career in the premiership, and in his last great speeches, in the House of Lords on his retirement in July and at the great Edinburgh reform banquet in September 1834, he stressed the finality of his achievement and the need for stability and consolidation in the immediate future. His resignation speech, brought about by confusion and dissensions in the ministry over the Irish Church, was "most powerful and affecting," according to J. C. Hobhouse. The chamber was crowded for the occasion, and the cheers which greeted him on his rising to speak lasted for several minutes, during which he was too overcome by his emotions to begin. His review, and justification, of his premiership and the achievements of his ministry was powerful and wide-ranging, concluding with a declaration that

I have not shrunk from any obstacles, nor from meeting and grappling with the many difficulties that I have encountered in the performance of my duty . . . I leave office with a fortune not more than sufficient to support my rank and station in society . . . and certainly with a fortune not improved by the emoluments of place. I leave office not retaining one shilling of the public money, either for myself or any of my connexions . . . I shall continue to attend in Parliament as an individual peer, and to assist in promoting those wishes which I conceive to be the best for the general interests of the country.

Creevey declared that "all agree that it was the most beautiful speech ever delivered by man."[15]

Grey's last great speech was at the Edinburgh "Grey Festival," held in September 1834 to celebrate his lifetime's achievements and especially the passage of reform.[16] Here he expressed the profoundly conservative nature of his principles and of the Reform Act itself—the principles of "strengthening and preserving all the settled institutions of the State" and abstaining from "all extreme and violent changes." He concluded by speaking of "the great truth, that, for the sake of liberty itself, the peace and good order of society must be preserved—the authority of the law must be restored—and that the power which, for the good of the subject, must belong to the Government, should be supported." Foremost among those "settled institutions of the State" which Grey believed must be preserved and protected was the House of Lords itself, and in a paradoxical way it was Grey's Reform Act which ensured that it was.

The House of Lords which Grey knew in those years was a body of some 300 hereditary peers together with 26 Bishops, and sixteen Scottish and 28 Irish elected Representative peers, though the actual daily attendance was of course far smaller.[17] The power of the House in Grey's time was not, in truth, to be explained so much by what went on inside the chamber as by the role played by its members in other areas of the political system. Grey's cabinet in 1830 was exceptional, but by no means unique, in the proportion of members from the titled aristocracy. But even outside the ranks of government the peerage exercised an influence over the workings of the political system out of all proportion to their numbers. In particular, before 1832 the peerage dominated the return of members to the House of Commons to an extent that rendered that House largely subservient to the Lords. The upper House had little need, and few occasions, to block or seriously amend bills sent up from the lower because legislation had already been framed and molded in accordance with aristocratic interests. This applied even to financial matters on which, by custom dating from medieval times and confirmed by a Commons resolution of 1678, the Lords did not seek to interfere with the exclusive right of the lower House to legislate. This caused no real problems until the first decade of the twentieth century, when the Lords' opposition to Lloyd George's "People's Budget" precipitated a constitutional crisis which was resolved only by the passage of the Parliament Act to restrict the Lords' power of veto.

If, however, the result of the Lords' influence over the Commons before 1832 was to smooth the path of contentious legislation and maintain the harmony of the constitution, it was that very circumstance that gave rise to the demand for reform of the House of Commons and the electoral system in the early years of the nineteenth century. The radical demand that the House of Commons should be made more representative of the people at large grew up in the late eighteenth century as a consequence of the American and French revolutions and their doctrines of the liberty and equality of all men.[18] The real target of the movement was not the power of the Crown. Dunning's famous resolution of 1780 demanding the reduction of the "influence of the Crown" was already out of date for that influence was fast diminishing and it was already in any case virtually under the control of the aristocracy. Far more radical was the demand in the 1790s and 1800s for the reduction in the influence of the peerage over elections to, and members in, the House of Commons. Christopher Wyvill's "County Association" movement of reformers in the 1780s was a movement of the "clergy, gentlemen and freeholders" of the counties, designed above all to free them from aristocratic influence.[19] In 1792–93, Grey's own Friends of the People, an Association for Parliamentary Reform which he helped to form and whose spokesman he became, identified the widespread influence of the peerage over returns to the Commons as the principal evil to be addressed. The Friends' Report on the Representative System declared in 1792 that no less than 164 English and Welsh MPs were returned by the influence or nomination of 72 peers. In 1816 T. H. B. Oldfield, the reform propagandist, calculated the figure as 249 (including Scottish members) who owed their election to peers, compared with 151 returned by the influence of Commoners and sixteen by the Treasury. Of the 100 Irish MPs added to the United Kingdom Parliament by the Act of Union in 1801, 51 were said to be elected by peerage influence. In 1832 it was estimated that 354, or 54 percent of the lower House owed their election to peerage influence. In addition, many relatives of peers sat in the Commons, not all for those seats under peerage influence or control. In 1832 257 MPs were Irish peers, or sons, fathers, brothers, cousins, grandsons, nephews and uncles of 169 peers.[20] The propaganda of parliamentary reformers focused on these figures and their significance: not only the middle classes but the people at large considered that their interests were being denied by the preponderance of aristocratic power.

It might thus seem ironic that Grey, the most aristocratic of men, should have identified himself throughout his active career with a movement which was substantially anti-aristocratic. How could he reconcile his aristocratic principles and status with a movement which, in the eyes of many of its supporters, was fundamentally democratic and devoted to the principle of political equality? These doubts affected the attitude of many popular radicals in the period after 1809, when Grey was frequently accused of deserting or betraying his earlier commitment to parliamentary reform. In turn Grey attacked the radical leaders like Burdett, Hunt, and Cobbett as being extremist demagogues who would destroy the social fabric as well as the political system. Yet he never deserted the cause of reform altogether, and though he confessed in 1810 that he no longer pursued the objective with "the ardour of youth" he assured his hearers that he had not changed "the general opinions" he had formed in his earlier days. He averred that he had embraced reform not to destroy the system but to restore it, to purge it of corruption and error, by a "temperate, gradual, judicious correction of those defects which time has introduced," and so to make it acceptable to men of moderate views.[21]

These disclaimers, pronounced from the House of Lords itself, did little to convince his radical critics: but in 1830, when the reform issue suddenly blazed up again, Grey took up once more the mantle of leader of the reformers. On this occasion he had two motives: one, to use the issue to defeat Wellington's government and climb into office, taking advantage of the duke's ill-advised declaration in the House that he would never agree to parliamentary reform, and secondly in the hope, which he had professed in 1793, that reform, if introduced by responsible men on moderate principles, could be made to satisfy its respectable advocates while preserving the essentials of the aristocratic constitution and attaching the middle classes to the Whig party. Reform, therefore, was to be a palliative rather than a surgical operation, to restore confidence in the existing constitution rather than create a new one, to prolong the aristocratic age into the era of rising democracy rather than give way to the tide.

It was in this sense that Grey reconciled the provisions of the Reform Bills of 1831–32—which even many reformers found astonishingly radical—with his devotion to aristocratic principles. It also explains why it was unnecessary to apply any of the principles of the bill to the House of Lords, and possible to ignore the demands of the more extreme radicals that the House of Lords should be reformed or even abolished. The stress now was to be upon the *useful* functions of the upper House in revising legislation that might have passed too hurriedly through the Commons, or in giving time for calm deliberation or questions on which the lower House might be unduly pressured by its constituents. Even *The Times*, the outspoken advocate of the Reform Bills, admitted in October 1831 when the Lords were holding up the progress of the second bill, that "among the uses of an Upper Chamber ought to be accounted that of checking occasionally the too impetuous flight of popular impulse, and subjecting that which may be but a light or transient caprice, to the test of calm, laborious, and reiterated deliberation."[22] It was therefore fundamental to Grey's idea of reform that the House of Lords should retain its proper constitutional powers unaffected and that it should continue to be nominally at least an equal partner in legislation with the Commons.

However, there was one obstacle in the way, and that was the House of Lords itself, or the Conservative majority in it. After seventy years of "Tory," or at least non-Whig, domination of government and patronage, the Whig party constituted a small minority in a House of predominantly Tory disposition, particularly among the more recently-created peerage-holders and the bishops and representative peers who had been appointed or chosen under government influence. The Reform Bill had passed the Commons after a six month struggle and a general election in which the people had given a resounding verdict in its favor. By the autumn of 1831 all eyes had turned to the upper House, and the question "What will the Lords do?" was on everyone's lips. The answer came in October when they rejected the Bill by forty-one votes after five nights of intense debate. The country erupted in riots and demonstrations against the Lords, and particularly the bishops, whose numbers had virtually decided the outcome. Several were burnt in effigy on 5 November, and in Bristol, Derby, Nottingham, and other towns there were violent riots, fires, and loss of life.[23] The demand arose that the Lords must be made to accept the will of the people, if necessary by introducing a sufficient number of new ministerial peers to overcome the majority.

This was to be Grey's greatest test. Would he accede to this demand, so reducing the House of Lords to the political tool of any government in power by the use of the royal prerogative to create peers on any occasion?

Would he agree to water down the Reform Bill, as the king urged him to do, in the hope of finding a compromise acceptable to the more moderate conservative peers? Was there any other course?

Grey's own feelings were not in doubt. He made it clear to his cabinet colleagues that he was averse to forcing the House of Lords if it could be avoided, but that he was also determined to honor his pledges to the country. He had quoted to William IV the significance of the 1831 election results, when the people had returned a verdict strongly in favor of reform by giving his government a sweeping victory—the first virtual national referendum on a single issue in British politics. He believed that the House of Lords ought to accept the people's wishes, not because they were the people's wishes, but because to defy them would lead to an irresistible demand for the abolition or drastic limitation of the powers of the Lords, or at the very least to a more radical reform bill including the secret ballot and universal manhood suffrage—measures which his moderate Reform Bill was designed to avert. In the end, he was prepared to force the king and the Lords in order to save the country from the revolution he feared would otherwise follow, but he hoped that wiser counsels would predominate. He received with willingness, if considerable skepticism, the attempts of Lords Wharncliffe and Harrowby to find a compromise solution which would not substantially water down the bill but would be acceptable to some of the "waverers" in the opposition. The search for compromise was never likely to succeed and when the House of Lords resumed its discussions in the spring of 1832 the government was again defeated on an amendment in committee.

Grey had told Althorp in March that he had an "extreme repugnance" to making peers pass the bill because it was "a measure of extreme violence," but he also declared to the king that modifications to the bill would antagonize the public and reopen the demand for more extreme measures.[24] In the end, he was forced to demand a pledge that William IV would create as many peers as might be necessary to pass the bill, even as many as 50 or 60. He pointed out in the House that the "checks and balances" of the constitution required that all these components, king, Lords, and Commons, must submit to some limit on their powers, and that, as the king held the power of dissolution over a recalcitrant House of Commons, the Lords must also submit to a legitimate exercise of the royal prerogative in case of deadlock. The Reform Act was to ensure that in future the prerogative would be used to enforce the will of the Commons and not, as in the past, of the Lords.

The king's failure to find an alternative ministry which would pass a modified bill meant that the House of Lords had to give way or face a revolution. Nevertheless, the Lords' resistance and the virtual coercion applied to the House damaged its standing in the public estimation. *The Times* forecast that "they can never replace the House of Peers on its old foundations in the respect and confidence of the people." Francis Place and Daniel O'Connell, among others, campaigned for reform or abolition, O'Connell declaring that the Lords were "mad, stark mad, to dare to fly in the face of popular sentiment" and foretelling the abolition of the hereditary peerage. John Wade, editor of the radical *Black Book*, declared that the work of reform was unfinished while the Lords remained in existence. Further obstruction by the Lords to the Whig governments' reform program in the period after 1832 aroused more resentment among radicals, fanned by O'Connell during a speaking tour of Scotland and the north of England in 1837. Two attempts in the House of Commons to commit the House to reform of the Lords only narrowly failed.[25]

Yet in the end Grey's cautious and reluctant tactics succeeded. He, and his successor Melbourne after 1834 refrained from forcing unwelcome measures down the throats of the Lords, preferring concession and retreat to confrontation, while on the opposition side Wellington restrained his more turbulent followers from seeking a collision. Wellington and Peel both quickly realized that the Reform Act had created a new situation because, in the event of deadlock, the king could not use his power of dissolution either to force the Commons to give way or to secure a new House more favorable, through the use of electoral influence, to the Lords' position. William IV tried to do so in 1834 but Peel's failure to win a majority at the general election was decisive for the future, and no later monarch attempted those tactics. It followed that if a government had the support of the Commons backed by public opinion, it was useless for the Lords to defeat it since they could not replace it by one more favorable to their views. Wellington's and Peel's recognition of this fact signified that for the future the House of Lords was to be the inferior partner in the political system and that its primary function now was to be that of a revising and delaying chamber, rather than having an equal voice in the legislative process. Wellington's success, in the long term, in imposing this view on the Conservative majority in the House meant that the political temperature of 1831–32 rapidly cooled after 1836 and so did the public agitation against the continued existence of the Lords.

Some commentators, like de Tocqueville or Lord Morley, believed that this fading of the objections to the House of Lords was due to an ingrained characteristic of the English people, a wish to preserve the aristocracy as a necessary part of the stability of society. De Tocqueville distinguished between popular criticism of particular peers or measures adopted by the House of Lords, and hatred or envy of aristocracy as such; Morley asserted that the House had the support of "the great mass of the property and intelligence of the country." Carlyle believed that

Our Aristocracy are not hated or disliked by any Class of the People—but on the contrary are looked up to—with a certain vulgarly human admiration . . . by all classes, lower and lowest class included.[26]

Others attributed the virtual end of the agitation against the House of Lords by 1837 to the recognition that the political contest lay not between the two Houses as such, but between two parties, Conservative and Liberal, whose formation was to a large extent due to the Reform Act itself. Before 1830, the predominant temper of the House of Lords was conservative in the sense that the majority of peers, on all sides, tended to see the role of the House as a brake on constitutional change, and a supporter of the Crown. The peerage was still the ornament and supporter of the throne and its prerogative, and though party politics were never absent from the upper House the large majority of its members looked to the king rather than to a party leader. This was well illustrated by the history of Catholic emancipation in the period after 1812. Despite his earlier friendship with Fox and the Whig leadership, George IV as regent and king followed his father's precedent in opposing any change in the religious establishment. In this he was going against the tide of political opinion which was moving in favor of relaxation of the political penalties on Roman Catholics. On a number of occasions between 1812 and 1828 motions in the Commons in favor of emancipation were either narrowly defeated or actually passed, and the fact that after 1812 emancipation was an "open" question in the cabinet—meaning that ministers and official men were free to vote according to conscience or personal interest—meant that the government, as such, did not support the royal prejudices or attempt to make its followers do so. Grey, and the Whig party in general, however, adopted emancipation as a "bond of party" and consistently voted for it in both Houses, as did Canning and his followers.

Nevertheless, majorities against emancipation in the Lords continued to be substantial. It was openly admitted that the Lords were acting less out of religious prejudice than in support of the Crown, and that emancipation would not be feasible unless there was a change in the royal sentiments. When, however, the Irish crisis of 1828–29 forced Wellington and Peel to take up emancipation as a government measure on the grounds of necessity, to avert an Irish rebellion, the king was compelled by Wellington to retract his opposition and to allow it to be known that he approved, politically if not personally, of the introduction of a Relief Bill. He had no alternative, since the Whigs and the Canningites, the only major groups outside the administration to whom he could turn, were committed to emancipation. Despite the resulting split in Wellington's Tory following, when the "Ultras" who refused to support emancipation effectively seceded from the party and voted against it, the Lords, as Wellington had foretold, turned about face and the previous majorities of up to 181 against the proposal were transformed into a majority of 107 for the bill. This reflected the tendency of the upper House to respond to royal and executive influence, illustrating the feelings of duty and loyalty which governed the conduct of many peers. Wellington nevertheless depended on Grey and the Whig peers in the Lords' debates: Ellenborough remarked that "he . . . fights the whole battle for us."[27]

After 1830, however, the situation rapidly changed. The defeat of Wellington's government in the Commons in November 1830 led inevitably to its resignation, despite its continued majority in the Lords, and to the appointment of Grey as prime minister with the king's agreement to reform as the principal measure of the new administration. The Reform Bills created a deep political division in both Houses. Reform was seen as a fundamental matter, affecting the balance of the constitution as well as the interests of all classes in society, and the widespread and general support of the electorate, as evidenced by the 1831 general election, brought the Lords majority face to face with the public. Beyond the constitutional issues which were now raised, there also lay a political question. The Reform Bills would—and were probably designed to—destroy the political power base of the Tory party in the pocket boroughs and inaugurate a period of Whig or Liberal supremacy in the Commons. Both sides in the long struggle of 1831–32 were aware of what was at stake, and the ferocity of the conflict derived largely from it. The contest took the form of a conflict between the two Houses, for the Lords were still the same House that had supported Tory administrations throughout Grey's lifetime, while the Commons had been forced to follow the will of the electorate and to pledge themselves to "the whole Bill, and nothing but the Bill." Nevertheless, the battle was a party one, between Whig/Liberals and Tory/Conservatives: it merely chanced that the balance of the parties differed in the two Houses. The withdrawal of the main opposition in the Lords after May 1832 was a strategic retreat, not a complete rout, and for the remainder of the decade the Tory majority in the Lords continued to harass and trouble the Grey and Melbourne administrations.

This, as Charles Greville remarked in 1835, intimated "a great practical change in the constitutional functions of the House of Lords."[28] No longer did the House provide a reliable backstop for governments who were in difficulties in the Commons. The majority in the House, who had previously been natural supporters of the ministers chosen by the monarch, were now their opponents. During the lifetime of William IV, who had quickly become disillusioned with his new ministers and who feared that they had carried reform too far, the opposition in the Lords could relieve their consciences by the argument that the ministers had been forced on the king against his inclinations and their opposition to government was therefore designed to support the monarch. This was the principle on which the Lords had acted in 1783, when they rejected Fox's India Bill and brought down the Fox-North coalition at the insistence of George III himself. In 1834–35 William IV tried to repeat his father's former tactics by installing Peel as his minister and calling a general election to give him a majority in the lower House. This time, because of the changes brought about by the Reform Act, the plan failed, Peel did not get a majority, and despite the Conservative majority in the Lords Melbourne returned to office. If this encouraged the Conservatives in the House of Lords to continue to oppose the Liberal government's policies in the belief that they were still acting out their traditional role of supporting the Crown, however, the accession of Queen Victoria in 1837 cut that ground from under their feet. The young queen was undoubtedly a Whig partisan, influenced by her personal admiration for Melbourne, and consequently opposition in the House of Lords was shown to be motivated by party and not by constitutional principle. Greville declared that it was "a departure from the character and proper province of that House to array itself in permanent and often bitter hostility to the Government, and to persist in continually rejecting measures recommended by the Crown and passed by the Commons." Thus, for the first time, "there is no party in the House of Lords supporting the Crown . . . , but all are either Tories or Whigs arrayed against each other and battling for power."[29]

This transformation of the character of the House of Lords was one of the most important consequences of Grey's Reform Bills. Party spirit had not been absent from the House before 1830, but now it was the major characteristic of politics in the chamber.[30] Grey's and Melbourne's difficulties in passing legislation through the Lords showed that there was no longer a standing majority in the House for the king's or queen's government; they were dependent on the efficiency of their party organization and the strength of their numbers, while the opposition similarly acted as an organized political party following their own principles and interests rather than sheltering behind the fiction of the royal leadership of government. The retreat of the monarch from active political leadership was the inevitable consequence: as Wellington had foreseen in 1831, the Reform Act had made it impossible for the *king's* government to be carried on. Henceforward government was by party, and both Houses were dominated by it.

Parties in Parliament did not act spontaneously. They had to be organized and directed, and this became more necessary in the Lords after 1830 as a consequence of the increased importance of party. While Grey was prime minister, his regular attendance, skill in debate, and grasp of business made him an effective leader of the government party. He was aided by the duke of Richmond, a member of the cabinet, who acted as government chief whip. In addition to the management of government business in the House, Richmond was responsible for ensuring the attendance of government supporters and the registration of proxy votes. After Grey's resignation in 1834, Melbourne, his successor, was less diligent and effective, and tended to leave management in the hands of his chief whips, Lords Stafford, Duncannon, and Falkland in succession. They too were less effective than Richmond had been, and were more easily deterred by the reluctance of great aristocrats to submit to party discipline. Lord Hatherton, who became a peer in 1835 after several years' experience of the stricter whipping system in the Commons, was appalled by the comparative laxity of the whips in the Lords and the poor attendance of government supporters. The Conservatives in opposition, despite their superiority in numbers, were more strongly disciplined by Wellington and his chief whip Lord Rosslyn—partly to counter the internal divisions on the Tory side which were deeper and potentially more damaging to the effectiveness of the opposition, and partly because of the need to keep up a constant pressure against the pace of Liberal reforms sent up from the Commons. On both sides of the House, eve-of-session dinners, circular letters, and the organization of proxy votes for important divisions were given increasing attention, reflecting the escalation of party conflict in the 1830s and 1840s. Wellington noted in 1837 that "Parties in Parliament . . . are now placed as two opposing armies"; government by party had displaced government by the Crown, and the House of Lords was even more affected by the change than the Commons.[31] As long as the Whigs or Liberals held a majority in the Commons there were bound to be difficulties with the permanent Conservative majority in the Lords: these difficulties diminished after 1841 because the Conservatives came into office, and also because the Liberals, from the mid-1830s onwards, were becoming more conservative. Melbourne's well-known wish to "let it alone" may have been rooted in indolence, but it also reflected the increasing conservatism of his predecessor and the shadow over his shoulder, Grey.

Not only, therefore, did Grey, by his tactics over the passage of the Reform Bill, make a substantial contribution to the preservation of the House of Lords with powers that were at least constitutionally unaffected, but he also, in the last decade of his own career, helped to ensure that the conflicts of 1831–32 were not repeated in the period before his death in 1845. His speech at the great dinner held in Edinburgh in September 1834 to pay tribute to him on his retirement as the "champion of reform" was couched in terms which would not have earned dissent from Peel. It was the language of Peel's "Tamworth Manifesto" rather than of radical reformism, and it strongly predicated the continuing importance of maintaining the House of Lords as an essential element in the constitution. And as the House of Lords was even more the principal forum for the expression of aristocratic interests after 1832 than before, with the diminution of the dependence of the Commons on the upper House, its necessary role as a defender of an important national interest was secure. Grey would not have dissented from Wellington's view that the Lords were the ultimate guardians of the constitution and its balance, but that they should use their power with discretion and only in case of urgent necessity. Their very presence was in normal circumstances enough to keep the House of Commons from rushing to extremes: in times of crisis their strength would be preserved for use if necessary. In practice it almost never was, and if it had been used the situation of May 1832 would almost certainly have recurred. The Lords were generally wise enough to realize that their strength was greatest when it was not used, and that if used it would be diminished. Grey taught them that lesson, and Wellington ensured that they did not forget it. That the Lords remained an essential part of the process and furniture of government throughout Victorian times owes more than a little to the man who is remembered more as a reformer than, as he was, a true conservative.

CHAPTER 6

The Duke of Wellington and the Resurgence of the House of Lords

R. W. DAVIS

It is accepted wisdom that the Great Reform Act of 1832 strengthened the House of Commons and the electorate against the monarchy and the House of Lords.[1] Of the monarchy, this is certainly true. In a sense, as E. A. Smith demonstrates in the previous essay, it is also true of the Lords. Thus one can safely say that after 1832, when the House of Commons was backed by public opinion, at least that part of it that voted, the Lords had no choice but to give way before their combined force. The difficulty, as Professor Gash has observed of the plight of the Whig government after 1835, was to bring about the winning combination: in fact the government's position weakened with each general election after 1832 until it was decisively toppled by the election of 1841.[2] As a result of declining public support for the Whig regime, from 1834 the Lords were able to curb the government with impunity. Perhaps never again did the Lords enjoy such an unbroken run of success, but they remained very powerful at least up to 1911.

Yet, if on the one hand the decline of the Lords' power after 1832 was a great deal less than is sometimes supposed, such decline as there was had in fact occurred before 1832. Indeed, a diminution of the Lords' power was advanced as justification for the passage by the duke of Wellington's government of 1828–30 of those great religio-political reforms that historians such as Jonathan Clark consider at least as significant as the parliamentary reform act several years later.[3] That is to say, the destruction of both the Anglican constitution by the repeal of the Test and Corporation Acts in 1828 and of the protestant constitution by Catholic Emancipation in 1829 was seen as necessary by contemporaries, among other reasons, because the House of Lords was no longer capable of protecting the old constitutional arrangements. Speaking of the repeal of the Test Acts, Wellington told the duke of Montrose, though he put the words in the rather unlikely mouths of the bishops, that "As public men they felt for the consequences of a difference of opinion between the two houses on a question on which the House of Commons would have been supported by the public opinion."[4]

Nor was Wellington alone in advancing this explanation of why the government and the Lords had to give way on Repeal. Writing in January 1829 about the question of Catholic Emancipation, the Whig-Radical Lord Durham said of Wellington:

He . . . would not, I dare say, be displeased if he was greatly forced, as on the occasion of the Repeal of the Test Act. The only hope now is, that the question will come up to the Lords with such an overwhelming majority that he will be justified in advising a compliance on their part with the sense of the House of Commons so decidedly expressed.[5]

The Canningite ex-premier Lord Goderich took the same view. He could "not help thinking . . . that a strong demonstration of opinion in the House of Commons would produce the same effect upon the Government and the House of Lords that was produced last year in respect to the Test Act."[6]

Public opinion, as distinct from Irish militancy, was not much invoked on the government side in 1829. But public opinion, in its most tangible form of electoral opinion, did figure in one of the arguments for settling the Catholic question. As Peel told the bishop of Limerick, putting it first in a list of considerations for settling the issue: "There has been a division between the House of Lords and the House of Commons on this subject that has now endured 16 years." What he described to the king as "the evil of continued division between two branches of the Legislature on a great constitutional question" had to be removed.[7] This division, which by 1829 had persisted through five Parliaments and four general elections, had been a source of acute embarrassment to the government since the early 1820s; and there can be no doubt that it was a major factor behind Wellington's enunciation the previous year of a new convention regarding the relationship between the two Houses.[8]

If, however, Wellington's had become the accepted convention by 1828–29, how does one explain the unyielding Tory opposition to parliamentary reform, with Wellington prominent in the lead, for more than a year after the general election of 1831 had given a clear endorsement to the Whig program? The answer the duke gave just before the Lords threw out the Reform Bill in the autumn of 1831, was that public opinion on the bill was by then wavering, and—anticipating an argument that would be powerfully and effectively advanced later by Lord Salisbury—Wellington held that such a situation imposed a special constitutional duty on the Lords. In a 21 September draft of a letter to the marquis of Bath, then in the country, Wellington said:

We here think that there is a very prevailing change of opinion in the country upon the subject of the Bill. At all events we think that the House of Lords ought to give the country a chance of being saved by affording further time to consider of this question, [and] that in taking this course the House will perform its peculiar function and fulfill its duty in the Constitution.[9]

Meanwhile, Wellington was busily trying to create proof of the change of opinion he claimed, writing to W. J. Bankes of the pending by-election in Dorset: "I cannot express to you how anxious I feel that your father should stand. His success would be the most complete answer to the *vapouring* about the continued eagerness *for the Bill*."[10] Buoyed by the success in Dorset he worked so hard to bring about, Wellington may have convinced himself. Others were more skeptical, including his closest friends. On 21 December 1831, Charles Arbuthnot wrote to his wife: "the Duke is convinced that there is already a great reaction. I believe there is some—I am not sanguine enough to think that it is great."[11]

As the events of the following spring were to prove, that was putting it mildly. But the question is not whether operating constitutional assumptions were always based in reality, but rather what they were. In Wellington's case, it is clear that even in the autumn of 1831 he still continued to invoke the rule that, if the public persisted in backing the government and its majority in the lower House, the Lords would necessarily have to give way. Indeed, according to his argument (one that would be developed fully in Salisbury's doctrine of the mandate) far from their standing in the way of public opinion, it was the Lords' special function to make sure that what was expressed was indeed the authentic opinion of the public.

No single individual was more responsible for the remarkable recovery of the House of Lords after 1832 than the duke. In theory, leader of the opposition, save for Peel's brief ministry in 1834–35, the duke was in fact leader of the House throughout the decade. It was a position from which it would have been easy to push too far, and there were tremendous pressures on him from within his own party to do so. But he did not yield to those pressures. Neither, however, did he sacrifice the powers of the House of Lords, or let the government or anyone else forget they existed. He used them sparingly, but with devastating effect. His was a game which required political skill of a high order. "There never was a more crafty villain than my brother Arthur," the Marquis Wellesley affectionately remarked to Lord Holland in the autumn of 1831, after the Lords had thrown out the Reform Bill. George Lamb, unrestrained by family feeling, entirely agreed about the marquis's brother: "He is so d—d cunning. People don't know him, he is the cunningest fellow in the world."[12] At any rate, he was cunning enough.

Wellington was deeply pessimistic about the fate of the country and its institutions after the passage of the Reform Act. Not until August of 1834 did he begin to feel reasonably safe about the institution of which he was a member, observing to the earl of Aberdeen: "I consider the destruction of the House of Lords to be now out of the question; and that we have only now to follow a plain course with moderation and dignity in order to attain very great, if not preponderating influence over the affairs of the country."[13] In the meantime, however, the duke had already been following since the beginning of the reformed Parliament a course of "moderation and dignity" in what would prove to be the successful effort to assure the Lords that "very great influence" over the country's affairs.

Early in the first reformed Parliament Wellington laid down a proposition that he would develop and elaborate in years to come. As a result of the Reform Act, he told the earl of Roden in March 1833, the Lords had become "an assembly still powerful in legislation; but without political influence." What he meant by "political influence" was, in fact, electoral influence. The peers' electoral influence, he contended, had been destroyed by the Reform Act, leaving them without this means of bringing the Commons around to the Lords' way of thinking. The Lords had, however, been left with their legislative power: without their approval bills did not become law. But, as the events of 1831 and 1832 had shown, such power could be very fragile. Wellington went on to tell Roden that "the Lords' character it is the object of the malevolent press of the day and of those who wish to destroy our institutions to pull down, because they feel that the destruction of the character of the House of Lords will lead to the destruction of their power as a legislative body and remove the only barrier to the attainment of their [i.e. the Radicals'] objects."[14]

Wellington had no intention of giving the malevolents any aid or comfort in their destructive scheme. He therefore wished, as he told Roden (and as he would tell countless others in years to come), "to afford no ground for the charge of 'faction'."[15] What Wellington saw as "faction" many others saw as the legitimate role of opposition; and he baffled and infuriated, particularly the so-called Ultra Tories led by the dukes of Cumberland and Buckingham, by his efforts to avoid the appearance of faction. Thus though he always came up for the opening of Parliament, he also always opposed an amendment to the Address, long a standard opposition ploy. More than that, with the opening ceremonies completed, the duke hurried back to Stratfield Saye, where he usually remained until after Easter. With their leader absent, opposition initiatives were not easy: which, of course, was precisely what Wellington wanted. When discussion was called for, Wellington always preferred a call for papers to a resolution, which demanded meeting the issue head on, and the effect of which could be reversed by an embarrassing resolution of the Commons in the other direction. Only after Easter, when bills were usually sent up from the Commons—that is to say, only when there was real legislating to be done—was the duke prepared for the Lords to take action. But it must not be frivolous action. Like the good general he was, Wellington had no intention of dribbling away his forces in minor skirmishes. Rather, he tried to save his troops for battles they might win, or from which they might at least retreat in good order, and with honor.

Wellington took great care in choosing the issues on which to take a stand, and he chose them with more tender regard for public opinion than is often supposed. In February 1836 the duke admonished the earl of Winchilsea who wished to move an address protesting the mode of proceeding against the Orange Society: "The House of Lords must take care . . . not only to be quite in the right, and to have a just cause to complain, but likewise to have a case in which the country at large manifests an interest and will approve of their proceedings." Wellington did not think the Orange Society qualified, repeating advice that he had given before, "to drop the qualification of *Orangemen* and assume that of Protestants, as being more likely to gain the support of the people of England." [16]

This incident shows not only the duke's concern for public opinion, but also the sort of issue he thought would attract public support. Kitson Clark has remarked on the strange phrase Wellington used after the defeat in the Lords in 1834, by a majority of 187 to 85, of a bill for the admission of Dissenters to the universities. The duke told a meeting of Conservative peers at Apsley House that they had shown what a great majority they were "in the country." [17] All one can say with certainty of such a statement is that the duke had the country on his mind. But what he probably meant was that the Lords had taken an action of which a majority in the country would approve. Clearly, he and other Conservatives were greatly bolstered by the strong Anglican reaction which set in in 1834 in response to Dissenting militancy and government suggestions of appropriation of any surplus that might exist in the Irish Church.

It was at the end of the 1834 session that Wellington confided to Aberdeen his conviction that the House of Lords was now safe. A month later he wrote another revealing letter to Aberdeen.

To tell you the truth, I am inclined to believe that that which for the last fifty years has been allowed to have such weight in public councils, I mean public opinion, was in fact the opinion of the party in opposition to the government, or, in other words, of the Dissenters from the Church of England. It is quite certain that in every remarkable instance in which the public opinion, as it was called, prevailed in deciding the course taken in public councils, the Dissenters were of that opinion.

The Anglican reaction of 1834, with its two massively signed petitions by laymen and clergy in support of the Church, showed that there was a public to whom the duke and his party could appeal.

What did Wellington mean by "public opinion," and how did he go about determining what that opinion was? A precise answer is impossible. Like his contemporaries, the duke used the term fairly loosely and gained his impressions from a variety of sources: his correspondence, what he read in the newspapers, by-elections etc. In this instance, however, he did have something more precise in mind. He went on to observe to Aberdeen that the Anglican public did not behave in such a way as to make its positions immediately recognizable as public opinion. Wellington charged that the Dissenters, pursuing their own political objects for which they wanted government support, were willing to overlook all sorts of abuses

which would have occasioned noise enough if we had been in office. But our friends, and the Conservatives in general whatever may be their opinions and feelings upon what they see going on, are not accustomed to notice such matters in the way in which we have known them to be noticed by the public.

The models he instanced were the anti-slavery agitations, the peace movement during the wars of the French Revolution and Napoleon, and the recent parliamentary reform campaign. In short, what he meant was organized agitation, which promoted public meetings, rained petitions on Parliament, and churned out other sorts of propaganda aimed at exerting pressure on the government.

While such agitations were anathema to the duke, he had, as he admitted, himself succumbed to them in the past, from the repeal of the Test Acts through parliamentary reform. Such manifestations were not, he believed and indeed hoped, to be expected of Conservative opinion. Nevertheless, Conservative opinion had its uses. As Wellington remarked to Aberdeen about a series of Conservative meetings in Scotland that autumn:

> They remind the world that there is such a thing as a Conservative party remaining in this country; and if they don't like the destruction of the institutions of the country they will find some of the same opinion as themselves. I don't think that any meeting can do much more than that. However, the numbers tend to show that there is a change of opinion in the country; or, what is I believe more near the truth, that there were many more opposed to the destruction of the old constitution of the country than was imagined, or than dared to avow their opinion.

Either way, Conservative opinion was finally making itself evident, and in the long run it would tell at the hustings.[18]

This is not to argue that the discovery of active Conservative opinion in the country induced Wellington and his followers to take up any issues they would not otherwise have championed. It was in the nature of the party that they would have defended the Church and/or protestantism, as indeed they had done in 1833 and 1834. But from 1834 onwards the Conservatives advanced these issues with a new confidence and authority. Religious issues became the Conservative showpieces, the ones on which there was no surrender. And, if at all possible, other issues were sheltered under a religious guise. Thus, in the spring of 1837, when it seemed that the Whig government was about to resign, Wellington wrote to Peel:

> It is very desirable that the public should understand clearly what the difference of opinion between the parties is: That you are determined [to maintain] the Protestant religion [and] the Church of England in Ireland as well as England. That you are determined to maintain the independence of a House of Lords. I think that a debate upon the third reading of the Irish Corporations Bill might bring out these points very forcibly.[19]

In other words, the question of municipal government in Ireland was not whether the Irish deserved similar institutions to those recently established in England, but whether protestants should be subjected to government by Catholics. And who had so far prevented this enormity? The House of Lords. The religious cloak was an ample one, and much could be sheltered beneath it.

In the main, the duke succeeded in his policy, and with excellent effect, not only for his party, but for the power of the House they dominated. But success was not achieved easily. The party was not a docile one to lead, and sometimes the duke's Ultra critics, and even more frequently the duke himself, denied that a party existed at all. Wellington, however, triumphed in the party as well; and it was in this triumph, over his own followers, that he demonstrated perhaps his greatest cunning. Lord Holland noticed that when a particularly delicate question arose, Wellington began to indulge in violent language—on some other topic, usually religious. In 1838, Holland praised the duke for his support of the government over its problems in Canada, a support that was highly unpopular in his own party. And, Holland went on to observe, the duke "was obliged . . . to keep the Tories together and he was disposed sometimes, by the nature of his general opinions to gratify his eager partizans by a warm speech of censure, such as he made on sundry questions relating to the Ecclesiastical establishments in England, Ireland, and Scotland."[20]

Holland had noted similar behavior on the duke's part earlier, and then he had not been so admiring. In mid-July 1835 he remarked that Wellington had begun to adopt a much more decided tone of "High Church politics," and that he set the example to his colleagues in "high Orange and Protestant language." But Holland went on to report:

Some however who know him well imagine that such compliance with the prejudices of the more wrongheaded of his party is one of his *straight forward* manoeuvres for acquiring authority and thereby checking the impatience of his unruly types whom he is anxious to restrain from any direct assault on the second reading of either the Municipality [that is, Municipal Corporations] or the Irish [Tithe] bill.[21]

A final example comes from an impeccable Tory source, the earl of Rosslyn, the Tory whip. Towards the end of the debates on the Irish Church Bill in July 1833, Wellington moved an amendment which would have made the abolition of ten Irish bishoprics dependent not on the proposed act of Parliament, but rather on royal pleasure. Lord Grey immediately made clear that this was an amendment the government would not accept. Rosslyn reported to Mrs. Arbuthnot:

The Duke, unwilling to hazard the consequences, was disposed to give up or rather modify the amendment. Our friends and even some of the reasonable ones showed great dissatisfaction, and the Duke agreed to divide. This was fortunate, for the division reconciled many of our friends, and happily we were beaten, several of our friends not voting. I went to the division with the less anxiety that I was pretty confident we were in a minority.[22]

The amendment was little more than a bone thrown by the duke to his supporters. Doubtless he would have been happy had the government accepted it, but he had made sure from the beginning that he could prevent it passing if he wished.

In the spring of 1841 there was general consternation in the Conservative leadership when the duke suggested that he would not join the next Conservative government. Sir James Graham wrote to Arbuthnot that Wellington's presence in the cabinet would be "indispensable." He added: ". . . and while he lives, no other man can quiet the House of Lords."[23]

There can be little doubt that Graham was right. The duke quieted the Lords for their own good; steadied them for the Radical onslaught. It came, and it broke. Or, to adapt Professor Gash's metaphor: in the later 1830s what he calls the "Lords Reform locomotive" slid harmlessly to a stop on the Wellington siding.[24]

It may, however, be asked whether this essay does not give too much credit to the duke. After all, after 1835 Peel was the leader of the party; and, as the leader in the House of Commons, he would always have had great influence. How much control would Wellington actually have had over Conservative policy at Westminster? The answer is that as far as broad questions of strategy for a parliamentary session were concerned, what to oppose and how much, though the duke was usually consulted as a matter of course, he did not, nor did he expect to, exercise a dominating influence. He recognized that policy in the Commons and Lords must be coordinated, and that the Commons must have the dominant voice. At the same time, however, he firmly believed that it was the Lords' right and bounden duty under the constitution to modify and improve legislation sent up from the Commons. He also naturally insisted on deciding the tactics to be used in the Lords. Questions of what amendments should be passed, or at what stage a measure should be thrown out, and how, left ample room for conflict between the leaders of the Conservative party in the two Houses, and for the leader in the Lords to exercise considerable influence on the party, particularly when the Conservative majority was in his House.

The first difference of opinion over legislation came in connection with the Irish Church Bill of 1833. Here Wellington appears to have engaged in another of what Holland called his "straightforward" maneuvers. On 3 June the duke proposed and carried over strong opposition by Grey an address calling upon the king to enforce the declared policy of neutrality in the civil war in Portugal. Lord Ellenborough noted in his diary: "It is strange that the Duke, after so much fear of driving Ministers to make peers by opposing injurious Bills, should all at once dash at a measure like this." It did indeed seem strange and had precisely the outcome Wellington had predicted for such measures: the Commons passed a resolution neutralising that of the Lords, and the king backed his ministers.

Peel was annoyed, and Lord Palmerston rejoiced over the duke's "grand mistake."

On 21 June, however, the duke's actions took on a rather different light. Citing the danger of a collision with the Lords, the government on that day in the Commons dropped the appropriation clause from the Irish Church Bill. Ellenborough noted in his diary the next day: "All feel that the humiliation of the Government is extreme, and the triumph of the Lords, for this concession is the effect of our vote on Portugal."[25] To have managed to get rid of the provision most objectionable to the Conservatives before the bill even reached the Lords was no mean achievement. Nor was there, in fact, much danger in the course Wellington pursued. There was much less likelihood of a creation on an issue on which the government had another recourse than there would have been in the event of a major confrontation over the Irish Church Bill, which would certainly have come in the Lords had the offending clause not been removed. To fire a warning shot across the government's bow was in every way prudent. And, though Peel continued to be baffled by the duke's ploys, the rest of the Whig bill proceeded through the Lords largely unscathed.

Peel probably disapproved of the Lords throwing out the Irish Tithe Bill of 1834 on the second reading. Aberdeen, who often acted as an intermediary between Peel and the duke, gently hinted that the action might have been precipitate. Wellington replied that the bill would have been lost in the end, and therefore the reaction in Ireland would have come anyway. Furthermore, the duke said: "I could not have commanded our majority if I had allowed the second reading to pass unopposed."[26] When there was nothing to be lost by giving the Conservative majority its head, it was both wise and useful to do so.

The duke gained substantially in the estimation of some of his followers in the Lords by giving them their head over the Municipal Corporations Bill the next year. The result, however, was a direct clash with Peel, which Peel won. As often happened in the relationship between the two men, there was insufficient preliminary discussion, with the result that, though they both professed a belief that some sort of bill ought to pass, what sort it ought to be was left unclear.[27] When Lord John Russell actually introduced a bill early in June, Wellington wrote a highly critical memorandum which he sent to the king. The king, or Sir Herbert Taylor, obviously had the impression that the duke was advocating rejection of the bill.[28] But Wellington did not say so explicitly, nor did he so act. On 27 July a meeting of seventy or eighty peers at Apsley House agreed to allow a second reading of the bill unopposed, subject to a hearing of counsel on the facts of the case, which was according to precedent. On 3 August another meeting at Apsley House voted to hear evidence against the principle of the bill. Since the point of the second reading is the acceptance of the principle of a bill, this resolution was much more serious, and it was passed over the duke's strenuous opposition. Lord Stanley remarked: "It was entirely against the Duke of Wellington's opinion, who was outnumbered at a meeting at his own house, held without previous concert with Peel, who is furious—and with very good cause—and I have no doubt it was caused by a systematic intrigue led by Lyndhurst and the Duke of Cumberland."[29]

The 3 August meeting is usually taken as the occasion on which, in the words of Disraeli, who is the authority for the report: "The Duke . . . formally resigned to [Lyndhurst] the leadership of the House of Lords."[30] If so, it was surely the shortest leadership on record. Wellington continued to send out calls for attendance at the committee on the bill. And one week later, on 10 August, at a meeting of about a hundred peers at Apsley House, he successfully urged that the bill be allowed to go into committee, while Lyndhurst outlined the amendments he intended to propose.[31] Wellington had a high opinion of Lyndhurst, who had been lord chancellor in his government as well as Peel's. Though not much encumbered with principles (not necessarily a disadvantage from the duke's point of view) Lyndhurst was a first-rate lawyer and a brilliant debater. The former lord chancellor often managed bills in the Lords, especially those in which complicated legal questions were involved.[32] There was therefore nothing particularly unusual about the situation that prevailed over the Corporations Bill, except the degree of publicity given to differences of opinion at a party meeting at Apsley House.

On 12 August at a small meeting, made up of those peers who had been in the recent Conservative government and Lord Fitzgerald, it was decided that the duke should give a general endorsement to corporation reform, and specifically to reform based on a ratepayer franchise, as the government bill proposed; and that on this basis he should oppose a proposed motion by the duke of Newcastle against going into committee. Wellington himself would have preferred giving the Conservative peers a free vote on Newcastle's motion, but gave way to the opinion that the Conservative peers should be advised to vote with the ministers. That evening the duke duly gave his speech endorsing the broad principles of the government measure. Fitzgerald wrote Peel that Wellington quite picked up after he had given it. "Up to that time he seemed to me painfully overexcited and depressed."[33]

Very likely he had been both. The duke believed that the bill carried the possibility of a very real menace. As he told Lady Salisbury on 8 August:

The worst of the Corporation Bill is that it will form a little republic in every town, possessing the power of raising money. In case of anything like civil war, these would be very formidable instruments in the hands of the democratic party.

Beyond that he was troubled by his differences with his old and trusted legal adviser Lyndhurst and by the latter's doubts, shared by the other Conservative judges, about the legality of the government's proposed legislation.[34] Lyndhurst, however, overcame his scruples and drew up his amendments, which were carried by the Lords and sent down to the Commons on 28 August. Wellington set great store by these amendments, as doing much to make the bill safe. In any case, they represented all the Lords could do under the circumstances. As Wellington explained to the duke of Northumberland:

The House of Lords cannot resist the principle proposed by the Ministers of the Crown and agreed to unanimously by the House of Commons. All the House of Lords can do is to regulate its application, to provide as well as circumstances will permit for vested rights and interests, and to prevent the mischief which would result in the government of all these towns by the sudden change from the restrictions of the old system to the relaxation of the new.[35]

The ministers were bound to be unhappy about the amendments. But Peel would prove an even more formidable opponent. While the Lords were debating the bill he had retired to the country in order to separate himself completely from their actions. Nor did he communicate with the duke except through third parties, mainly Aberdeen, Ellenborough, and Fitzgerald. This kind of treatment was not calculated to put the duke in a good humor. He wrote stiffly to Sir Henry Hardinge, one of Peel's main lieutenants in the Commons, that "I understand that Sir R. Peel does not approve of the course which the House of Lords has taken upon the Corporation Bill." He would not dream of suggesting that any member of the Commons should say a word in approbation of that course contrary to Peel's opinion. But he did hope that "if the Ministers should feel an interest in increasing a good understanding between the Houses, and in passing the bill sent down by the House of Lords they may be supported by the votes of those supposed to be our friends."[36]

The ministers did prove to be conciliatory. Russell was prepared to accept some of the Lords' amendments. Peel backed most of the rest, but not the most important one. The Lords had proposed to add aldermen serving for life as a check on the elected councils. Peel sided with Russell and accepted his compromise suggestion that aldermen should instead be elected by the council for a term of six years. When the bill came back to the Lords, there was much anger. But at a meeting at Apsley House, after first allowing free discussion, the duke finally came down on the side of concession, and his followers obliged, with even Lyndhurst agreeing to lead in conceding as he had led in the onslaught. The duke, however, remained very angry, writing to Alderman Heygate:

The House of Lords . . . cannot stand alone. We must have some support in the House of Commons, and you will have seen that there was not one man in that House to stand up in defence of the rights, principles, and systems which it was the object of the amendments of the House of Lords to secure.[37]

It was the evident truth, and Wellington gave way before it.

This must count as a defeat for the duke, and for the Lords, at the hands of their own friends. But to say, as is usually said, that the duke lost control of the Lords is inaccurate. Lyndhurst carried a point against him at a party meeting that seemed to put in question the principle of the bill. Yet Lyndhurst then proceeded to work on amendments to that very same bill, thus acting in direct opposition to the point he had carried. Nor did either the duke or Lyndhurst ever actually suggest throwing the bill out. True, Peel did not like some of the Lords' amendments; indeed, he seems to have disliked them more than the government did. Yet his opinions on the specific amendments seem never to have been conveyed either to Wellington or to Lyndhurst. At any rate, they were not prepared for the strength of his reaction when he finally returned for the Commons debate. But, then, he was out of town and not in direct communication with either through the whole period when the amendments were being drafted and discussed. What is true is that Wellington led less decisively on this occasion perhaps than on any other. He was personally deeply opposed to the bill, yet felt he could not oppose it. Therefore, he did his best to defang it; or rather, he turned to someone else he thought could do the job better, Lyndhurst. But it was Wellington who had entrusted Lyndhurst with the amendments, and, if he followed the latter's lead, it was because he chose to.

Lyndhurst would also be in charge of the Irish Corporation Bill the next year; but this campaign went much better for all concerned, save, of course, for the bill's supporters. Angry though he was, the duke saw that the division between the party in the two Houses was dangerous for the party, and in his opinion for the country. He therefore swallowed his anger and seized upon the pretext of an Irish representative peerage election to reopen communciation with Peel. General consultations grew out of this opening, and the Conservatives went into the 1836 session more united than they had been for a long time, except during the brief period of Peel's government. Aside from an Irish Tithe Bill which the Lords emasculated of its appropriation clause and the government laid aside, the main measure of the session was the Irish Corporation Bill. Lyndhurst's device to deal with this measure was simply to abolish the Irish corporations, without replacing them, thus leaving them to be governed under the ordinary institutions of county government. This satisfied his party, but once again the government abandoned its bill. Wellington was lavish with his praise of Lyndhurst: "You have established yourself not only as the first speaker in the House of Lords, but as the first in your own profession, whether in Court of Law or Equity, or in the House of Lords." But basically the duke's admiration was sincere; he wrote to do his best to assure that the former lord chancellor would be back for the beginning of the next session.[38]

The last session of the Parliament elected in 1835, in the spring of 1837, also saw close cooperation between the Conservative leadership in the Lords and Commons. Stanley and Sir James Graham were anxious for a settlement of the Irish Corporation question. To this end, Stanley suggested that if the government produced acceptable bills on two other Irish questions, tithes and a Poor Law for Ireland, the opposition should agree to pass a Corporation Bill. Peel was well inclined towards such a solution, and he was also eager for a junction with Stanley and Graham. But, as Kitson Clark has said, he showed throughout these negotiations "a very nervous and sensitive loyalty to the Lords."[39] Clearly, he did not look upon his 1835 victory as in any way definitive, or significant beyond the issue involved. Unfortunately, Lyndhurst was in Paris, but Peel was careful to confer with Wellington and the other leading Conservatives in the Lords. He believed that he had got a commitment that the Lords would not throw the Corporation Bill out on the second reading. He also thought that Wellington had undertaken to bring Lyndhurst around on this point, and to bring him into consultation with Stanley and Graham. There was a nasty moment in April when it became apparent that the duke's understanding of what had been agreed earlier in the session was somewhat different:

I certainly recollect that I stated that I would endeavour to prevail, and that I thought I should succeed in prevailing, upon Lord Lyndhurst to abandon his wish to throw out the Bill upon the Second Reading; particularly if the whole case was left open. But I did not consider that any thing was settled till he should come to England; when he and I were to meet Lord Stanley and Sir James Graham.

But Wellington laid the misunderstanding to his bad hearing: "The fact is I don't hear half that passes."[40] And he cheerfully accepted Peel's version of what had passed at the meeting. Lyndhurst too was duly brought round. There was, however, no final settlement of the interlocked Irish bills, as the two Houses were still maneuvering when the death of William IV ended the life of the Parliament as well.

The first session of the new Parliament in 1837–38 saw a continuance of the generally good relations between Peel and the duke. But the latter angered many of the rank and file of the party in both Houses by what Disraeli called "his damned generosity and all that" towards the government and its difficulties arising out of the Canadian rebellions.[41] The session also saw the passage of an Irish Tithe Bill, shorn of an appropriation clause, and an Irish Poor Law. The Irish Corporation Bill, however, did not pass because of a franchise that Conservatives generally found too low.

Though Wellington had grown very deaf and had other health problems late in the decade, there is no indication that they seriously affected his powers of leadership. He lost neither his shrewdness nor his cunning. He certainly became very cautious, almost timid, in his view of the prospects for a Conservative government. But if he erred here, he erred in the right direction; for there were many more, especially in the Lords, all too ready to make a mad dash for power on the slightest pretext, or none at all.

Wellington's caution helped to dictate his strategy on the government's Canada Bill of 1839. Peel opposed the inclusion in the bill of an endorsement in principle of a union of the two Canadas that in practice was to be put off for several years. Wellington agreed in wishing to put off the endorsement of the abstract principle. He was also afraid that Lord Brougham, who had made himself the leading critic of his former colleagues' Canada policy, would make another attack in which he would be joined by Conservative peers also anxious to bring down the government. The duke wrote to Peel:

The course which I would recommend to you is that you should call to your discussion of your course upon that Bill the Lords named below. If they should hear that they could not afterwards take any course with Lord B upon it merely for the annoyance of the Government.

The duke named Lords Lyndhurst, Ellenborough, Wharncliffe, Haddington, Ripon, Aberdeen, Ashburton, Abinger, and Manners. It was a carefully chosen group, including the party's leading experts on imperial and colonial affairs (Ellenborough, Haddington, Ripon, Aberdeen, and Ashburton); and law (Lyndhurst, Abinger, and Manners). It also included leading debaters and/or peers influential in the several sections of the party: Lyndhurst, to whom it would have been likely the Ultras would turn; Ripon, the former Canningite prime minister and now Stanley's leading ally in the Lords; and Wharncliffe, another influential moderate. The duke's was a plan for a complete co-option of anyone to whom those wishing to oppose the measure could possibly have turned for a champion. As Wellington accurately observed to Peel the next day: "The suggestion which I made to you in my note yesterday is the best for keeping the House of Lords quiet and in a state to be managed."[42] And so it proved: the bill passed easily through the Lords.

On the eve of the 1840 session of Parliament Peel wrote to the duke that he expected pressure from the party for some "hostile movement against the Government," and that he felt they must give in to this pressure. Wellington disagreed, because he believed that the country's defenses desperately needed building up, and that the Whigs were more likely to get the necessary support in the country and in Parliament than the Conservatives; because he believed that the reformed electoral system was not yet likely to return a sufficient majority to allow the Conservatives to govern; and because of the hostility of the queen, so recently demonstrated in the Bedchamber Crisis. But Wellington went on readily to concede that the decision was not his to make. As far as the Lords were concerned: "The House of Lords ought to take, and I don't doubt that the majority will take, the course which will be most convenient to our leaders in the House of Commons."[43] It was a clear recognition of the primacy of the House of Commons, by a very confident leader in the House of Lords.

The 1840 session would be the last before the next Conservative government came to power in which the Lords was an important arena of political action. Wellington was true to, and able to deliver on, his promise that the Lords would be guided by the convenience of the party leaders in the Commons, but at considerable personal cost. He and Peel had a series of sharp differences of opinion during this session. One was over Hansard's publishing rights, backed by the House of Commons, but questioned by the Court of Queen's Bench. Peel strongly backed the privilege of the House of Commons, while Wellington and much of the rest of the party took the other side. When the Parliamentary Papers Bill came up to the Lords, however, the duke gave up his personal opinion and managed to get it through unopposed. Much more serious was the clash over another Canada Bill, which now formally proposed the union of the two

Canadas. Wellington was convinced that the union of the two provinces would be but a prelude to independence, and entered into strong opposition to a bill Peel supported. Without consulting the duke, Lord Hardwicke gave notice of a motion to oppose going into committee on the bill. Wellington himself had given notice of a motion to hear evidence. Peel responded to these notices by a memorandum, which said in effect that the Lords could do as they pleased, but that he would do the same. Then, as he done in 1835 under similar circumstances, he refused to have any further communication with the duke. This rather extraordinary mode of proceeding was no more helpful now than it had been then. To Stanley and Graham, who were anxious to talk to him, the duke addressed similar communciations. To Graham:

I have always endeavoured to keep the House of Lords in a position to be useful whatever might be my opinion upon a question under discussion.

I have done so upon this question and will continue the same course as long as I am able to take any part in political affairs.

I have nothing further to say upon the enclosed paper.[44]

This was written on 4 July. The next day Aberdeen reported to Peel that he had met with the duke and Lyndhurst to discuss the position on the Canada affair. Wellington agreed to give up his notice of moving to hear evidence. He would also support going into committee, in opposition to Hardwicke if necessary. He would call a meeting of Conservative peers and outline the course he proposed to follow. Though he would personally persist in his objection to the union of the two Canadas, he would recommend to his followers that they not oppose the government's bill. Aberdeen hoped that the duke "would be so far successful as to prevent any open division."[45]

He was, as Aberdeen explained in a letter to Arbuthnot on 14 July. The meeting at Apsley House took place on the morning of Hardwicke's proposed motion. Aberdeen described the duke's speech:

of all the admirable statements I have heard him make at these meetings, I was never so much struck as on this occasion. The effect of his address was like magic; and although we had many present who were obstinate, violent and wrongheaded, not a syllable was said in opposition to the Duke's suggestion. He treated the whole subject with the utmost dexterity and skill; and when he spoke of his own position, it was beautifully done, and the effect irresistible. I am happy to think that he was pleased with the conduct of the peers. Indeed, I have never known such an instance of his power and influence. Under the very peculiar circumstances in which this question was placed, that he should only have found ten persons refractory is most wonderful.[46]

Aberdeen was, of course, writing to one of the duke's closest friends and may well have expected that the letter would be passed on (which it seems not to have been). Nevertheless, the results speak for themselves. Against his own well-known opinion, reiterated at the meeting, the duke had managed to swing the party in the Lords behind the position of a much-disliked leader in the Commons.

"It was a curious position for the victor of a thousand fights, but a man must be in a curious, and tragic, position when his influence ought to be more important than his opinions." Thus Kitson Clark on the whole affair.[47] But this is perhaps too lugubrious a judgment. At the 5 July meeting with Lyndhurst and Aberdeen at which the duke agreed to reverse his course, Aberdeen had noted that "The Duke was in perfect good humour throughout—remarkably so, with everything and everybody, except with the government." He had told Graham that "I have always endeavoured to keep the House of Lords in a position to be useful whatever might be my opinion upon a question under discussion," and that he had done so on this occasion.[48] This was perfectly true. A motion to hear evidence might have increased pressure on the government, but it would have committed the Lords to nothing. Increasing pressure on the government was presumably Wellington's intention, in the hope of extracting concessions. The government had much to thank the duke for, not only his early support in the Canadian crisis, but also his help in sorting out a number of delicate questions connected with the queen's marriage. And, in fact, Melbourne cheerfully accepted such amendments as the Lords did propose, with the object of delaying the implementation of the measure.[49] Peel himself had managed to influence government policy on the previous Canada Bill. Why not the duke on this one? Naturally any attempt to bring a major change in government policy brought the possibility of the government's resignation. Given their discussions before the session began, there was no reason for Wellington to suppose that this was something to which Peel was averse. When that became clear, the duke would have been a much greater fool than he was, and totally irresponsible, which he never was, to have proceeded with the course he was pursuing. The fact was that Peel had a strong tendency to go off half-cocked over what he *thought* were the duke's opinions, and then by refusing to communicate with him to put himself in a position where it was as difficult as possible to find out what those opinions actually *were*.

In a broader sense, it had in fact always been the case that the duke's influence was more important than his opinions, though these were by no means unimportant. Whatever the case in war, in politics Wellington's greatest moments were when he was leading a retreat, over the Test Acts, Catholic Emancipation, parliamentary reform, the Corn Laws. To a lesser extent perhaps, this was also true within the party, as in the case just noticed. But, whether he was winning or losing, the duke's major function within the party was to preserve a sense of continuity. If Peel had actually been able to bring his party around to the newer and more liberal views represented in the Tamworth Manifesto, it would have been different, but he was not. The 1840s demonstrated conclusively that the bulk of the party remained more Tory than Peelite Conservative. This was certainly the case with the Lords in the 1830s, and it is difficult to imagine who besides Wellington would have been capable of keeping the party united. Genuinely Tory in his own convictions, the duke was able to maintain the pride and spirit of his followers even when he led them in retreat. In 1835 Wellington signalled his course on the Municipal Corporations Bill by putting himself in opposition to the duke of Newcastle's proposed motion against going into committee. Yet on 5 September of that year, Newcastle writing to say that, if convenient, he would like to leave town before the end of the session, concluded:

If however your Grace has the slightest wish that I should remain you have only to say—Stay and I will cheerfully remain at my post. After the noble fight which your Grace has made, I will not desert my leader.[50]

The strong, even violent, rhetoric which so agitated Peel, reassured the Tory peers and made them ready to believe the duke when he told them that the odds were insuperable; that they had fought a noble fight, and could retire with honor. By allowing the Tory peers to maintain their self-esteem, the duke kept the party together. Peel could never have done it.

As for the House of Lords, the duke managed to exercise its powers in such a way, and with sufficient drama, as to make it respected, even feared. The Whig retreat over the Irish Church Bill of 1833 is a good example. At the same time, Wellington was able to restrain the Lords from indulging in excesses that might have brought a successful attack on their powers. Even his defeats were useful in this respect, because what his followers saw as battles to the last ditch, others viewed as statesmanlike withdrawals. Wellington's influence was indeed more important than his opinions. No one knew it better than the duke. Nor did it trouble him unduly. It was his influence that enabled him to perform his duty to monarch and country; and, if any man has ever put his duty before his opinions, it was the duke of Wellington.[51]

The Old Whigs: Bedford, Fitzwilliam, and Spencer in the House of Lords, 1833–1861

ELLIS ARCHER WASSON

"Cradle to grave" only mildly overstates the poles of the political *cursus honorum* enjoyed by the heads of great aristocratic families in nineteenth-century Britain. Magnate heirs generally entered the House of Commons soon after their 21st birthdays. In some cases, including that of the Earl Fitzwilliam of this study, first election actually came before the age of majority was attained. Barring accident or disease an inevitable translation to the House of Lords usually occurred in mid-career. In some cases, as in that of the duke of Bedford discussed here, heirs were called to the upper House in their fathers' lifetime. More commonly the vagaries of fate decided the date of elevation. For many peers entry into the Lords made little difference in their habits as legislators. The luxury of the proxy system relieved them from the necessity of pairing, presuming they took party discipline seriously in the first place. Those with their wits about them (and even some who did not) were considered fit to be members of the cabinet whether as lord or MP. Only in the twentieth century did a peerage become a serious liability for the premiership.

Pushed by proud parents into the political arena at the earliest possible moment, the three subjects of this study followed careers fairly typical in form, though not necessarily in substance, of grandees of the first rank. In a society still dominated by the landed nobility, the seventh duke of Bedford (1788–1861), the fifth Earl Fitzwilliam (1786–1857), and the third Earl Spencer (1782–1845) stood at the apex of what Lord Grey called "the high aristocracy."[1] Two things other than their titanic wealth made these men unusual. First, they applied themselves to political life with rare sedulity for magnates of leviathan status. A recent study puts two of the three in the top ten percent of the most active MPs during their years in the Commons.[2] Secondly, they had a passion for progressive ideas and political reform.

Vast acres of corn and coal, not personal talents, made these men important, though Spencer's gifts of character raised him to exceptional heights as Grey's indispensable lieutenant in the early 1830s. Bedford, if he is remembered at all, is known only as Lord John Russell's brother. Fitzwilliam's campaign of verbal terrorism against the Corn Laws is his principal claim to fame. Nonetheless, Bedford, Fitzwilliam, and Spencer were a formidable team who shared emotional bonds and like opinions in religion, agriculture, economics, estate management, science, and politics. They helped to set the Whig agenda for a generation or more. Elsewhere I have described the kinship, intimate friendship, and advanced ideology of "the Young Whigs" during their days in the House of Commons. The purpose of this chapter is to analyze the changes, as they became "Old Whigs," in their activities, opinions, and influence after they were swept inexorably to the upper chamber. Some recent experts on Whiggery have suggested that they "retired" upon elevation to the Lords.[3] Unquestionably, they devoted less time to parliamentary duties in the precincts of Westminster. Did membership in the Lords hinder their activities or sap their will to rule? Did they give up in disgust? To what extent did other responsibilities make it impossible for them to continue at their former pace? Did they exercise political influence at the national level? What future did these men see for a legislative chamber that had become a wet blanket cast upon reform, darkening a constitution that they had labored for three decades to make less oppressive and more responsive to public opinion?

I

In 1809 Bedford was the last of the threesome to enter the Commons and in 1833 the first to leave.[4] His attendance record, when marquis of Tavistock, was never good. In part this was due to his passion for foxhunting and horseracing (he won the Derby three times, once with an unnamed horse!) and in part to recurrent bouts of serious bronchial trouble that drove him to Devon and Cornwall for many winters. In 1824 he was briefly taken into custody for failure to attend a call of the House but then excused on the grounds of illness.[5] He admitted: "I want both talent and practice for public speaking: and when my mind is full of matter, I am unable to express it, and leave unsaid half what I wish to say."[6] Even his doting father acknowledged Bedford's delivery was "irksome."[7]

He fell increasingly silent and his last speech in either House of Parliament was delivered on the Catholic Question in 1829.[8] The Russells may through the centuries have produced able statesmen and philosophers, but they also tend towards nervousness and eccentricity. In Bedford's day they spoke with such odd pronunciation that it was parodied even within the family circle. The sixth duke felt "an utter inability" to debate. The eighth became a recluse. Before he shot himself the ninth duke also proved a hopeless speaker who was liable to break down entirely after five minutes on his feet in the House of Lords.[9] Thus, there is no surprise in the seventh duke's silence during his long tenure in the Lords. He was called to the upper House in his father's barony of Howland of Streatham in 1833, probably at his own request. His elevation helped to bolster the Whig minority in the Lords, and Lord John Russell could be relied upon to keep the family banner aloft in the Commons while their father had lapsed into a life of inattentive dissipation leaving the eldest son true chief of the tribe in the House of peers.[10] Bedford attended sittings of the House, but was sometimes inattentive. He once failed to turn up for a crucial vote when his brother's government lost by a narrow margin.[11] As we shall see, however, the placidity of his public persona belied an active political life that increased in intensity and importance after his entry into the Lords.

Fitzwilliam, as Viscount Milton, was first among equals in the House of Commons as MP for Yorkshire (1807–31).[12] He was the richest man regularly active in the lower House for nearly three decades. His father had inherited Rockingham's estates and was Burke's patron, and the son edited the first edition of the sage's correspondence. Hence Fitzwilliam was the heir to some of the most central and potent traditions of Whiggery as well as one of the greatest fortunes in the kingdom. He was also intelligent, articulate, hard working, and ready on his feet. His failure to attain office was due to an assumption that anyone who disagreed with him was either immoral or stupid, and Fitzwilliam felt that no man, even a Whig prime minister, had the right to tell him what to do.

Though temporarily stunned into inactivity by the unexpected early death of his wife in 1830, Fitzwilliam gradually recovered from the blow and continued to speak regularly after he moved to the Lords upon his father's demise two years later. He and Bedford entered the chamber within three weeks of each other. Fitzwilliam spoke at least once in every session until his own death, regularly attended sittings and carried on a series of campaigns to educate his fellow members about the iniquity of the Corn Laws, the failure of government policy in Ireland, and many other topics. His obsession with the Corn Laws earned him the derisory sobriquet among his peers of "Corncrake."[13] In fact his views were often sensible and humane. He cared passionately about Church reform, economic development, and the abolition of slavery. The trouble was that he did not believe the rules of parliamentary procedure applied to someone of his august lineage. He spoke out of order and sometimes became a serious impediment to the business of the House. Because the Lords lacked a powerful Speaker he could trample over their conventions at will.[14] The word compromise did not exist in his vocabulary. Sadly, Fitzwilliam seems to have understood, as he admitted in the House, how "very offensive he made himself to their Lordships," but he was unable to cease calling his brother Irish peers "criminals" or enraging the Archbishop of Canterbury, not to mention the whole bench of bishops, by referring to the Church of England as a mere "sect" like the Baptists or Unitarians.[15] He acknowledged late in life: "I am still irritable—in my irritation I am vehement, even violent, in my violence I attack others, and, though I cannot charge myself with harbouring a particle of ill-will towards any human being, I am well aware that I judge others severely."[16] Hence Fitzwilliam's influence at Westminster remained far beneath what his ideas and abilities merited, though in large regions of England and Ireland he remained respected and even popular with the electorate.

Spencer's entry into the Lords a year after that of his friends indicated the exceptional role he had played in the great Reform Ministry, when he was known as Viscount Althorp.[17] On his father's death in November 1834, Spencer's resignation as Leader of the House of Commons precipitated the collapse of the government. There had been talk of calling him to the upper House in his father's lifetime to pilot the Reform Bill through the Lords and bolster Whig leadership there. But Grey, who called him "my right arm," could not afford to lose him in the Commons. The impact of his eventual departure demonstrated the accuracy of this judgment.[18]

Spencer attended and spoke infrequently in the upper chamber. In part this was due to his well-known dislike of London and desire for the peace of the countryside. However, since he went on in his "retirement" to found or become president of several national organizations, which obliged him to reside regularly in the capital, this cannot explain his absence at Westminster. The problem was that his following among Liberals and Radicals was large, and they remained ardent for his leadership. If he appeared frequently in the Lords many MPs would assume Spencer was preparing a direct challenge to Melbourne's government and a bid for the premiership.[19] Spencer was politically ambitious, despite his many statements to the contrary, but he had a genuine horror of the highest office, which he rightly felt was beyond his capacity. Other factors, discussed below, also made an active career in the Lords impossible. Hence he lodged his proxy with a minister to indicate his support of the government and rarely appeared thereafter.[20] However, by no means did he fade from the national scene. It was said that Spencer's conduct in the Lords was "Sir R[obert] Peel's ideal—rare appearances for serious purposes and without compromise generally to the independence of his personal habits." Gladstone, who told this story, said that "this was possible in the House of Lords but only there."[21]

II

Certainly, the customs and ambiance of the House of Lords gave much greater personal freedom to grandees than did the Commons. Some career politicians saw moving to the House of Lords as a kind of involuntary retirement and were reluctant to depart from the lower House.[22] Brougham, whose elevation to the peerage Spencer had made a condition of his own acceptance of office in order to break the lawyer's dangerous power in the Commons, wrote that he was "doomed" to the Lords that "odious House."[23] The physical facilities were unpleasant. When the old Houses of Parliament burned down in 1834, the peers moved to the surviving medieval Painted Chamber, which Greville aptly called "a wretched dog-hole." Pugin's triumphant new chamber did not open until 1847 and even then the acoustics were bad.[24] However, the old House of Commons had been at least as unpleasant; indeed it was a stinking hole when the chamber was full on a hot night at low tide. Uncomfortable conditions in the House of peers did not keep the Old Whigs from their places. Nevertheless, they did make a radical shift in the allocation of their time. Inheritance of a great estate, for men to whom the ideal of Christian stewardship was a matter of cardinal importance to their immortal souls, meant reordering their personal lives and activities. Moreover, they were members of a generation that paid increasing attention to agricultural development and innovation. Hence territorial responsibilities consumed more time than they would have in the schedules of the previous generation.[25] In addition Augustans of their fathers' ilk spent money as if there was no tomorrow, and all three estates were heavily in debt.

Debt, of course, is a relative thing. John Evelyn called Althorp Park a palace with state rooms "as may become a great prince." Woburn Abbey was called even by aristocratic visitors a "princely mansion" with an estate that formed "a little Kingdom." Dinner was presented "pretty much in the

Windsor Palace [sic] style; but, of the two, more formal." Wentworth Woodhouse, was probably the largest private dwelling in the British Isles, and the estate was called a "principality." Fitzwilliam also had another huge seat in England and large Irish estates, coal mines and an industrial empire.[26]

Bedford was an active and good manager. He supervised a team of 450 estate workers in Bedfordshire, copper mines in the West Country, Covent Garden Market and a large London estate. He was an enthusiastic agricultural improver, and declined to help administer the royal estates "because the management of his own affairs left him no time to attend to others."[27] He read agricultural literature, introduced steam driven machinery to farm work, attended sales and shows, and presided over meetings. Above all he struggled to reduce a debt of over half a million pounds left by his father. Fortunately, the Russell resources were deep and within fifteen years he had freed his inheritance completely, but at the cost of careful and time consuming management.

Fitzwilliam's estates were even larger and more complex. The Earl played an active role as policy maker and executive. He had 700 employees in his coal mines and iron works alone in 1833.[28] The far-flung nature of his holdings meant that Fitzwilliam was often on the road or crossing the Irish Sea. He was also active in agricultural affairs. Moreover, the Fitzwilliam debt stood at £800,000 in the 1840s. One third of his income was swallowed by interest. But the Earl's wealth was also expanding. He did not always make astute management decisions but he succeeded in passing on his inheritance safely.

Spencer's estates were smaller and less diverse than those of his friends. However, he was the most active agriculturalist and faced proportionally the most serious crisis in his finances.[29] His duties as president of the Smithfield Club and the Royal Agricultural Society, which he founded, kept him frequently in London. He was an innovative and successful cattle breeder and managed every aspect of this business personally. His succession to the earldom led to a decade long struggle to save the Spencer family from catastrophe. Interest consumed over three-quarters of his income on a debt of over half a million pounds. Again, judicious management saved the estate, although Spencer was forced to sell large blocks of land.

The struggle to right the listing barks which kept afloat dynastic honor and power meant many hours spent at the pumps. Retreat to the country, or more accurately, the estate offices, colliery board rooms, and even auction houses was not retirement, but a necessary shift of priorities (and not any less unpleasant than work at Westminster) if these great Whig families were to rule in future generations. A significant number of peers of both parties were in similar financial circumstances, but few had an automatic right of entry to the inner circle of power in the way Whig grandees did.

III

No one thought much about giving office to Fitzwilliam, but both Melbourne and Lord John Russell tried to bring Bedford and Spencer into government. The duke was offered the rule of Ireland or India in 1839 and his brother tried to persuade him to join the cabinet in 1845. In 1847 Ireland was again mentioned. However, Bedford turned down even the ceremonial appointment of master of the horse despite heavy lobbying by the queen.[30] Spencer made it clear to Melbourne immediately after his succession to the earldom that further office-holding was unlikely. He had been badly frightened by his narrow escape from the premiership in July 1834. He declared later that only the question of the "*salvation*" of his immortal soul could induce him to consider Downing Street again.[31] Even so Melbourne tried to bolster the Whig party's popularity by inducing the earl to rejoin the cabinet and in the late 1830s he offered the rule of Ireland or Canada. However, the financial crisis engulfing his estate precluded Spencer's acceptance.

Although the Old Whigs assumed heavy managerial responsibilities on succeeding to their titles, political retreat was not on their agenda, nor would their colleagues in government allow them to fade from the scene. Whiggery was an hereditary circle of great families which required the active interest of grandees as its source of direction and *raison d'etre*. Bedford, Fitzwilliam, and Spencer were related by blood or marriage to virtually all the key personnel in the party, knew everybody else, exercised great territorial power in the provinces, and headed various organizations of national importance that shaped policy and promoted progress. Inevitably, they helped to direct the future policy of the Whig party as well.

Bedford loved to be in the center of things even though not in the limelight. He boasted to Charles Greville, truthfully, "there is no great affair of my own time I have not been well acquainted with." He spoke with relish about "my heaps of interesting political letters." Lord Clarendon called his letter writing, begun at four or five in the morning and continued until ten or eleven, almost a "mania."[32] In the 1840s and 1850s Bedford played a role akin to Lord Duncannon's in the 1820s: a quiet reconciler, negotiator, news gatherer, go between, and keeper of the flame. He had the enormous advantage of possessing Woburn Abbey, a kind of party headquarters close to London. Even jaded country house visitors were struck by Woburn's luxury and comfort. The hunting and shooting, the fishing and strolling, the library and art collection, and the food and company attracted a horde of visitors who shared their secrets with the duke. This, after all, was the first private house to which the young queen paid a personal visit at the outset of her reign. The duchess was the one who gave England the afternoon habit of taking tea. The leader of the Whig party was a younger son of the house. Bedford's father had erected a Temple of Liberty near the lake which housed the statues of Whig heroes of the past. The social influence of such a place was overpowering and provided a key center for the mixing of various strains of Whiggery and the gradual absorption of liberal Tories into the Whig fold. The house became even more a Whig holy of holies than Holland House had been, without the intellectual distinction.[33]

Melbourne consulted the duke about appointments. At moments of political crisis Bedford was liable to be center stage. He was drawn into the Bedchamber Crisis in 1839 through his wife's role in the affair. In December 1845 he met with the other senior Whigs at Chesham Place to decide whether Lord John Russell should form a government. He advised against the attempt, although it was upon Lord Grey's objections that the plan foundered. The queen asked Bedford's advice about who to send for if Derby resigned, and Woburn was the site of the secret meeting in December 1852 which investigated options for a coalition at the behest of the Prince Consort.[34]

The most significant avenue of Bedford's influence lay through his brother the prime minister with whom he had an excellent and affectionate relationship. They did not always agree and on crucial decisions Russell took his own counsel, but he relied on the duke emotionally and intellectually as well as financially.[35] Lord John's precipitate nature and inability to manage people were nicely balanced by Bedford's bonhomie and common sense. In terms of policy the duke thought Melbourne's government too aristocratic and not liberal enough. With Fitzwilliam and Spencer he goaded the ministry to go further with reform. He put considerable pressure on Russell to join the Aberdeen Coalition in a subordinate position. He wisely warned his brother to avoid open attacks on O'Connell. When he was premier, Lord John's arrogance and stubbornness could only be overborne by Bedford. Greville noted that Russell "receives everybody ill who goes to him to tell him what he does not like to hear, and nobody but the Duke . . . will go to tell him what he ought to hear."[36] In general the duke held a moderate line which encouraged the more timid of his magnate cousins in the Lords to support reform.

Fitzwilliam, too, was intimately acquainted with all the Whig prime ministers of the time. A regular stream of comments and criticisms flowed from his pen to Downing Street. Topics might include anything from money markets and railways to minor matters of patronage. He treated Lord John Russell like a schoolboy. He accepted the Whig whip only when it came in the prime minister's hand, but even then he was liable to add caveats and exceptions. Nonetheless, he was carefully consulted. The official leaders of the party wrote to him about parliamentary strategy.[37] He was a colossus too big to be ignored and all too ready to speak his mind in public. He did just that in the House of Lords on the state of Ireland, spraying indiscriminate but sensible criticism on governments of all shades of opinion for their incompetence, inhumanity, and lack of vision. He advocated vigorous and radical reforms in Ireland to overcome the "tyrannical oligarchy" of the Ascendancy. Fitzwilliam understood, as most Englishmen did not, that the problems of Ireland had as much an economic basis as a religious one. In the latter sphere he favored full legal and economic equality between the protestant and Catholic churches. Not only did he make his own estate a powerful example of humane management during the Famine, but also he denounced the poverty of the English response to the catastrophe. The great question Fitzwilliam kept repeating over and over again was how to sustain and reorganize life in Ireland without the potato. He knew that intervention on a massive scale was necessary to break the downward cycle of the economy. Infusions of capital, railway building, land reform, and commercial farming would all be needed for the salvation of the country. He even declined the Garter, the one bauble many magnates would kill to acquire, in part because of his disagreement with Russell's Irish policy.[38] He helped to educate his colleagues, and Whig lords lieutenant in Dublin hastened to listen to his views. His old friend, Lord Ebrington, wrote as he began his tenure at the Castle: "I am very anxious to set myself and the Government right with you as far as I can, for I know no man in Ireland whose good opinion I feel a greater desire to obtain than yours, in all things relating to the Administration of affairs here."[39]

The man Whig ministers were most anxious to stay on good terms with in the 1830s and 1840s was Earl Spencer. He was popular both in the Commons and across the nation, particularly in Liberal urban strongholds. "Pray never fail to let me know any thing you think material," begged Melbourne, who did not want to be blindsided by an angry earl.[40] Lord John Russell is said to have respected his opinion more than any other man's.[41] They had worked closely for many years in the Commons, and as Russell's predecessor as leader of the party there Spencer well understood the challenges of the job. Russell consulted the earl frequently on technical issues relating to the Poor Laws, leases, tithes, the budget, and especially on tariff policy. Spencer tried to persuade Lord John to be more sympathetic to Dissenters and Radicals, advised the chancellor of the exchequer on currency and bank questions, and corresponded regularly with the President of the Poor Law Commission, who was the family lawyer.[42] Spencer remained active in electoral affairs, contributing funds, suggesting tactics, and proposing candidates. He made himself available as a debater in the Lords when required. Melbourne turned to him to move the deathbed Address in 1841, which turned out to be one of the most memorable speeches of Spencer's career.[43] In 1843, after he publicly announced his adamant opposition to the Corn Laws, what Spencer feared most if he became too active politically began to happen. Speculation arose that he was positioning himself for a return to office, and the press began to sniff the wind. Indeed, although the queen was frightened by his extreme opinions, she told Bedford to tell the earl to hold himself in readiness should Peel's government fall. Even if he had overcome his own reservations about the premiership, however, Spencer's health would not have allowed him to act. He was feeling more and more like an old man and made it clear to Russell that no challenge to the latter's ambition would come from him.[44]

IV

Bedford, Fitzwilliam, and Spencer had corresponded regularly and frequently acted as a unit when they were the lion cubs of the Whig party. That intimacy and unity continued into old age. They were seen in the 1840s as the most important of the active politicians among the grandees of the party, and when they acted in unison made a formidable force.[45] For example, they had been in the most advanced wing of the party on the subject of parliamentary reform, and had made it clear that change would not end with the 1832 act. They strongly disapproved of Russell's "finality" speech in 1837. Bedford felt his brother's comments unduly restricted the party's ability to maneuver and ruined Lord John's chances of becoming a popular leader.[46] Fitzwilliam, originally the most reluctant reformer of the three, had, as was his nature, become radical on the subject in the early 1830s. He later advocated universal manhood suffrage in Ireland as a means of breaking the power of the Ascendancy. He felt the next reform bill in England ought to establish universal suffrage.[47] Spencer believed the Great Reform Bill had merely been a first step, and supported both the secret ballot and universal suffrage from the 1820s onwards.[48] One of the most significant aspects of their careers in the House of Lords was ensuring that no one could say in the 1840s or 1850s that the Whig magnates stood against change. The most active politicians among the great landed proprietors in a profoundly aristocratic party were advocates of continued, indeed radical, parliamentary reform.

One of the most decisive interventions made by the troika during their years in the House of Lords was in foreign policy. They had strong pacifist leanings based on religious feelings, wanted cheap government, and disliked Lord Palmerston, still a distrusted Canningite in their eyes. They became thoroughly aroused when the sultan's vassal in Egypt, Mehemet Ali, led an insurgency against the Porte in Syria in 1839. France supported Ali. In concert with the tsar, the emperor, and the king of Prussia (three Whig bogies of the first water) Palmerston, the foreign secretary, threw Britain's support to the sultan. War with France became a possibility. To Spencer France was the nation "most fitted to be our friend by situation, institutions, and civilization."[49] He rallied his friends and they launched a letter writing campaign among the senior leadership of the party to undermine Palmerston. The latter was furious. "Spencer may know more about a cow than I do," he complained in outrage, "but I do not think he is so good a judge of foreign politics as I am." However, he was forced to grovel and mince, barely salvaging his policy with promises of a peaceful resolution.[50] Palmerston blotted his copybook again in 1842 when he attacked Aberdeen's attempts to improve relations with France and conclude the Canadian boundary treaty with the United States. It was harder to discipline Palmerston since the Whigs were now not in office, but Bedford's brother would later find it possible to drive from government for a time a man whom the grandees saw as a crypto-Tory.[51] They were not, of course, able to block Palmerston's ascent in later years, but by then Spencer was dead and the Russells outmaneuvered.

The most significant issue facing the Whigs in the 1840s was agricultural protection. Bedford was the least enthusiastic about repeal. He did vote for Fitzwilliam's motion for reform of the Corn Laws as early as 1839, although it was not until Lord John's Edinburgh letter in 1845 calling for total repeal that he embraced the cause wholeheartedly.[52] Spencer and Fitzwilliam, more intellectually curious and alert than Bedford, had read

Smith and Ricardo and become strong converts to free trade in the 1820s. However, they disagreed over the tactics needed to achieve their objective. Spencer was constrained by his membership in the Grey cabinet (the prime minister was a vehement advocate of protection) and then by his leadership in national agricultural organizations (farmers were strong supporters of the Corn Laws) from publicly espousing his views. Fitzwilliam was never constrained by anything and began to browbeat the landed interest in what he called "the battle of commercial Freedom."[53] He carried his campaign into the House of Lords with vigor and even abandon, much to their disgust. Spencer worked behind the scenes and lobbied Russell. He also became more vocal in public with his concerns in the early 1840s, delighting Fitzwilliam with a major attack on protection in a speech at Northampton in 1843 that caused a national sensation. Spencer and Fitzwilliam were not able to use their position in the Lords to convert the country to free trade. Yet, as with constitutional change, leading Whig magnates, highly visible on the national stage, were advocating reform throughout a time of great political and social unrest. It must have been reassuring to the more conservative patricians, who knew that Spencer was in deep financial difficulty and relied almost entirely on corn rents for income, to hear him promise that there was no danger to aristocratic solvency in repeal. Within the party in the Lords, the leadership of Bedford, Fitzwilliam, and Spencer was extremely helpful in swinging the rest of the reluctant Whig magnates behind Russell's lead in 1845.

V

In the end, of course, the House of Lords surrendered over protection, as it did in 1829 and 1832 on the great constitutional questions of reform. In the eighteenth century the Lords may have been "the bulwark of the King's government," and in the nineteenth the "citadel of the great fortress of reaction," but their lordships knew the story of King Canute. This is not to say that they gave up without a struggle. Spencer found the atmosphere unbearably dim, calling it the "Hospital for Incurables." "In the House of Commons I might possibly have done some good," he lamented, "out of it I cannot possibly do any."[54] Fitzwilliam, too, gloomily ruminated on his situation a few months after his elevation, "surrounded with the impenetrable darkness of the House of Lords." His particular anxiety was their lordships' apparent indifference to manufacturing and commercial interests. Even bringing in new blood did not seem to help. He turned on the ennobled banker, Baring, despairingly: "Every drop of commercial blood had oozed from the noble Lord since he had changed his character from that of a merchant and a liberal politician to that of a great landowner and an aristocrat."[55] The Whigs added seventy peers to the House in the decades immediately after 1830, but this did little to redress the balance in a chamber where they could lose crucial divisions by nearly a hundred votes. In addition, there was great difficulty imposing the Whip on patricians, as Fitzwilliam's own case exemplified, and the squeamishness in party councils about requiring the attendance of grandees was enough, the new and minor baron, Lord Hatherton, confided to his diary, "to break one's heart."[56]

What was to be done with the House of Lords? "The people of England cannot submit to their uncontrolled dictation," declared Spencer, but he had no remedy. There was a republican twinge to Whiggism not wholly dead even in the nineteenth century. It was once rumored that the earl would prefer to be "Mr. Spencer."[57] Fitzwilliam denounced the coronation as "little better than idle and ridiculous pageant," fit "only for barbarous ages." However, the marquis of Londonderry powerfully riposted that if Fitzwilliam did not want the crowning, he supposed the earl was then prepared to move "that there be no Lord Fitzwilliam at all."[58] And in truth the old Whigs could not imagine a world without king and peers. Spencer wrote: "whatever may be the case some years hence, this country is not yet fit for a Republic, and could not be converted into one without bloodshed and the most appalling evils." Their belief in republican virtue derived in part from a deep distrust of the executive, which an independent aristocracy could check.[59] Indeed, Fitzwilliam felt indigent noblemen "are as injurious to the constitution of the House of Lords as the rotten boroughs are to that of the House of Commons."[60]

Canning had presciently pointed out in 1822 that those Whigs who advocated reform of the Commons on the grounds of past misconduct were by implication accepting the need to reform the Lords as well. Hallam had noted that Whigs "deemed all forms of government subordinate to the public good, and therefore liable to change when they should cease to promote that."[61] Increasing the number of peers was the simplest way to make a change. The Old Whigs had pressed hard for a massive increase in the peerage to overcome resistance to the Reform Bill in 1831 and 1832. Spencer advocated this procedure a second time in 1833 to ensure a secure Whig majority in the upper House. Bedford, too, called for another full scale confrontation between the Commons and the Lords in 1834 to make the latter submit to the will of the former. Fitzwilliam did recommend some years later, as he had in 1831, that reform of the Commons be effected by issuance of writs to newly enfranchised boroughs without even sending a reform bill to the Lords.[62] They did not, however, suggest organic change, which some Radicals and a few Whigs believed necessary.[63] Even if they had been willing to contemplate a massive infusion of life peers or outright abolition, the Whigs held too few votes to make the changes anyway.

VI

When Fitzwilliam's contemporary, the third duke of Northumberland, moved from the Commons to the Lords he switched from voting Whig to Tory. The earl, on the other hand, even near the end of his life offered solutions to political problems that were as or more radical than those he advocated half a century earlier. The common assumption is that the onset of old age tends to make people more conservative and that the acquisition of great wealth is likely to reinforce the desire to protect property. In the case of Bedford, Fitzwilliam, and Spencer, however, no Percian about-face occurred when they went to the Lords. They pursued a steady line. It is impossible to detect any significant variation in their opinions after their change of chamber. They remained devout Whigs.

The problem, of course, is what did being Whig mean in the mid-nineteenth century? Protracted debate, recently quite active, has not yielded an agreed answer. One school holds that the Whigs' "congenitally undemocratic" nature resisted any infusion of radicalism, and without moral purpose or any real doctrine they clung to power with an uncertain and increasingly palsied grip.[64] Lord Grey saw no distinction between himself and Wellington, and the reform program simply petered out. The duke of Argyll noted contemptuously: "the Whig mind was then destitute of any fresh idea."[65]

According to one authority, wilting Whigs "had grown tired of the partisan nature of politics" and increasingly felt more at ease with their conservative opponents than with Radical and Liberal supporters.[66] Peel is given most of the credit for the important legal, economic, and social reform of the era. Indeed, it is argued that Melbourne's government only survived on Sir Robert's sufferance. "There was a future for Liberalism," Norman Gash has magisterially pronounced, "but none for Whiggery."[67]

On the other hand, Peter Mandler finds the Whigs in rude good health, vigorous, robust, and powerful reformers. He has refurbished Careless Davis's notion that Whiggery thought aristocracy only a means of government not an end. He has identified a resurgence of the Whig patrician spirit in the years after 1830. They were bent on proving the usefulness and responsiveness of the aristocratic state. This self-confident paternalistic style accomplished a wide range of important changes and it was Peel who blocked social reform. Whiggism had a coherent philosophy, economic doctrine and moral earnestness.[68] In yet another interpretation this latter quality is seen at the heart of Whiggery after Grey's departure from the leadership. Boyd Hilton, J. P. Parry, and Richard Brent argue forcefully for seeing Evangelical and Liberal Anglican religious feelings as paramount in the development of Whig economic, social, and political reform. The old fashioned view that Whiggism was more of a way of life, a "temperament," has been revived with Foxite glitter replaced by Clapham grey.[69]

In truth, there were many mansions inside the Whig house. The varieties of Whiggism were almost endless. The Whigs never became the votaries of one doctrine. They could not even agree on a name. This is well-illustrated by the subjects of this essay, who stood closer to each other than to any other members of their party. Fitzwilliam prefered "Whig," because "I like old words best." Bedford spoke of his "Whig and Liberal principles." Spencer called himself an "ultra-Whig," although after 1834, when the term began to become common, he called himself simply a "Liberal."[70] The history of the party was littered with factions: Grenvillites, Portland Whigs, Holland House, Canningites, the Devonshire set, Foxites, et cetera. Graham and Stanley were for many years Whigs of good standing. Evangelical and Liberal Anglican Whigs had their own bent. Fitzwilliam and Spencer viewed the economy "as an arena of great spiritual trial and suspense." The former openly referred to the Corn Laws as immoral and unchristian. On the other hand, Whigs such as Melbourne detested this approach and had an "absolute loathing" for any attempt to enlist religious feelings against protection.[71]

Whiggery was held together by two forces, and Bedford, Fitzwilliam, and Spencer were central in the operation of both of them. The Whigs, Sidney Herbert once observed, were incurably "superstitious about ducal houses." The Russells, Spencers, and Wentworth Fitzwilliams were all of ducal descent, and with only three or four other families constituted "the blood-royal of the Whigs."[72] The aristocratic system was central to the party ideology and identity. New men might be helpful with oratory and magazine articles, but the inner councils of policymaking remained blue-blooded until Whiggery was no more. Such practice inevitably meant that the most patrician and broad-acred received special deference. Had they not the whole foundation on which the party rested would have been made nonsense. Once Stanley crossed the aisle and Durham the Atlantic only Lansdowne and later Morpeth were more active than Bedford, Fitz-william, and Spencer among the Whig leviathans. The dukes of Devon-shire, Grafton, Norfolk, Sutherland, and Westminster were not disposed or able to perform a like role. Those who had the will to rule shaped Whig politics. The existence of an aristocratic coterie willing to promote party interests and give national leadership helped keep Whiggery alive. No more than a couple of dozen men dominated Whig affairs between 1820 and 1850. They held key offices in government, rallied party spirit on the opposition benches, and shaped aristocratic thinking on current issues by means of correspondence, country house visiting, and meetings in London. Bedford, Fitzwilliam, and Spencer remained at the center of this group throughout the period. Their switch from one House of Parliament to the other made no difference in this process. The Old Whigs had no intention of "retiring" after entering the Lords and did not do so. Each of them died in the traces, working, often at considerable personal cost, to promote party interests and the national welfare as they saw it. No man of Fitzwilliam's sensitive spirit would have subjected himself to the public abuse he regularly received around the country at agricultural meetings unless he had a passionate attachment to political principle. Spencer re-mained a leading figure in Whiggery and national life until the day he died, broadening the scope of his activities as the years passed and contrib-uting to election funds even in the years of his acutest financial crisis. Bed-ford supported his brother's work, saw Woburn replace Holland House as the central gathering place of Whiggery, and bustled tirelessly around London on one political mission after another.

The other unifying Whig characteristic was the Old Whigs' under-standing that reform was essential to their survival as a class and a party. There was, even in the mind of the most desiccated Foxite, some sort of notion that government was a moral and ethical activity. Whigs identified virtue with enlightenment and progress. Public virtue and the moral wel-fare of the people was grounded in the nation's stability and prosperity.[73] It was this broad concept, often variously defined or understood, that linked eighteenth-century Whigs with the Gladstonian Liberalism associ-ated with the party at the end of its existence late in the nineteenth cen-tury. Bedford, Fitzwilliam, and Spencer had been among the most ardent advocates of these views in their years in the Commons, and Russell con-tinued to lead the party under this flag from the benches in the lower House. In the Lords, where the spirit lived a muted and flagging existence within the breasts of the aging and cranky Grey, the cool and listless Lansdowne, and the Canningites Melbourne and Palmerston, the Old Whigs carried the still fresh and idealistic core values of Whiggery into the citadel of Toryism.

One can see this best in the Old Whigs' attitude towards public opinion, to which they became increasingly sensitive as it became more and more a force in politics. One finds frequent references to "public opinion" and the "voice of the people" in their correspondence and speeches.[74] They acknowledged that "the democracy" could be fickle and passionate. Precisely where the line lay between what Fitzwilliam called "the great *calm* body of thinkers," the national intelligence, and the mere popular will was hard to define. But it is clear from their thoughts about Ireland that they were contemptuous of an aristocracy which "had no community of feeling with the people."[75] Hence Lord Fitzwilliam lectured Melbourne in 1839 on the virtues of the Chartists, who, he said, were not just reckless and profligate radicals but sober and temperate men with real grievances and moral and religious feelings. He understood too "the efforts of the Anti-Corn Law League would have been powerless unless they had found a response in the feelings of the great mass of the people." Although he did not join the League, he did appear on the same platform with Cobden and even invited him to stay at Wentworth Woodhouse.[76]

VII

Ill health, ennui, self-indulgence, and a sense that they were out of step with the spirit of the age had ended the political careers of the Old Whigs' fathers a quarter of a century or more before their deaths. Querulous about parliamentary reform, opposed to free trade, and unable to summon the energy to do more than collect books, build holiday cottages, or ornament their parks, they drifted so far from the center of things that even the charisma of their names was unable to keep them influential as elder statesmen. "I am but a fireside politician," Bedford's father noted with satisfaction. "The part of an active Politician is not at all suited to my health and disposition," complained old Earl Spencer. For the last thirty years of his life, Fitzwilliam's father regarded himself more "as a counsellor from a distance and the representative of Whiggism in Yorkshire than as an active leader in the House of Lords or in party assemblies in London."[77] The senior generation had succeeded to their titles early in life, one while still a child, and none of them had the extensive experience in debate or business in the Commons that their sons acquired.

The careers of their sons in the House of Lords were very different.

They entered with reputations established and careers made in the Commons. To be sure, they could be timid and were certainly unimaginative. Their patrician world view could, especially in Fitzwilliam's case, lapse into arrogance and was likely to emphasize moderation. But stoically, honestly, and sometimes generously, they set examples of aristocratic accommodation to change and even vigorous reform. The Radicals were divided and weak, and the liberal Peelites often stymied by reactionary ultra-Tories. Throughout the difficult decades after the passage of the Reform Bill a handful of Whigs, some Canningites, some new men, some Foxite patricians, and some younger sons, worked to achieve and sustain a national equilibrium in a period of economic and social upheaval. Bedford, Fitzwilliam, and Spencer have been dismissed as "retired" or at best "gadflies" on the fringes of this effort. In fact they stood in the core of the Whig reactor, which continued to glow. Halévy called them, even in their later years in the Lords "the leaders of the Whig aristocracy."[78] Bedford and Fitzwilliam never fulfilled the promise of their youth in the Commons where each of them had once been seen as a candidate for the leadership of the party there. Spencer did attain that post but held it only until he was obliged to go to the Lords. After the inevitable translation from one House to the other, they proceeded with even greater territorial weight, no longer just "heirs," to be the leading grandees of their generation in the party of aristocratic reform. As "Old Whigs," they helped to ensure that at least two more generations of Whig peers would be able to play a leading role in national government. The aristocratic nature of Whiggery remained intact until no more Whigs existed. The stability, economic growth, and political reform the Old Whigs worked for in the Commons and in the Lords unfolded not always as they imagined but peacefully and progressively. Later Russells, Fitzwilliams, and Spencers continued the tradition of family influence in liberal politics. Spencer's heir remained a leader of the Liberal party into the twentieth century still seated upon the front bench of an as yet unemasculated House of Lords.

CHAPTER 8

Lord Derby

ANGUS HAWKINS

The fourteenth earl of Derby participated in parliamentary politics for 48 years. He was the first British statesman to become prime minister three times, in 1852, 1858, and 1866. He remains the longest serving party leader in British political history.[1] As a member of the House of Lords he led the Conservative party for the 22 years between 1846 and 1868. These facts alone testify to the continuing importance, despite the increasingly democratic nature of Victorian politics, of both the upper House and the aristocracy in nineteenth-century Britain.[2] Indeed, born in 1799 as Edward Geoffrey Stanley, Derby's political career, until his death in 1869, lay at the center of contemporary political change. As Britain became an increasingly complex, urban, and diversified society made up of new social interests, how were the historic relations between aristocracy, landed property, and the established Anglican church to be adjusted and preserved?

Shortly after Derby's death Benjamin Disraeli paid his long serving party leader an eloquent tribute and in doing so summarized his career. Derby had, Disraeli declared, abolished slavery, educated Ireland, and reformed Parliament. Yet this memorial owed as much to an emergent vision of Disraelian Conservatism as to Derby's own priorities and achievement. Derby did introduce the Irish Education Act in 1831, pass the Abolition of Slavery Act in 1833, and oversee the second parliamentary Reform Act of 1867. But to compose his long career around the single *leit motif* of legislative reform is to impose one simple pattern on the rich intricacy of Derby's public life. The main themes of that career lay, rather, in the circumstances of Derby's birth. They prefigure that complex process of adaptation, played out in the institutional focus of Parliament, experienced by the nation's traditional elite involving the power of landed property, and the status of the established church.

Stanley was born on 29 March 1799 at the family seat of Knowsley Hall, Lancashire. The owners of 60,000 acres in the county and the patrons of seven Anglican livings, the Derbys enjoyed a lineage going back to the twelfth century, traced through the family portraits, hanging alongside Rembrandt's "Belshazzar's Feast" and Reuben's "Death of Seneca," at Knowsley.[3] Set in the largest park in the county Knowsley itself, framed by ornamental gardens and a large lake, lay close to the commercial bustle of Liverpool. The proximity of the leafy comforts of Knowsley to the urban dynamism of Liverpool, in which the Derbys had further economic and political interests, forcefully represented the challenges facing Britain's aristocratic elite.

During Stanley's youth Knowsley was under the forceful sway of his grandfather, the twelfth earl of Derby; a man who epitomized the high ideals and low pursuits of Regency Whiggery.[4] A political devotee of Charles James Fox the twelfth earl endured the long years of opposition to which this allegiance condemned him. At the same time he was able to indulge his passions for horse racing and gambling. The twelfth earl's speeches, their rhetoric hardened in adversity, warned of the executive tyranny implicit in the royal prerogative, proclaimed the importance of a vigilant aristocracy in checking arbitrary rule, and framed the shibboleth of civil and religious liberty within a firmly hierarchical social vision. The sanctity of property was enshrined in the broad acres of a landed elite, upon whose rank and breeding rested a public duty to govern in the common interest of the nation. From his cock-fighting, to his long tenure as Lord Lieutenant of Lancashire, to his parliamentary denunciations of arbitrary government, the twelfth earl embraced the full spectrum of Foxite tastes. Conviviality, worldly sophistication, an elevated rhetoric exalting liberty, and a cosmopolitan manner were all there.

Stanley's father, who became the thirteenth earl of Derby in 1834, was a far less forceful presence who, though returning loyal Whig votes in parliamentary divisions, found ornithology and zoology more fascinating than politics.[5] The thirteenth earl's wife, his cousin Charlotte Hornby, brought an intense piety to the Knowsley household that contrasted strikingly with the worldly mores of her parents-in-law. Her early death at the age of 39 in 1817 left her reclusive husband the more devoted to a daily routine of copious zoological notes and observations. It was, therefore, under the influence of his grandfather that Edward Stanley came and from whom he imbibed deep drafts of Whig orthodoxy.[6] It was also a robust and self-reliant personality that emerged during Stanley's early years that sounded an hereditary echo of the paternal line.

Sent to Eton like his father and grandfather before him, Stanley survived the often savage regime of the infamous headmaster "Flogger" Keate. Self-confident, impatient of criticism, and not given to easy familiarity with those outside his own social rank, Eton honed Stanley's resilient and hardy personality. It also sharpened his evident intelligence and unusual powers of concentration, giving him an intimate knowledge of and abiding love for the classics. Keate himself was a brilliant classical scholar. Stanley also joined the newly formed Eton Society, later known as Pop, a debating society which proved the nursery of some of the nation's greatest orators.

In 1817, from the unreformed Eton of Keate, Stanley went up to the reformed Christ Church, Oxford, created by Dean Cyril Jackson. In that ethos of intense, if narrow, diligence Stanley's intellectual abilities, grounded in his classical studies at Eton, were affirmed by his winning the chancellor's prize for Latin composition in 1819. But, not unusually for a son of the peerage, he left without taking a degree. On coming down from Oxford it was to the cultured third marquis of Lansdowne that Stanley looked for an education beyond the classics.

Lansdowne, with Stanley's grandfather, was to be a most profound influence on the public doctrine and political beliefs of the young statesman. It was under Lansdowne that Stanley was groomed for greatness. In the library of Lansdowne's country house, Bowood, Stanley absorbed the particular brand of Whiggism of his mentor, while also adopting the old Whig uniform of a blue coat with brass buttons and a buff waistcoat worn by his host. This Bowood inculcation was a wider, less clannish, training than that to be had at other Whig salons such as Holland House.[7] Lansdowne had studied at Edinburgh University under Dugald Stewart, digesting a rich academic diet of David Hume and Adam Smith. Lansdowne thus came to form an intellectual bridge between the literary sophistication of "Grand Whiggery," as represented by the Foxite *illuminati* of Holland House, and the liberal impulses of the Scottish Enlightenment, as expressed in the new social sciences and the maxims of political economy. Stanley also acquired from Lansdowne a future philosophy of action rooted in a particular view of the English past. This, in turn, informed his understanding of the British constitution.

The grand historical narrative in which Stanley now immersed himself highlighted the emergence of the unique genius of the English national character evident in past politics.[8] Under the destructive Stuarts Englishmen's ancient legal liberties had been threatened. They were finally rescued from arbitrary rule by the Glorious Revolution of 1688. Central to their continued protection was the sovereignty of Parliament left at full liberty to legislate for the good of the country. It was from calm debate between the estates of the realm in Westminster that the true national interest emerged, while a tyrannical prerogative, violent demagogues, and an ungodly mob were held at bay. From his reading of the Elizabethan Sir John Davies's *Tracts* on Ireland Stanley found affirmation for his belief in the sanctity of private property, particularly landed property, as the necessary condition for civil order and progress. Finally, he saw arising from this historical scheme an important practical truth; that the pertinacious and destructive powers of conflicting social interests had to be avoided by expedient and timely reforms. Politics did not define society, but rather provided the means by which differing social interests, transformed by the force of progress, might be harmonized. The authoritative arena for this amelioration of social interests was Parliament.

Parliament was the seat of constitutional sovereignty from which the executive, as organized in the cabinet, drew its authority. It was necessary that the cabinet both enjoy the support of the majority of the Commons and be able to marshal that support. Parliamentary parties were a requirement and a virtue; in part because they protected parliamentary sovereignty from two rival subversive sources of authority, namely the prerogative and the people. Governments should not be the product of a popular mandate or the royal prerogative. Executive authority was derived from parties in Parliament. Such associations were, moreover, to some extent the product of legitimate influence as well as shared principles. Legitimate influence reinforced the natural authority of the aristocracy; an influence all the more legitimate because, Whig argument ran, the English ruling class was a more open elite than, for example, the closed privileged caste that had existed in France before 1789. The discernment of the national interest occurred in Parliament, through calm deliberation not popular pressure, within the framework of a social hierarchy in which a responsible aristocracy provided national leadership, responding to genuine grievances, checking an arbitrary prerogative, and withstanding the subversive clamor of demagogic fervor. All this was encapsulated in the phrase "responsible reform." The function this constitutional view prescribed for Whig aristocratic leadership was essentially one of mediation; balancing competing social interests on the fulcrum of private property, neither initiating demands nor denying legitimate grievances, both of which might be ultimately destructive. This constitutional model formed the bedrock of Stanley's public doctrine. On it he built his reading of Adam Smith (Lansdowne recommending *The Wealth of Nations* as "an admirable example of clear reasoning upon difficult and obscure subjects"[9]), thereby leavening Whig orthodoxies with the liberal nostrums of Scottish political economy. This blend, reflecting Lansdowne's particular brand of Whiggism, had two important implications for the future. First, it distanced Stanley from those Foxite Whigs gathered at Holland House. Second, it established potential sympathies with liberal Tories such as George Canning. When he entered Parliament in 1822, as MP for Stockbridge, Stanley was already a distinct and complex type of Whig.

Stanley's tutelage under Lansdowne also encouraged the young man's interest in Ireland. The Derbys owned an estate at Ballykisteen near Tipperary. Stanley's interest in Ireland was direct and personal, while Lansdowne, by the early 1820s, was becoming drawn into the problems of the economy, church and government of Ireland. To these issues Lansdowne brought a broad cool intellect little animated by any strong passion. The difficulties of education in Ireland also interested the older man and to these topics Lansdowne directed Stanley's reading. Davies's *Historical Tracts* on Ireland argued that the subduing of Ireland by England required the replacing of a native system of personal law with a system of property law as the precondition for civilized social order. The protection of property was a prior necessity for civic order and social progress. Gratton's speeches were prescribed as essential reading as was the life of Curran by his son. Finally, an 1820 pamphlet, "full of excellent sense and good eloquence," on the education of the Irish Peasantry was recommended as supporting an enlightened non-sectarian reform of Irish education. This too became seen as a requirement for bringing Ireland to the full benefits of civilized order.

Young Stanley's public doctrine provides the crucial context for understanding his subsequent political career. For Stanley, national politics were parliamentary politics. He remained largely immune to the development of extra-parliamentary organizations and a popular and increasingly powerful press. The authoritative arena of national political life was party affiliation within Westminster. Parties in Parliament were necessary for cabinets to govern. Yet they also had to be parties, or political associations, of a particular kind in order to preserve parliamentary sovereignty. They had to be associations cohesive enough to fulfil the needs of stable ministerial existence; parties sufficiently strong to authorize an executive, without the cabinet being reliant upon the royal prerogative. Yet they had to be associations loose enough to prevent the executive being merely the product of an electoral mandate; parties sufficiently weak to leave open the possibility of ministerial defeat without a dissolution. It was Parliament, not the monarch or the people, who chose the government.[10] It was this constitutional understanding that framed the young Derby's view of political leadership. Throughout his life it described the setting and helped to define the purposes of his public actions. Party support raised parliamentary leadership to power creating strong mutual obligations. In 1847 he told Lord George Bentinck that "Peel's great error has always been disregarding the opinion of his party, whenever it did not exactly square with his own; and I am confident that no man these days can hope to lead a party who cannot make up his mind sometimes to follow it."[11] Mediating those political opinions, created by changing times, within Westminster and reconciling them to existing structures was the essence of statesmanship. Derby repeated more than once a conviction which, he said, had been forced upon him early in public life: "that real political power was not to be had in England: at best you could only a little advance or retard the progress of an inevitable movement. [A]n English minister had more responsibility, more labour, and less authority, than the ruler of any people on earth!"[12] As the force of progress transformed society it became the responsibility of the nation's leaders to maintain the equilibrium of social interests.

Derby inherited a profound sense of the duty of the aristocracy to uphold that equilibrium. In 1849 he lectured Disraeli:[13]

He who has put his hand to the parliamentary plough cannot draw back. I do not speak, of course, of the great majority of members of both Houses, who act as parliamentary units, giving numerical strength and nothing else, to the party to which they attach themselves, but of those whom talent, or station, or accident has placed in the foreground and enabled them to exercise, whether they will or not, an influence over numbers of their brother members. For them there is no retreat.

Private conviction, however, was often masked in public by a flippancy entirely characteristic of Derby's class. Power was not an object of ambition, but the obligation of birth. It was a duty, moreover, to be carried lightly. One did not strive for success. While complaining of the "weary work of politics," Derby could declare that he "*never* was *ambitious* of office."[14] Yet this was the expression of a habitual indifference to self-exaltation; a formal pose of unambitious and selfless devotion to the common weal. It was an indulgence in a rhetorical convention shared with other aristocrats such as Lord Grey, Lord Melbourne, and Lord John Russell. It was expressive of social status and a belief in a Whig vision of parliamentary government in which a responsible aristocracy dutifully recognized its guardianship of the nation. It was *not* expressive of private motive or real purpose. A carefree manner was not to be confused with

carelessness. To some Derby's *blasé* bearing suggested idleness or inca-
pacity; particularly to those excluded by a bluff social demeanor, a blunt
sense of humor, barriers of class, or disconcerted by levity when seeking
gravitas. Derby had, like Lord Palmerston, Lord Hartington and Lord
Rosebery, a passion for horse racing, gaming, and field sports among
much else, and never pretended that absorption in politics excluded all
other interests. Homer, Newmarket, and pheasant shooting were as inte-
gral to his personality as Westminster and clubland. But those who read
Derby's passion for such activities as indicative of a casualness towards
public duty or disregard for public issues completely misconstrued his
character.

Derby's remarkable single-mindedness, emphasized such traits and social conventions. He was very fond of the expression "one thing at a time."
Again and again he demonstrated an extraordinary capacity for total concentration on the matter at hand. His close friend Lord Malmesbury
remembered: [15]

[Derby] was the keenest sportsman I ever met; whilst he was in the field his whole
attention was in the present pursuit, and woe to him who attempted to divert him
to politics at this time. When over, he would divest his mind completely of the
sport and sit down at once to write the longest and most important paper straight
off, in a delicate hand and without a single erasure—so completely could he in a
few moments arrange his subject in his mind. I have often witnessed this intellectual *tour de force* both in and out of the cabinet.

This single-mindedness sharpened Derby's intelligence. Disraeli admitted
that Derby astonished him; "his mind always clear, his patience extraordinary, he rises in difficulty, and his resources never fail." [16] Bulwer Lytton,
impressed by the speed with which Derby conducted business and his
recognition of the main points of a complicated case, thought him "the
cleverest public man he had ever met. Others had more genius, more
knowledge, more pure intellect, but no one seemed to rival Derby's cleverness." [17] Thus Derby seemed "a host in himself. He has marvellous acuteness of intellect and consummate power in debate. There is no subject
which he cannot master thoroughly and lucidly explain." [18]

All this gives credibility to the acclaim heaped upon Derby as a young
man during the 1820s. He was described as "the only brilliant eldest son
produced by the British peerage for a hundred years." [19] Interestingly, in
1829, it was Huskisson who called him "the hope of the Nation." [20] Such
comment from that source is testimony to the political position Stanley
established in his early parliamentary career. His apprenticeship under

Lansdowne, his claim to Canning's mantle in 1828, his governance of Ireland from 1830 to 1833, and his vision of parliamentary pre-eminence in 1835, all shaped the convictions, habits, and reflexes of the later Conservative leader. The seeds of 1867 came from the library at Bowood and Canning's political legacy, which had quickly taken root in the fertile soil of Derby's youthful vigor.

Derby's first major statement to the Commons, in 1824 as Mr. Stanley, was a spirited defense of the property of the Church of Ireland, threatened with an enquiry by the Benthamite radical Joseph Hume.[21]

He would not assert that there might not be circumstances which would justify an interference with the property of the Church, but he would maintain that no such circumstances could exist which would not equally justify an interference with landed, funded and commercial property.

The speech made his grandfather ill and split Whig ranks. Stanley's diagnosis of the actual causes of Irish distress was the want of a resident gentry, want of capital, want of employment, and the lack of adequate education.

The secular nature of this analysis was confirmed when, under something of a cloud, Stanley visited North America during 1824–25. He found in Canada similar violent political tensions over provision for the protestant and Catholic churches. But in this case he opposed an establishment replicating the Irish situation of a Catholic population under a protestant church. Upon his return to England he told Spring Rice that he wished the Irish situation "had never existed, and I am unwilling to renew the experiment in the Trans-Atlantic world."[22] Stanley favored Catholic Emancipation and the provision of property for the Catholic church in Canada. In the case of Ireland, however, he was a staunch defender of the property and status of the protestant establishment because the despoiling of its legally designated property would be a violation of a legal right fundamental to civic order. It would, moreover, be a breach of the sanctity of property irrelevant to the real causes of Irish suffering. It was social and economic factors that were causing Irish destitution, and while responsible political reforms could remove religious disabilities, abuse of property would only undermine the legal authority upon which civil society stood. What the miseries of Ireland required was the firm establishment of the force of law which, once done, would allow reforms to be introduced.

During 1826–27 Stanley faithfully supported Whig proposals for Catholic Emancipation, while also concurring in the reform of the Corn Laws proposed by Liverpool's government. This established sympathies with liberal ministerial Tories such as Canning and Huskisson and suggested that, should they be prised away from their ultra-Tory colleagues on the front bench, congenial company might be found among some on the opposition benches. Liverpool's debilitating stroke in early 1827 and resignation in April threw political alignments into review. Canning formed a government which did not include any of the anti-Catholics of Liverpool's ministry, Wellington, Peel, Eldon, Bathurst, and Westmorland. Lansdowne led Whig negotiations with Canning, eventually joining Canning's cabinet. This was a lead Lord Grey, Lord Althorp, and Lord John Russell declined to accept. But Stanley faithfully followed his mentor's course being offered a Lordship of the Treasury. Yet within a month the 56-year-old Canning was dead and the dithering, henpecked Goderich succeeded as prime minister desperately attempting to hold Canning's coalition together. In September 1827 Stanley became under-secretary for the colonies, but by January 1828 Goderich's unconvincing effort to preserve Canning's ministry came to an end. Between January and May 1828 Wellington, as prime minister, also sought to retain Canningites as ministerial colleagues, but from the beginning both Lansdowne and Stanley refused to have anything to do with a Wellington administration.

By 1828 Canning's memory formed the template for Stanley's ambition. He characterized Wellington's ministry as a strange medley of men and principles; Catholic Emancipation being regarded by ministers, with the exception of Huskisson, with either indifference or bigotry.[23] Canning's policy of moderate liberal reform, Stanley repeatedly declared in the Commons, was the only course for the nation to adopt. "The old and stubborn spirit of Toryism," he pronounced, "is at last yielding to the increased liberality of the age."[24] Such a policy was to be defined in terms of firm commitment to Emancipation; piecemeal, not radical, parliamentary reform; and the establishment of the Corn Laws on a sliding scale. In April 1828 Stanley again raised Canning's standard by espousing the dead statesman's 1827 plan for Corn Law reform. In May Stanley delivered a panegyric on Canning's liberal policy of keeping pace with the spirit of the age, not going in advance of it, while judiciously ensuring that Parliament did not lag behind it.[25]

In 1828 Stanley clearly saw the opportunity to establish himself at the head of a centrist Canningite movement in the Commons, decrying atavistic Toryism and holding in check dangerous radical reform. For a man not yet 30 years of age this was an ambitious plan, reflecting his own self-confidence and the high regard he had already won from some of his contemporaries. Once those Canningites who had initially agreed to serve under Wellington resigned from office in May 1828 circumstances appeared all the more promising. Sir James Graham, for one, informed Stanley that "you will find a strong and respectable body willing to act under you." There appeared to exist a "golden opportunity of forming a party in the House of Commons on some broad intelligible principle," upholding Canningite ideals and recommending moderate reforms.[26] The broad principle that stood as the touchstone of Canningite policy was Emancipation.

The success of Stanley's strategy was dependent on two considerations. First, that Wellington's ministry, under Peel's leadership in the Commons, would continue to act as a reactionary foil, opposing Emancipation and blocking reform. Second, that rival young Whigs, such as Russell and Althorp, who had held aloof from Canning, be marginalized; their advanced views being tainted with radicalism. In the event, during 1828–29, both strategic requirements were denied. As a consequence Stanley's ambitious conception of a centrist Canningite party, holding the parliamentary balance of power, collapsed. Most importantly Emancipation was passed under the aegis of Wellington and Peel. The touchstone of Stanley's policy was removed and the reactionary foil to moderate reform dissolved. Moreover, Russell's repeal of the Test and Corporation Acts in 1828 succeeded in mobilizing a Commons majority that confirmed Russell's place in the mainstream of Whig opinion. This left Stanley no ground on which to stand. The one consolation was that Emancipation had also torn apart the fabric of that Tory hegemony which had dominated government, almost exclusively, since 1794.

The final collapse of Tory government in November 1830, after Wellington's emphatic refusal to countenance reform, brought Lord Grey, at the head of a coalition ministry, into power. Whigs, Canningites, and Ultras, galvanized into common action by Wellington's obduracy, formed the most aristocratic government of the century, united in the belief that only parliamentary reform could now preserve the legitimate influence of territorial magnates and the essential status of property. Stanley accepted the office of chief secretary for Ireland in Grey's government and for the next three years Ireland was to dominate his thought and sap his strength. As an historical warning Ireland had already driven Pitt from office in 1801, as well as the "Ministry of All the Talents" in 1807 and, in the form of Emancipation, had scattered Tory ranks in 1829.

Ireland tested the very basis of Whig doctrine. Whiggery expounded the commitment to careful reform within a context of social stability. Upon the bedrock of legal authority and property rights progress was ensured through timely political concessions to emergent social interests. All had to be based, however, on the rule of law and the legitimate operation of social influence. Thus a responsible aristocracy could affirm an identity of interest with a growing middle class. In the English context, by December 1830, Whigs had little problem in arguing that concession was required to the powerful and respectable interests pressing for parliamentary reform. But Ireland painfully teased apart the strands of Whig thought. Ireland was an overwhelmingly agrarian society, without a substantial middle class, where the religious divide between Catholic and protestant exacerbated the social chasm and violent conflict of interest between landowner and peasant. The month Grey took office these grievances found a natural and explosive focus in the question of the tithe. A widespread "tithe war" was creating further contempt for the law which, in turn, raised the dilemma which cut through to the very root of Whig doctrine. What degree of respect for civil authority was necessary for concessionary reforms to be either appropriate or responsible? As Althorp was bluntly to formulate it in August 1832, was Ireland "fit for free government?"[27]

Stanley's secular analysis of Irish problems, the absence of a resident gentry, want of capital, want of employment, and a lack of adequate education, complemented Grey's pronouncement in December 1830 that, more than anything else, Ireland's difficulties would be solved by "a good system of government."[28] Stanley warned Melbourne, Grey's home secretary, that resistance to the tithe had to be considered as a prelude to resistance to the payment of rents; a direct assault on property rights. Stanley, as well as Duncannon, Palmerston, and Spring Rice, were all members of the government with extensive Irish estates. It was a further complication that Irish leaders such as Daniel O'Connell were embracing new methods of populist agitation putting even greater subversive pressure on the rule of law. It would, therefore, be a gross historical distortion to see Stanley's policy in Ireland from 1830 to 1833 arranged around landmarks of legislative reform. The legislative reform exists. An Irish Education Act was passed, lords lieutenant were appointed for the Irish counties to help reform the magistracy, a Tithe Composition Bill was introduced, as well as a measure imposing a graduated tax on Irish benefices. But Stanley saw his primary purpose as reinstating the force of law in Ireland. Only then would far-reaching and permanent reforms be possible.

Stanley's determination to enforce the law, as a precondition to reform, not only brought him into direct and bitter conflict with O'Connell and other Irish MPs. Stanley's putative superior, the lord lieutenant of Ireland, Lord Anglesey, also came to believe that Stanley was tainted on Irish affairs. Anglesey favored more extensive reform than Stanley believed prudent. By 1832 relations between the two had deterioriated so far that they could no longer discuss Irish business with each other, Stanley privately maneuvering to have Anglesey removed from office, while Anglesey made public his frustration and despair at Stanley's unswerving resolution.[29] Stanley's priorities also angered and alienated ministerial colleagues, particularly Russell, Althorp, Brougham, Lord Durham, and Lord Holland. As a member of Grey's cabinet, after June 1831, Stanley faced constant criticism and pressure from more advanced Whigs decrying his apparent reluctance to introduce remedial reforms. His main ministerial ally, apart from the duke of Richmond, Graham, Ripon, and on occasion Palmerston, was the prime minister. Grey used Stanley as a counterweight to restrain Russell's impetuosity. Throughout 1831 and 1832 Grey protected Stanley, giving him a strong voice in cabinet counsel, and upholding Stanley's defiant insistence that law had to be firmly installed in Ireland. His parliamentary and cabinet enemies, Stanley told Anglesey, "may succeed in throwing me out . . . but they shall not bear me down."[30]

In January 1831 Stanley had O'Connell arrested for sedition, though O'Connell later, much to Stanley's annoyance, avoided having to face trial. Later in the year he armed the Irish Yeomanry and attempted to introduce an Arms Bill. Stanley insisted on an Arrears of Tithes measure requiring the collection of unpaid tax. This, Anglesey complained, left the lord lieutenant "carrying, at the point of a bayonet, an odious measure."[31] In 1833 Stanley secured the passage of an Irish Coercion Act. All these actions were derived from Stanley's unshakable faith that law and property were the prerequisites to civilized progress and the blessings of reform. The properties and revenues of the Church of Ireland were enshrined in the inviolability of legal status.

It was to be appropriation, the use for secular purposes of Church of Ireland revenues, that finally shattered Grey's coalition ministry. In April 1833 Stanley had been promoted to Colonial Secretary and secured the passage of the slave emancipation measure, though he remained much involved in the discussion of Irish affairs. In May 1834, during Commons discussion of the Irish Tithes Bill, Russell publicly exposed cabinet differences over appropriation and prompted a crisis which, by the end of the month, saw Stanley, Graham, Richmond, and the earl of Ripon (formerly Goderich) resign from the government. The explosive issue of the Church of Ireland's property, which had lain buried at the heart of Grey's cabinet since 1830, detonated, scattering fragments of Grey's cabinet across the floors of both Houses.

Stanley's departure marked the failure of the strategy Grey had consistently pursued since 1830 of using Stanley as a counterbalance to the extreme reformers within the government. The loss was all the greater as during the reform debates of 1831–32 Stanley had won all the accolades for his oratory, culminating in his demolition of Croker in December 1831. Stanley established himself as the most effective orator the government had, his triumphs of eloquence repeatedly rescuing the ministry from Commons defeat. Such triumphs, in turn, reinforced perceptions of Stanley as a future party leader, facing Peel across the chamber. Stanley's departure from Grey's cabinet created new possibilities for party alignment in a situation in which reform, the issue which had formerly cemented Grey's ministry, was removed. How would party connection arrange itself in the post-1832 political landscape?

During 1834–35, as in 1828 though with far greater reason, Stanley again entertained "visions of the helm."[32] And if Emancipation had been Stanley's key reference point for mapping out party alignment in 1828, in 1834 it was the Church of Ireland. Once again Irish affairs were to be the touchstone of parliamentary politics. Stanley's aspirations were encouraged by William IV, via his secretary Sir Herbert Taylor, who made known his strong wish for a moderate government under Stanley. In July 1834 a tired and disillusioned Grey resigned, handing over the premiership to Melbourne. In November 1834 William IV dismissed Melbourne's ministry. In December 1834 Stanley declared magisterially in a speech delivered at Glasgow University (which, uncharacteristically, he took great pains to ensure was accurately reported in the press):[33]

His will be a great destiny who knows how to direct and turn into the proper channels the energies of the people, and to conduct with propriety, at this period, the government of this great nation; but if he shall imagine himself capable of stemming and abruptly resisting its force onwards, he will be swept along with the torrent.

During the winter of 1834–35 Stanley glimpsed himself as a man of destiny delivering progress with propriety.

During late November and early December the country awaited Peel's return from Italy to take up his commission to form the next government, as the leader of the opposition designated by Wellington. In country retreats and the clubs politicians busily speculated on events. Stanley had extensive discussions with Graham and Ripon, the "Derby Dilly" as O'Connell had dubbed them. They decided they would wait for an invitation to join Peel's cabinet and reject it, leaving Peel to his ultra-Tory supporters.[34] As a result Peel's administration, trapped by the Ultras' prejudices, would be short-lived and a centrist government headed by the Derby Dilly would succeed it. The possibility of an election, Stanley calculated, would only hasten the process. On 11 December, as planned, Stanley declined Peel's offer of office.[35] Stanley then prepared to make the occasion of his installation as lord rector of Glasgow University, on 21 December, the platform for announcing his general policy, the "Knowsley Creed." In his speech Stanley declared his readiness to remove the blemishes and deformities in the great institutions of the country, while energetically opposing those who intended not to reform but to destroy.[36]

The machine must move forward for good or evil—for it cannot be stopped; like the fire it may purify, if properly kindled by a skilful hand, but if it should be impetuously and recklessly accelerated, destruction and overwhelming wreck must be the inevitable consequences.

While espousing reform of civic institutions Stanley made it clear that he regarded protection of the established church as the test of responsible, as opposed to destructive, reform. Safeguarding the Anglican church while giving power and privilege to intelligence and new wealth, was the definition, at the core of the Knowsley Creed, of progress with propriety.

Yet in politics, as in chess, success is dependent upon the anticipated moves of opponents, whose own strategies can never be precisely predicted. Three days before Stanley delivered the Knowsley Creed at Glasgow, attempting to stake out the center ground of moderate reform, Peel published his Tamworth Manifesto. By doing so Peel skilfully pre-empted Stanley's characterization of Conservatism as the immovable obstacle to progress. Peel made it clear he had no intention of being trapped by his Ultras, rather committing himself to "a careful review of institutions, civil and ecclesiastical, undertaken in a friendly temper, combining, with the firm maintenance of established rights, the correction of proven abuses and the redress of real grievances."[37] This theme Peel repeated, two days after Stanley's Glasgow speech, at a Mansion House dinner. Graham could only observe that "it is hard to say where an old Tory is to be found."[38]

In the elections of January 1835 Stanley maintained that he and his supporters, standing between two extreme parties, represented sound and conservative reform. Some estimated the Stanleyites number at 86 MPs in the new Parliament, with nearly 180 Whigs and Radicals facing a minority Peel government. Stanley told the Dilly MP John Denison.[39]

I think it not undesirable for the country that when there is likely to be much of violence on both sides, there should be an avowed intermediate party, acting with no factious views, but sufficiently strong, and if possible, sufficiently compact, to act as a check upon the other two, to aid the government in their resistance to mere party motions and to dangerous measures, but also to keep them up to the collar in measures of sound reform, and lastly to be a *corps de reserve* upon which, in the case of accidents, the King might be able to fall back.

Yet, while the *corps de reserve* waited expectantly for Peel's resignation, his Tamworth Manifesto and subsequent official rhetoric increasingly poached on Stanley's ground. Russell's success in forging an alliance between Whigs, Radicals, and the Irish further undercut Stanley's position. The Lichfield House compact of February 1835 and a second meeting of Whigs, Radicals, and Irish in March, called under Russell's auspices, galvanized a united opposition to Peel. By March 1835 Stanley's "visions of the helm" were beginning to dim. As in 1828 Peel and Russell's success dashed Stanley's hopes. Neither Peel nor Russell allowed themselves to be marginalized, pushed to the periphery by their extreme supporters.

When Melbourne, at the head of the Lichfield House alliance with Russell as his leader in the Commons, replaced Peel as premier in April 1835 Stanley's ambitions were firmly checked. In the immediate years after 1835 the trajectory of Stanley's career was in decline. Between 1835 and 1837 he and Graham drifted into Peel's Conservative party. In 1841 Stanley resumed the position of colonial secretary in Peel's second ministry, the same office he had left seven years before in Grey's cabinet. As a member of Peel's cabinet he dutifully attended to the continuing problems of Canada, war with China, diplomatic tensions with the United States, and the difficulties of New Zealand. In 1844 he was elevated to the Lords as Lord Stanley of Bickerstaffe. So it was from the upper House in 1845 that Stanley watched the growing crisis which, once again, was to propel him to the forefront of parliamentary politics.

Stanley's arrival in the House of Lords, immediately prior to the fateful events of 1846, emphasized both the strengths and weaknesses of his character and political style. As a landed aristocrat, possessed of powerful rhetorical gifts, he enjoyed a strong body of natural support. His talents and acumen ensured an immediate ascendancy and easy pre-eminence in the upper House. Yet his elevation accentuated his arrogance and aloofness towards those not of his own class, a bluff robust manner keeping the commoner at a distance. It also highlighted his lack of sympathy with extra-parliamentary forms of support, such as the press, affirming his sense that what really mattered was that which occurred in Westminster and clubland. Stanley's standing in the Lords, therefore, not only gave him a powerful vantage point from which to shape the parliamentary politics of the mid-Victorian period; it also threw into starker relief the assumptions and nature of his instincts and constitutional beliefs. The force of his talents was formidable; the parameters of his skills increasingly apparent.

Peel's proposal to repeal the Corn Laws and the momentous split in the Conservative party this caused, in circumstances very different from those anticipated in 1828 or 1835, brought Stanley party leadership. Stanley resigned from Peel's cabinet in December 1845 in protest at the prime minister's intention to repeal the Corn Laws. Not that he was a dogmatic Protectionist. Stanley's final statement in cabinet was that "we cannot do this as gentlemen."[40] He believed that Peel's great crime was the premier's callous violation of the trust placed in him by his back-benchers. In 1852 Stanley warned Disraeli that "to take office with the purpose of throwing over, voluntarily, the main object of those who have raised us to it is to follow too closely an *exemplar vitiis imitabile* to which I can never submit."[41] It was Stanley's constitutional beliefs that were outraged by Peel in 1846. As leader of the Conservatives after 1846, it was those Whig principles of parliamentary government learnt from Lansdowne in the 1820s that framed Stanley's public actions and policies.

Though party sentiment was not as intense in the Lords as in the Commons, nonetheless, among politically active peers party feeling was very real. Certainly Stanley continued to see party alignment in both Houses as the essential constitutional dynamic defining policy and power. Under his leadership during the 1850s and 1860s, the Conservatives remained the single most cohesive party in Parliament, manifesting greater unity than Peelites, Liberals, and Radicals in the division lobbies. During his 1852 ministry Stanley, as Lord Derby, received a daily report of attendance in the Lords.[42] In 1859 the Liberal leader in the upper House, Lord Granville, observed that the close attendance of Derby's supporters, both in and out of office, "was very remarkable."[43] Granville attributed this to strict discipline and Derby's personal ascendancy within his party.

The Corn Law crisis of 1846 shattered the natural majority Conservatives, under the duke of Wellington, had commanded in the Lords. During the late 1840s and early 1850s Peelite peers held the balance of power. This, alongside the disruption of party connection caused by the Corn Law crisis in the Commons, by 1847 brought Derby to contemplate an imminent elemental struggle between democratic and aristocratic principles. Characteristically Derby was haunted less by the extra-parliamentary specter of Chartism than the dangerous forces of populism he saw existing within Westminster. In particular the Peelites in the Commons, with Peel himself as "the apostle of expedience" contemptuous of party obligations, he saw as espousing a reckless executive power, unfettered by party constraint, acting in the name of a national interest and opinion distinct from that expressed in Parliament.[44] In this view of affairs "the old Whigs," such as his former mentor Lansdowne and Lord Grey in the Lords and Sir George Grey and Sir Charles Wood in the Commons, for example, Derby saw as more conservative than the Peelites. It was the incipient populism of Peelism that alarmed Derby. It was the victory of aristocratic principles over such dangerous populism that had to be secured; a victory consolidating the authoritative status of Parliament, with responsible peers and their party colleagues redressing genuine grievances.

The House of Lords, therefore, held a special place in Derby's public doctrine. The Lords, he believed, should provide a leadership prepared to preserve the essential features of Britain's constitution which had, since 1688, safeguarded progress and encouraged prosperity and liberty within a legal framework of civic order. At the same time, in recognizing and carrying out their duty to the commonweal, leading peers should also adjust and reconcile through expedient and timely reforms those powerful forces of conflicting social interests created by continued progress. Thus the onward movements of political, social, and economic improvement could be harmonized through the vigilant arbitration of a responsible aristocracy knowing when to concede and when to protect. This Whiggish vision defined Derby's view of the Lords and affirmed the constitutional importance of the upper House. In personal terms it framed Derby's party leadership, exercised from the Lords after 1846, and provided a view of Conservative politics which espoused responsible and necessary, as opposed to destructive and reckless, reform. Through his twenty-two year period of Conservative leadership Derby consistently adhered to this view. By the late 1850s the traditional Conservative majority in the Lords had been re-established. Around the social hub of the Carlton Club Conservative peers, after 1858, reasserted their dominance in the upper House. A key figure in this process was the youthful tenth Earl Coville of Culross who, in 1852, Derby appointed as his chief whip; a post Coville was to hold with marked success until 1870.[45] Under Derby's leadership and Coville's discipline, in the Lords at least, a Conservative, though not reactionary, dominance was rebuilt as a responsible constraint on the dangerous forces of democratic populism.

For 18 of his 22 years of Conservative leadership Derby headed, from the Lords, a party in opposition. Throughout those years Derby followed a consistent strategy firmly rooted in the context of party dynamics within Westminster. Derby never believed that either the alignment of non-Conservative groups that faced him in the Commons or the Lords, Peelites,

Whigs, Liberals, an assortment of Radicals and the Irish Brigade, was a stable or secure alliance. He saw deep fissures between them which, through a strategy of "masterly inactivity," he sought to emphasize. Conservative passivity would create a void in which non-Conservative differences would come to the fore. In attempting to act together, in the absence of a Conservative foil, Peelites, Whigs, and Radicals would only discover their own incompatible differences. Thus, while keeping his ultra-Tory supporters firmly in check, Derby avoided irrevocable commitment to any one issue. During the late 1840s he believed this policy might draw penitent Peelites back to the Conservative party. By 1852, as this prospect faded, he believed it would prise Palmerston away from his Whig and Liberal associates. During the late 1850s and 1860s disillusioned Whigs, such as the third earl Grey, and moderate Liberals, such as the Adullamites, seemed candidates for adhesion.

This opposition strategy of passivity was not the expression of political bankruptcy, but a shrewd assessment of the implicit tensions within parliamentary opinion. During the spring of 1846 Stanley resisted the formal organization of a Protectionist party. The deepening division amongst Conservatives, however, was Bentinck and Disraeli's opportunity and achievement. Derby looked to a reconciliation after an election in 1847 and talked of building "a pont d'or for the penitent" Peelites.[46] Yet economic circumstances, which gave new substance to the Protectionist cause, and lack of back-bench enthusiasm frustrated Stanley's hopes. Nonetheless Stanley intervened to prevent Russell's defeat in 1848 over Pakington's amendment to the government's Sugar Duties Bill. In 1849 Stanley avoided appointing Disraeli as sole leader in the Commons because he was "the most powerful repellant we could offer to any repentant or hesitating" Peelites.[47]

Until 1851 Derby remained hopeful of Conservative reunion. Derbyites and Peelites came together to censure Palmerston for his defense of Don Pacifico. Derby urged Disraeli to take a prominent part in debate so as not to allow the attack to appear a purely Peelite enterprise. Yet Palmerston himself might, in favorable circumstances, be a powerful acquisition; particularly once Russell in 1848 revived the question of parliamentary reform. The Peelite refusal to support Derby in his attempt to form a government in 1851 marked a major turning-point in Derby's priorities. He declared "that we have nothing to look to from the leading Peelites but rancorous opposition."[48] Thereafter Palmerston increasingly became Derby's best hope of realignment; especially after Palmerston's resignation from Russell's cabinet in December 1851. Derby's initial reaction was to side with neither Russell nor Palmerston, but to let the factions fight it out amongst themselves, yet by February 1852 Derby was receiving "intimations that P. is not unwilling to join us."[49] Although, in the event, Palmerston did not openly associate himself with Derby, from 1852 onwards the potential alignment of Derby and Palmerston, as a consolidation of political restraint against a party of reckless reform led by Russell with Radical and Peelite colleagues, powerfully influenced all speculation.

Against such conjecture Derby adopted a studied non-commitment, for example, over the revived issue of parliamentary reform.[50]

My idea is that we should abstain from pledging ourselves to resist any and every measure which may be brought forward, at the same time that we deprecate the introduction of any extensive alteration as uncalled for by any necessity or any strong public feeling.

In reviving the issue Derby believed that Russell had put himself in the condition of a man who "having sold himself to the Devil, is anxious to cheat the Devil, and get himself out of his bargain. But I am afraid that the Devil will be too much for him."[51] Conservative evasiveness dramatically emphasized Palmerston and Russell's differences. At the same time Derby believed that reform was an issue over which any Conservative reunion with the *disjecta membra* of the Peelite section was "wholly out of the question, and that the attempt would only lead to misunderstanding and disappointment."[52]

Just as Derby adopted a strategy of non-commitment over the issue of reform, so as to stress Whig, Liberal, and Radical differences, so he sought to restrain, whenever possible, the Anglican fervor of his own back-benches. As early as August 1846 he was:[53]

apprehensive as to stimulating Protestant or anti-Catholic zeal. I should not like to hear an anti-popery cry got up in the hopes of neutralizing protestant dissenters . . . it seems to me that the grand error committed by all parties is that Conservatives consider favours shown to R. Catholics to be an injury to Protestantism, and that the Whigs think nothing can be done for the former without an accompanying measure of robbery on the latter.

Nonetheless, because of rank and file sensibilities, he did not support a measure for the relief of Irish Catholic clergy in 1847, although he privately approved of it. Nor did he support aid for Catholic schools, because it was unacceptable to the greater body of his followers. Over the Ecclesiastical Titles Bill Derby thought it better to:[54]

follow the stream, which is running quite strong enough, than attempt to take a lead of our own. I think the government are in an awkward dilemma from which they will find it very difficult to escape; and the more rope we give them the more chance there is of their hanging themselves at one end or the other.

Though it was inevitable that, to some degree, Conservative back-benchers were the champions of the established church, Derby was content to allow others to rush forward to its defense. Particularly if self-appointed guardians, such as Lord John Russell, brought on themselves political embarrassment.[55]

John Russell has not played his cards as well as he thought he had . . . I am clear that our policy is, while we lose no fair opportunity of protesting against the Papal aggression, to wait upon the Government and see, not what they say, but what they do.

Aware that militant protestantism was a rallying cry that could backfire on its proponents Derby acknowledged it with stoic and often reluctant caution.

Between 1853 and 1858 Derby again consistently pursued a strategy of "masterly inactivity" with Palmerston, rather than prominent Peelites, becoming the more attractive catch. The composite nature of the Aberdeen coalition seemed proof of Derby's belief in the incompatible differences of non-Conservative opinion. He found it "difficult to imagine how a government can go on formed of such discordant materials as that which Aberdeen has brought together."[56] Passivity could only enhance such differences while "the chance for Conservatism is the disruption of the cabinet from internal differences."[57] This was "killing [the coalition] with kindness." Derby's intention was clear: "Wait, don't attack ministers, that will only bind them together. If left alone they must fall to pieces by their own disunion."[58] Derby effectively smothered all of Disraeli's initiatives and in January 1853 informed his lieutenant:[59]

We shall have a difficult game to play. We must to a certain extent keep up the spirits of our party; but we must exercise, and get them to exercise, great patience and forbearance, if we do not wish, by an active and bitter opposition on our part, to consolidate the present combination between those who have no real bond of union, and who must, I think, fall to pieces before long, if left to themselves.

During the winter of 1854–55 Derby declined assailing the Aberdeen coalition on an outspoken patriotic platform over Crimean mismanagement. This avoided alienating Palmerston, but it also allowed Palmerston the opportunity to appropriate to himself the same cry. Derby, however, believed parliamentary reform rather than foreign policy, would be the cause of the coalition breaking apart.

The ministerial crisis of December 1853 again seemed to confirm Derby's expectation. Prior to Palmerston's brief resignation from Aberdeen's cabinet over reform Malmesbury felt "no doubt that many of our staunchest supporters would follow [Palmerston] as leader of the Commons."[60] Believing Palmerston's departure fatal to the government Derby immediately opened indirect negotiations to ascertain Palmerston's views on reform and foreign policy. It seemed that Palmerston wished to join "the old and discontented Whigs" with the Derbyites.[61] Only Lord Lansdowne's refusal to resign with him, Malmesbury believed, foiled Palmerston's plan. (Palmerston rejoined Aberdeen's cabinet.) In the event it was the Crimean conflict that brought down Aberdeen's ministry, but Russell's hasty resignation and Roebuck's hostile motion again seemed to affirm the reality of deep fissures within non-Conservative ranks.

In February 1855 Derby, like Russell, believed Palmerston was not a possible premier. Palmerston's unexpected success disrupted all plans and denied the Conservatives the patriotic cry deferred the previous year. In opposition to Palmerston, from 1855 to 1858, the Conservatives were therefore caught in the artificial position of confronting a possible ally. Yet Derby persevered in his patience policy convinced that a Whig-Liberal-Radical fracture was inevitable. Derby did not encourage Disraeli to force the issue of Russell's diplomatic differences with his cabinet colleagues in July 1855. Nor did he condone Disraeli's wish to exploit the political advantages of a peace movement. By November 1855 Disraeli concurred that "silence and inertia are our wisest course."[62] Eighteen months later, following the election of 1857, Derby provided Disraeli with an authoritative statement of his strategy:[63]

The Peelite and Manchester men are obliterated: but it would be a mistake to say that the House is divided into two parties only; among the Liberals there are two divisions differences between whom must shortly become more marked than they are at present. The old Whigs are far less numerous than the Radicals, and are proportionally afraid of them. Pam has ousted Johnny from the command of the Whigs, and the necessities of the latter's position will make him bid for the support of the Radicals with whom, however, he will never obtain a cordial acceptance. Palmerston on the other hand will not be sorry to see him take this course; and if he finds him committed to it, will take the line of great moderation, and lean upon Conservative support. To encourage this tendency on his party, if it exists, and to ferment divisions and jealousies in the Government majority must be our first objective; while we should carefully avoid multiplying occasions for their voting in concert, in opposition to motions brought forward by us.

Despite the horrifying news of the Indian Mutiny the pose of waiting and watching suited Derby and frustrated Disraeli for the remainder of 1857.

The increasingly prominent issue of parliamentary reform promised to bring to the fore irreconcilable differences between Palmerston, Russell and the Radicals.[64]

Similarly between 1859 and 1866 Derby saw Conservative inactivity as the catalyst for prompting a realignment of party, proving to Palmerston that his real enemies sat alongside, not opposite, him. In January 1860 it was reported that "P. had been beaten several times in his cabinet and was nearly wearied out," while "the impression of all the partisans of the government and of the foreign powers and Ministers here is that they will break up."[65] Parliamentary reform, abolition of the church rates and repeal of the paper duty provided ample opportunity to pursue the strategy. Conservatives did not attack the government collectively upon the withdrawal of the 1860 Reform Bill, while making it clear to Palmerston that if Russell resigned, followed by the desertion of Bright and the Radicals, he could rely on Conservative support. At the same time Derby ensured that "every obstructive notion came from the Liberal side of the House."[66] In private conversations during May 1860 Malmesbury ascertained that Palmerston would welcome Conservative assistance in defeating Gladstone's repeal of the paper duty. Disraeli agreed with Derby's stragegy: "The cards will play into our hands if we are quiet."[67]

In December 1860 Derby prompted Malmesbury's "quasi-negotiations" with Palmerston with an eye to the growing differences between cabinet moderates on the one hand and Gladstone and Milner Gibson on the other, the latter two being seen as the tools of the Bright and Cobden party.[68] In January 1861 Malmesbury gave a pledge of support to Palmerston, as long as the government did not touch parliamentary reform, or take part in a war against Austria on behalf of Italian nationalists.[69] This led Derby "to hope that the Radical party, in and out of the cabinet, will find themselves checkmated in the approaching session."[70] This, in turn, might force Palmerston "to break away from Gladstone, if not Russell."[71] It was these considerations that lay behind Derby's advocacy of "keeping the present men in, and resisting all temptations to avail ourselves of a casual majority."[72] This Malmesbury described as keeping the "cripples on their legs."[73]

During 1863 and 1865 Derby found the merits of inactivity enhanced by severe attacks of gout. Yet he never contemplated retirement and continued to reflect upon future ministerial appointments. This was in large part because of Palmerston's advanced age which, since 1855, had seemed to promise imminent realignment. In fact Palmerston's longevity did much to obscure the shrewdness of Derby's patience policy. The anticipation that

Palmerston would soon be removed from the scene deferred actions while his presence continued. Over the American Civil War Derby carefully avoided commitment to the cause of the South. Though the Schleswig-Holstein question provided a powerful cry Derby refrained from partisan activity during the critical month of May 1864. Meanwhile Disraeli was happy to note that, following Gladstone's welcoming of the visit of Garibaldi, the "smaller Whigs, Beaumonts, Ramsdens, and perhaps Lansdowne and Fitzwilliam may detach themselves."[74]

At the opening of the 1865 session Granville anticipated Derby lying "in wait for a few months, tranquilly expecting that the next parliament will see him wafted into office and enjoying the sweets which come with office."[75] Derby continued to instruct Disraeli "to support the moderate part of the cabinet and watch for every opportunity of widening the breach between them and the *honest* Radicals."[76] A severe attack of gout in August 1865 temporarily brought Derby to the low point of his opposition leadership, a period in which he communicated to Disraeli nothing but political gloom. Yet within six weeks Palmerston was dead. Derby was again talking of fusion and future Conservative governments. Yet he remained insistent that Conservative policy must be regulated by government action and continued to urge Disraeli to practice restraint in discussing the government's difficulties in Ireland and the suspension of Habeas Corpus. Upon reform he argued that if cabinet moderates quarrelled with the Radicals then Conservatives must do their best to "widen and perpetuate the breach." If the government "throw themselves with the extreme party, we must offer them a strenuous opposition relying on the aid of their moderate men to prevent mischief."[77]

For the eighteen years during which he led the party in opposition Derby consistently pursued a strategy of masterly inactivity. This policy was not a symptom of political apathy or indifference, but an astute judgment upon the alignment of party sentiment within Parliament. The events of June 1866, when Russell and Gladstone's Reform Bill was opposed by back-bench Whigs, seemed a vindication of Derby's strategy. But the achievement was more apparent than real, for he remained insistent that realignment must be represented by front bench figures that backbenchers would follow. The 40 Whigs who "ratted," in Bright's phrase, did not include those prominent names Derby desired. Indeed, it was Disraeli who encouraged "Adullamite" co-operation because of his own insecurity, his need to brand Gladstone a Radical, and fear that non-commitment would allow a Russell Reform Bill to succeed. Nevertheless, the positive significance of Derby's decisions while in opposition reside in what he chose not to do. It is noteworthy that on the three occasions when he came to power in 1852, 1858, and 1866 Derby took office as a result of splits in non-Conservative opinion, not Conservative offensives. In 1852 Palmerston attacked Russell, in 1858 Russell and the Radicals attacked Palmerston, and in 1866 the Adullamites attacked Gladstone and Russell.

The complement to Derby's passive strategy in opposition is his active policy in office during 1852, 1858–59, and 1866–68. In power, despite never enjoying a clear Commons majority, Derby displayed an unwavering commitment to moderate reform. In 1828 he had talked of "the old and stubborn spirit of Toryism . . . yielding to the liberality of the age." In 1835 he had talked of channeling the energies of the people forward with propriety through constructive reform, the great and unstoppable engine of progress moving onward. These statements echoed on into the declarations of official mid-century Conservative governments. As prime minister in March 1858 Derby struck the keynote of Conservatism in office: [78]

While we will fairly and strenuously maintain the great institutions of the country, we shall not hesitate to propose and support measures of undoubted improvement and progress, and to introduce safe and well-considered amendments, wherever amendments may be required . . . [T]here can be no greater mistake than to suppose that a Conservative ministry necessarily means a stationary ministry. We live in an age of constant progress—moral, social and political . . . [I]n politics as in everthing else the same course must be pursued—constant progress, improving the old system, adapting our institutions to the purposes which they are intended to serve, and by judicious changes meeting the increased demands of society.

It was Derby, not Disraeli, who "educated" the mid-Victorian Conservative party.

Much abuse was and still is heaped upon the makeshift Conservative ministry of 1852. But it should be noted that it was this government that relinquished protectionism as Conservative policy. It also carried a new Militia Bill (based upon a plan devised by Prince Albert), secured a new constitution for New Zealand, curtailed corrupt practices at elections by establishing commissions of inquiry, enacted several valuable legal reforms (streamlining common law procedure, remodelling Chancery practice, and generally revising the system of equity), as well as a supplementary budget with some free trade characteristics. A total of 88 public acts were passed during the session: not a totally contemptible record for ten months work.[79]

Delivered from the constraints of protectionism Derby's cabinet of 1858–59 energetically resumed a policy of moderate progressivism. Disraeli devised a "Gladstonian" budget as proof of Conservative financial wisdom. A new India Act completely revised the government of the Asian subcontinent. The government gave its countenance to a bill abolishing the property qualifications for MPs, and to legislation allowing practising Jews to sit in the Commons; the latter Act considered by one modern authority to be "the most symbolic religious liberty measure of the 1850's."[80] In 1859 a parliamentary reform bill was introduced that was more "liberal" than the scheme favored by Palmerston's Whig-Liberal cabinet the previous year. At the same time Anglo-French relations were calmed in the wake of the Orsini crisis; Anglo-American relations were soothed over central America; mediation was pursued in the affair of the *Charles et Georges*; the Cagliari incident was resolved; and a policy of neutrality was adopted in the growing Italian crisis.[81]

For a third time, in 1866–68, a minority Conservative government under Derby made plain that mid-Victorian Conservatism would not be atavistic bigotry and prejudiced obstructionism. In July 1866 Derby was hoping the question of Ireland might again be a basis for centrist fusion and thought an Irish land bill a necessity. By the autumn of 1866, however, despite Disraeli's reluctance, Derby was portraying parliamentary reform as the unavoidable priority.[82] In September Derby informed Disraeli that reform required his urgent attention. The next month Derby declared that he had arranged a cabinet meeting to discuss the question. Thus the Reform Act of 1867 became the single most important demonstration of Derbyite progressivism. If the passage of the bill owed much to the brilliance of Disraeli's short-term tactics, in the long term it owed as much, if not more, to Derby's perception of official Conservative policy. When introducing the Reform Bill into the Lords in July 1867 Derby declared:[83]

I did not intend for a third time to be made a mere stop gap until it would suit the convenience of the Liberal party to forget their dissensions and bring forward a measure which would oust us from office and replace them there: and I determined that I would take such a course as would convert, if possible, an existing minority into a practical majority.

The Second Reform Act was a fitting climax to Derby's long career. In February 1868, in almost constant pain from gout, he retired from politics.

Derby's historiographical fate has been one of neglect. In the first instance this tells us much about how the Conservative party has come to see itself. In particular it is testimony to the dominance of a tradition that has genuflected before the memory of Peel, Disraeli, and Churchill. Neglect began early. Disraeli, in his 1852 biography of Lord George Bentinck, treated Derby as "a secondary personage in the party and the legislature."[84] By the 1880s T. E. Kebbel was creating a "Beaconsfield tradition" and, as a Disraelian apologist, portrayed Derby as an apathetic leader whose dead weight frustrated Disraeli, the suppressed genius of the mid-Victorian Conservative party. The publication of Charles Greville's diaries in 1888 confirmed this view with a portrait firmly based on personal animus. Derby, Greville wrote, was "of all men, the one to whom I have felt the greatest political and personal repugnance."[85] Derby's fondness for port and horse-racing became the key to his whole personality. Derby became the representative truth of a retrospective belief that between the leadership of Peel and Disraeli the Conservative party was lacking in serious purpose and was doctrinally impotent. An affected nonchalance, which has done Palmerston's reputation no harm, has been seen as proof of a lack of seriousness and commitment. The inherited view of Derby has been of a man "lacking the qualities of ambition and dedication normally necessary for successful party leadership."[86] Because of historians' reliance on Disraeli's papers too often Derby has been framed within the view of Knowsley from Hughenden.

Yet this dismissal of Derby has not only distorted our understanding of the history of the Conservative party, making the 1867 Reform Act seem a maverick act and allowing Disraeli to appear the savior of Conservative party fortunes; and (with Peel) the architect of modern Conservatism. It has also obscured a crucial piece of our picture of the development of party and the constitution during the nineteenth century. The 1850s and 1860s witnessed the high point of Whig constitutional thought at Westminster, summed up in the term parliamentary government.[87] Of course, alternative and hostile views existed, Tory, Peelite, and Radical among others. But Peel's accidental death in 1850 removed the pre-eminent embodiment of older executive notions of government (their demise at Westminster admittedly not preventing their resurrection in the corridors of Whitehall as the ethic of a professionalized civil service). Radical voices, drawing on populist traditions, cried out on behalf of those excluded from power by unmerited privilege and aristocratic monopoly. "The People," Radicals cried, were dispossessed of their God-given rights and self-respect by Whig condescension and patronage. This focused Radical animus on the elevated sovereignty of Parliament, emphasizing issues such as the ballot and franchise extension as striking at the Whiggish root of oligarchic corruption. Yet the canonical statements of constitutional thought of the mid-Victorian years, the 1858 essay (unduly neglected by historians) written by the third earl Grey, *Parliamentary Government considered with Reference to Reform of Parliament*, Erskine May's *Constitutional History of England*, and

Walter Bagehot's well known *English Constitution* all described, with their own refinements, a Whig vision of parliamentary government. The dominance of this view was due, in no small part, to the fact that the Conservative party was led by a man imbued since birth with Whig constitutional orthodoxy. Leading Whigs and Conservatives were agreed on the rules of the game. Differences lay in the individual strategies each player pursued. Thus the 1867 Reform Act, arguably the last great Whig measure of the Victorian age, was passed by a Conservative prime minister.

For Derby policy and party leadership were defined within Parliament as part of the interplay of parties; parties at once cohesive enough to create a government, yet fluid enough to bring a government down. Parties were associations born of "voluntary subordination" not "unconditional obedience." As Derby described it in 1854, parties were made up of those who were in the habit of acting together.[88] A closely-knit social, political, literary, and cultural world, embraced the Pall Mall clubs, private dinner parties, the London "season," the drawing rooms of the great hostesses, and visits to country houses during the recess. This provided an easy social familiarity which, in the absence of formal organization, reinforced political ties and shared opinions. Notes sent to MPs by the Whips requesting attendance at a division were solicitous, in contrast to curt modern summonses, made not in the name of the party, but "for the welfare of the country." In hustings speeches MPs regularly engaged in conventional rhetoric about their independence, priding themselves on not being the powerless pawns of party. This was *not* criticism of party in principle, but the assertion (in the absence of tight formal organization) that allegiance could not be assumed, bought or coerced. Allegiance was a matter of voluntary agreement with the broad policies and opinions of a particular party. Hence Derby's conviction that no-one could lead a party who was not prepared at times to follow it. Party cohesion was also, therefore, dependent upon affection for and loyalty to the party leader. This was an attribute of party cohesion of which Derby was very much a beneficiary. In comparison to Peel, for example, Derby enjoyed two qualities of leadership his predecessor lacked. First, a rare ability to rally support by the force of his oratory. Second, high station and country habits congenial to back-bench Conservatives. Disraeli performed an important service in this context by providing an obvious target on to whom to deflect the frustrations and resentments created by Derby's own strategies and policies. Conservatives found it easier to despise Disraeli than be disloyal to Derby.

Precisely what was missing from Derby and the Whig's view of party were those modern requirements for party government adopted by the late-nineteenth century; namely, centralized party bureaucracies, extensive constituency organization and a mass membership, enforcing the expectation that MPs would speak and vote as a bloc in Parliament, seemingly demonstrating ideological homogeneity. Even at the moment of Derby's retirement in 1868 the assumptions and conventions of parliamentary government, which had framed and helped define his career and policies, were being challenged and discarded. During the 1850s and 1860s prominent non-Whigs, such as Palmerston and Gladstone, began using outdoor speeches and an emergent cheap daily press to exert external pressure on opinion within Westminster. Interestingly, in 1867 it was Gladstone, retaining a Peelite sensitivity for the independent authority of the executive, who criticized Derby for presenting to Conservative back-benchers, in a private meeting prior to the parliamentary debate, the government's Reform Bill. This showed at once Derby's awareness of the necessity of parliamentary party support and Gladstone's vestigial Peelism that saw this as demeaning to the executive.

After Derby's death in 1869 the basis of Victorian parliamentary government was swept away. An expanded electorate, centralized constituency organization, a cheap daily press, the assimilation of radicalism into the Liberal party, militant Nonconformity, Gladstonian Liberalism, popular speaking campaigns such as Midlothian, the emergence of programmatic politics, Disraelian Conservatism, the prominence of religious issues, and the social fragmentation of literary and political culture, among other factors, demolished the Whig constitutional structure and erected in its place the modern two-party system. National parties, rather than Parliament, became the autonomous elements in the constitution, making and unmaking governments. In the 1860s James FitzJames Stephen described Parliament as "the only real depository of all political power."[89] Thereafter the platform supplanted Parliament: elections selected governments not Westminster. In 1875 Leslie Stephen (James FitzJames Stephen's brother) suggested that "the floor of the House [of Commons] has ceased to be the exclusive, or even the most effective, standing-point from which to address the true rulers of the country."[90] The historian J. A. Froude dryly observed the same year that it was now becoming an assumption that the nation was wiser than its leaders.[91]

This was a political world very different from that inhabited by Derby. He had created a moderate Conservative party within a Whig constitution. The mid-Victorian Conservative party, both in its reform legislation and its limited perspectives, was a faithful reflection of Derby's public doctrine. Moreover that doctrine helped buttress the structure of mid-

Victorian parliamentary government whose architecture became enshrined in Erskine May and Bagehot. This achievement alone warrants our bringing Derby's renovated portrait down from posterity's attic and hanging it in that empty space between Peel and Disraeli alongside our other Victorian worthies. Yet that achievement, the creation of a moderate Conservative party within a Whig constitution, which he saw as the necessary response of his class to the changing nature of British society, also tells us much about the survival of aristocratic influence, the ordered nature of political change, and the prestige of Parliament in Victorian Britain.

CHAPTER 9

Lord Selborne, Bonar Law, and the "Tory Revolt"

CORINNE C. WESTON

Unionist fortunes were on the mend by 1914, but Andrew Bonar Law, Arthur Balfour's successor as opposition leader in the Commons, seemed no more effective than Balfour to a knowledgeable observer. According to the second Lord Selborne—imperial proconsul, political architect of the Union of South Africa, and a prominent figure in the 1911 diehard revolt—Bonar Law though honest and unselfish lacked such important leadership qualities as vision, initiative, and courage.[1] Selborne was writing in the midst of the First World War; and his portrayal of Bonar Law at this early stage in his political career is by no means typical. Roy Jenkins, a strong Liberal supporter, found that "from behind the sad eyes of Bonar Law the tide of quiet violence poured out"; and T. O. Lloyd, writing for a popular audience, wrote in the same vein when he commented with regard to Bonar Law's notorious Blenheim speech (29 July 1912) that "it would be hard to go much further in the direction of incitement to rebellion without giving direct orders to break the law."[2]

Yet the descriptions are reconcilable. Selborne had observed Bonar Law over the years whereas Jenkins and Lloyd describe him specifically in relation to Ulster during the third Home Rule Bill's passage (1912–14). That Bonar Law was an Ulsterman by heritage is the cardinal point. C. P. Scott, editor of the *Manchester Guardian*, went to the crux of the matter when he wrote of the Unionist party leader that he was "very reasonable and moderate up to a point. Then suddenly you touched something and he blazed up. At heart he was an Orangeman and the Orange fanaticism was there. He had brought it with him from Canada [where he lived for many years]. He might at any time, in defence of what he regarded as an attack on Ulster, lead a Tory revolt."[3]

To Bonar Law, the third Home Rule Bill constituted just such an attack on Ulster because it made the protestant majority in that province subject to Catholic Dublin's rule. Unsurprisingly, Bonar Law figures as the leader of a Tory revolt in George Dangerfield's much reprinted and highly influential *Strange Death of Liberal England* (1935). Under his leadership the Unionists are said to have exploited Ulster's "bigotry" to break the Liberal party, Parliament, and the constitution. The word "Unionist" fitted snugly around their mood "like an iron glove around a fist." Their activity had little to do with Ireland, a great deal to do with beating the Liberal party "into an irremediable mess of political blood and brains." Beginning in 1912, everything the Unionists did "was aimed . . . against the very existence of Parliament." Pledged to its protection, they had unconsciously sought its ruin; and the ultimate irony was that this utterly constitutional party "set out to wreck the constitution and . . . very nearly succeeded."[4] This is a broad indictment, going beyond the party leadership to the back-benchers in Parliament and making no distinctions within the leadership itself.

The Irish scholar, Ronan Fanning, reaches much the same conclusion. Bonar Law's succession to the party leadership brought with it a militant Unionism traceable to the diehard revolt, which became increasingly strident during the home rule crisis. He writes:

More and more Unionists (Carson, Milner and Willoughby de Broke were but some of the most prominent) despised the rules and conventions upon which Balfour's approach to politics reposed. But under Andrew Bonar Law rules would be broken, conventions abandoned, inhibitions scorned; the diehard style, if not the diehard policy, would triumph. In Bonar Law the party had now a man ready to supply the demand for forceful leadership that had created him; his speeches would not be qualified; moderation would hold no appeal for him; and under him the Conservative and Unionist party would adopt a course that for violence and extremism had no parallel in modern British history.[5]

Of the three Unionist leaders cited by Fanning as extremist, only Sir Edward Carson was in the shadow cabinet; and by himself he could not shape the atmosphere within which the leadership functioned.

Although Bonar Law's strong devotion to Ulster, coupled with his "new style of leadership," makes Dangerfield's and Fanning's characterizations of him plausible, their comments on the Unionist party are problematic. For there were in fact divided counsels at the highest level of the Unionist leadership, and that this was the case stands squarely in the way of a wholesale condemnation of that party. It also provides the central theme of this essay.

The place to begin a discussion of the Unionist leadership at this time is with Selborne's outlook as an influential member of the shadow cabinet. Should it appear that despite a deep hostility to home rule, a sentiment shared with Bonar Law, he acted with moderation throughout the crisis over the third Home Rule Bill, this finding would go far to demonstrate that the shadow cabinet, taken as a whole, was more in accord with Selborne than their leader. For Selborne's immediate past suggests that he would be supportive of Bonar Law's initiative on the Ulster question. He had after all been so conspicuous in opposition to the Parliament Bill of 1911 that contemporaries referred to the diehards as "Selborne and company" or "Selborne and friends," and he had taken the lead in founding the Halsbury Club that drove Balfour from the leadership.[6] In short, one would anticipate that he would be in Bonar Law's camp when the crisis over the third Home Rule Bill peaked in March 1914; and if he was not, then it is reasonable to conclude that disaffection was widespread within the shadow cabinet.

Before considering signs that Selborne was indeed more moderate in this period than Bonar Law, it should be pointed out that the present-day professional historian would write of the Tory revolt in different terms from those used by Dangerfield and Fanning. Witness, for example, the remarks of the Australian scholar, Patricia Jalland, author of a well-received study of the Ulster question in prewar British politics. She writes of a powerful Unionist campaign aimed at securing a general election before the bill became law but makes no reference to a "Tory revolt" as such. In her view both parties were at fault, the Unionists by urging the king to revive an obsolete veto to stop the legislation; H. H. Asquith, the Liberal prime minister, by failing to make special provision for Ulster when the third Home Rule Bill was being formulated. Many months would pass before he addressed the problem, and by the time he acted, events in Ireland had outdistanced him. Jalland attributes Asquith's inaction to his habitual lassitude in facing problems and a fateful underestimation of the opposition to the bill in Ulster. If the Unionists were more realistic, they were in no position to determine policy or rectify Asquith's mistake. Supported by the Irish Nationalists, on whom they were dependent after 1910, the Liberals were in complete control of the Commons; and the Parliament Act had effectually ended the Lords' veto.[7]

As the third Home Rule Bill passed effortlessly through the Commons, where the guillotine did heavy duty, and with the Lords sidelined, the Unionists found themselves in an unfamiliar world. No longer players at Westminster when in opposition and a minority chafing at their helplessness, they adopted extra-parliamentary tactics that brought civil war perceptibly closer in Ireland. It should be stressed however that the avowed Unionist objective was to secure an appeal to the electorate, either by a general election or a referendum before home rule could become law. Impressed by this facet of the party's policy, Michael Brock concludes that Unionist maneuvers as late as 1914 were "meant as the prelude, not to a rebellion, but to a general election."[8]

Yet Unionist policy at one juncture seems to support Dangerfield and Fanning. This was the moment when the Unionist leaders, desperate for some means of stopping home rule, contemplated using the Lords to amend or delay the important Army Act. Passed almost routinely every year, the act formed part of the sacrosanct Revolution Settlement (1689); and to amend it for political purposes, as the Unionists came close to doing, was to skirt treason because of the threat to national security. The purpose of what would have been a revolutionary action was to force a general election, and even if the Unionists failed to achieve this goal, the fact remained that the Liberal government would have no means of using force in Ulster if the deteriorating situation there required action.

Unsurprisingly, Bonar Law was the first Unionist leader in a position of responsibility to embrace the plan and the last to abandon it. From the very beginning of his tenure as party leader, it was clear that he stood for a new style in politics. At the time he declared: "I am afraid I shall have to show myself very vicious, Mr Asquith, this session. I hope you will understand." By April Asquith was angrily denouncing Unionist tactics; and in late July in a speech to a great Unionist rally at Blenheim Palace Bonar Law asserted that even if the Liberals carried their Home Rule Bill through the Commons, there were "things stronger than parliamentary majorities" and his party would not be bound by the considerations and constraints of any ordinary constitutional struggle. He then reverted to a political theory known as the referendal theory which the great Lord Salisbury had promoted in Victorian England. The government's usurpation of a despotic power made necessary an appeal to the people before the third Home Rule Bill became law. Should Asquith forge ahead without a general election on the issue "as part of a corrupt parliamentary bargain [with the Irish]," Ulstermen would be justified in a resistance *à outrance* by all the means in their power including force.[9]

At this point Bonar Law voiced Unionist support for Ulster's resistance in the most sweeping terms:

In my opinion, if such an attempt is made, I can imagine no length of resistance to which Ulster can go in which I should not be prepared to support them, and in which, in my belief, they would not be supported by the overwhelming majority of the British people.[10]

Even Lord Blake, Bonar Law's biographer, considered that the Unionist leader had gone far to break the conventions upon which parliamentary democracy was based; and on another occasion Blake wrote that in this period "the whole parliamentary process was beginning to be questioned to a degree unparalleled for two centuries." This was particularly the case on the right; but the Unionist party, nevertheless, did not become authoritarian on the continental model because its parliamentary tradition was so strong.[11]

Even as Bonar Law publicly pledged his party's support for Ulster's resistance, he may well have had in mind using the Lords to amend or delay the Army Bill. The evidence comes from his letter to *The Times* on 26 July 1911, almost exactly a year before the Blenheim speech, in which he gave his reasons for supporting the Parliament Bill rather than resist until the king, on the advice of the Liberal government, created the necessary peers to carry the bill. Condemning the diehard revolt as the height of folly, Bonar Law forecast that the Unionists would regret their action in six months if they forced a creation. This was a "hedger" position, in sharp contrast to Selborne's; and Bonar Law took it knowing as he did so that once the Parliament Bill was law, the next item on the Liberal agenda was home rule.

His reasoning is of great interest in the context of this discussion. As he saw the situation, the Parliament Bill, despite its restrictions on the Lords' power, would leave their House in a position to delay legislation for two years; and he believed that the two years could be put to good use. But more than this, he believed that the Lords would continue to have important powers. And he then came to his guiding consideration:

They [the Lords] can delay for instance the Expiring Laws Continuance Bill or the Army Annual Bill, and such action on their part would undoubtedly make the continuance of the Government impossible and compel an election. . . . It might or might not be wise to use this power, but if I am right in thinking that the House of Lords, would have the means of compelling an election before Home Rule became law that surely is not a power which ought to be lightly abandoned.[12]

Apparently by coincidence Lord Wolmer, Selborne's son and heir, brought forward on 15 August a similar proposal.[13]

The idea gained ground in Unionist circles as the third Home Rule Bill neared passage. This was evident when Hugh Cecil—Selborne's brother-in-law—discussed it at length in a memorandum of 4 June 1913. Although there is a copy in both the Selborne and Bonar Law papers, it was not until 10 February 1914 that the idea was introduced to the public in an important way. At that time Lord Willoughby de Broke, Selborne's ally and close associate in the diehard revolt, announced in the Lords that he would move an amendment to the Army Act though he took no further step. Dismissing the sponsor as "notoriously a fanatical diehard," Lord Blake points out that "what has not hitherto been revealed is the extent to which even responsible Unionist leaders were prepared to go—Bonar Law not least among them." But, unmistakably, Blake, and A. M. Gollin, too, the latter writing about Lord Milner, treat the Unionist leaders in the shadow cabinet as fundamentally different from Milner, his lieutenant, Leo Amery, and by this time Willoughby de Broke.[14] More likely, when the Ulster question was involved, Bonar Law was midway between his colleagues in the shadow cabinet and the extremist elements associated with Milner and Lord Willoughby de Broke.

As for Selborne, there is no evidence that he toyed before 1914 with the idea of using the Lords to amend the Army Bill for political purposes; and when he did so in March of that year it was only fleetingly. Almost a year into the passage of the third Home Rule Bill, he gave his view of the situation in a letter of 19 September 1912. Explaining that in every state there must be an ultimate authority, which differentiated a civilization from a barbarous state, he would place that authority in the partnership of the Crown and the people. The iniquity of the Asquith government's proceedings was that in settling the Irish question it was seeking to evade that ultimate authority. The Liberals were proceeding "without giving the people through the electors any opportunity of decision." In the circumstances Ulster's attitude was morally and constitutionally right, and he believed that the Home Rule Bill would not pass into the irremediable past until the people had an opportunity to pronounce upon it. He also discussed the idea of taking up arms if the verdict were against the Unionist party.

I will never say that it is always wrong to take up arms. I should myself take up arms without any hesitation for the monarchy against a republic, and I have already said that I think Ulster is wholly justified in her present attitude. But civil war is the *ultima ratio* and the last party in the world that ought to turn to arms if it can possibly avoid it *or go outside legal and constitutional forms* [italics added] is the Conservative and Unionist party. If they did so lightly, it is likely that it would mean the breaking up of society and the end of the nation, for it would remove all restrictions on radicals and socialists who are blind to the value of tradition and authority. Finally, it is not really the United Kingdom alone which would be affected but the whole empire.[15]

The tone of the letter is not that of a Unionist on the verge of a revolutionary step, and its contents are the more interesting because Selborne was writing to T. Comyn Platt, a friend of Carson's and close associate of Lord Willougby de Broke. Platt had assisted the latter when he was secretary to the Halsbury Club and was himself secretary to Lord Willoughby de Broke's British League for the Support of Ulster.

And then there is Selborne's reaction to Hugh Cecil's memorandum on amending the Army Act. It is of the first importance in the context of this discussion. His comment, written in the memorandum's margin, went directly to the point. Were the Unionists to adopt this course, the government "would dissolve and fight on the basis of our unpatriotic action."[16] If this was the intuitive reaction of the preëminent diehard leader two years after the diehard revolt, presumably other Unionist leaders reasoned similarly. But six months after the memorandum's appearance, Selborne's attitude stiffened as rival armies emerged in Ireland and the third Home Rule came closer to passage still bare of any concession to Ulster. In these circumstances, the Cecil memorandum was clearly more germane.

For the point to be stressed is that the Unionist attitude towards amending the Army Act habitually fluctuated with the Liberal response to the worsening situation in Ireland. By the middle of 1913 when Hugh Cecil prepared his memorandum, hope rose of a settlement excluding Ulster from home rule. Secret meetings followed between Asquith and Bonar Law, even a bipartisan conference; but by mid-January 1914 negotiations collapsed. Asquith's non-committal attitude heightened distrust; and in the background, bringing pressure to bear on both sides, was the dangerous situation in Ireland. Fearing lest the Liberals use the army to coerce Ulster into accepting home rule, Unionists now for the first time gave serious consideration to having the Lords amend the Army Act; and discussion of the plan continued, despite dwindling support, until 20 March. It will be recalled that the avowed objective was to force a dissolution of Parliament and a general election, which the party leadership promised to treat as binding whatever the outcome.

On 26 January Bonar Law brought up the subject with Lansdowne, who, however, doubted the wisdom of the course. How could the Unionists justify their position, Lansdowne wanted to know, unless Ulster made the same commitment to accept the results of a general election? He saw no signs of Ulster's willingness to do so. But convinced of the gravity of the situation, he would further examine the plan.[17] Both Lansdowne and Bonar Law were suspicious of Liberal intentions. The Liberals might turn to the royal prerogative to achieve their ends just as Gladstone had relied on it in abolishing army purchase. On this point the Unionist leaders decided to consult Sir Robert Finlay. Cautious and non-adventuresome, the latter reported that if the amendment were carefully prepared, it would not be overturned; and he supplied the shadow cabinet with the model of such an amendment.[18] Moreover, Bonar Law reported to Lansdowne on 30 January that the conviction was growing that the step had to be taken. "So far everyone to whom I have spoken," he wrote, "is of the same opinion, including the three Cecils, Selborne, Austen Chamberlain and Carson." Granted that the step was serious, it was less so than allowing the government to drift into a position of using force against Ulster. Further, this was the only step available "within the letter of the constitution."[19] Lansdowne too believed that the step might be necessary but rather dreaded it.[20]

Still to be consulted were two Unionist leaders of more than ordinary importance, Balfour and Curzon. At this time Balfour was unable to attend the shadow cabinet because of his commitment to a course of lectures at Glasgow University. For his information, Bonar Law sent him a copy of his letter to Lansdowne with the comment that of their colleagues, only Lansdowne doubted the wisdom of the step. As for himself, Bonar Law declared that he had been doubtful throughout though he had recently decided that to amend the Army Act was "the least of a choice of evils."[21] Unimpressed by Lansdowne's objections, Balfour put forward some of his own. The amendment would lead to a situation in which the army could not be used to protect Roman Catholics in Belfast from protestant bigotry and, in the future, might give rise to a dangerous precedent in a period of labor unrest. Notwithstanding, he would do whatever he could to support the shadow cabinet's course.[22]

As for Curzon, his position closely resembled Lansdowne's, so Bonar Law reported on 2 February. "He feels the seriousness of it, but has no alternative to suggest." Curzon was likewise fearful of being outmaneuvered and would consult a special authority. Bonar Law would enquire from Robert Cecil whether anyone had greater authority in the matter than Finlay. If this bore fruit, Bonar Law would pursue the suggestion but had confidence that Finlay's opinion, which he had in hand, was sufficient, the more so since Felix Cassel—a member of Parliament and Sir Ernest Cassel's nephew—agreed with Finlay, as did Carson.[23] Cassel's memorandum was circulated to the shadow cabinet. Bonar Law sent a copy to Lansdowne, and there is one in the Selborne papers. Since no immediate decision had to be made about the Army Act, the shadow cabinet on 4 February postponed action, referring the plan, in Lansdowne's words, to a "strong committee," which consisted of Finlay, Carson, Robert Cecil, the later lord chancellor, Sir George Cave, and Halsbury.[24]

The Finlay committee proved more than willing to amend the Army Act. Its report of 6 March "decidedly" favored the amendment; and Lansdowne was "pretty sure" that the forthcoming shadow cabinet of 12 March would be receptive. Informing Balfour of these plans, Lansdowne would admit the force of Balfour's argument against the amendment but added: "We have got to do something, and I do not see what else there is to do." Balfour again acquiesced. The objections to the proposed course were obvious though not conclusive. In revolutionary times revolutionary measures were necessary, he supposed, but they were nonetheless "rather against the grain."[25]

But three days before the shadow cabinet, Asquith offered a compromise, and the situation abruptly changed. On the very day of the meeting the prime minister made public a plan to exclude Ulster from home rule for six years. Four counties in northern Ireland, together with Belfast and Londonderry, would benefit. Asquith expounded only general principles, and an unusually brief white paper, issued on the same day, added little detail. Unwilling to accept a time limit, Bonar Law handled the matter badly. His rejection was too brusque for Hugh Cecil, who told Carson on 13 March that their success depended on winning a general election.[26] Presumably he was better satisfied when Bonar Law on 19 March offered to submit the Liberal plan to a referendum.[27] Though Asquith was unreceptive, he began three days later another private negotiation with Bonar Law. By then he had no alternative. On the night of 20 March word reached London of an army mutiny at the Curragh, and as quick as this the Liberals had no choice but to negotiate with the Unionists. Asquith's policy was in a shambles. That this was his understanding appeared when he wrote to Venetia Stanley on 22 March—the day he renewed negotiations with Bonar Law: "The military situation has developed, as might have been expected, and there is no doubt if we were to order a march upon Ulster that about half the officers in the army—the navy is more uncertain—would strike. The immediate difficulty in the Curragh can, I think, be arranged but that is the permanent situation, & it is not a pleasant one."[28]

The point to be stressed is that a week before the Curragh mutiny or incident, as it is sometimes termed, the Unionist leadership as a whole—Bonar Law and Lansdowne the great exceptions—had lost any enthusiasm they had for amending the Army Act. And of the two political leaders, Bonar Law was the energizing force. The decisive moment had come on

12 March when Asquith made public the Liberal plan to exclude Ulster. Any hint of a compromise undermined whatever support existed for the plan to tamper with the Army Act. On that day the shadow cabinet reviewed the Finlay amendment, and its deliberations make it manifest that Bonar Law had very little support for his policy. After this, though he would continue to press it, he surely knew that it had no future. Whatever happened afterwards, the shadow cabinet's verdict was decisive. Lord Balcarres, who went to the Lords as earl of Crawford after his father's death, was thereafter remote from the party's highest councils; but he attended the shadow cabinet of 12 March and left an invaluable account of its proceedings. This is what he recorded:

Conference at Lansdowne House, 12 March 1914. Absent Austen Chamberlain, F. E. Smith. Lansdowne and B.L. began by stating their decision, reluctantly reached, to amend army annual bill.

Curzon, *Selborne* [italics added], Derby indicated dissent.

Carson [member of the committee] said Ulster expected something of the kind, though he had never indicated such a course to the Unionist Council.

W. Long said he would support it, but deprecated precipitate action or announcement, as he considers the govt position untenable, and their proposals impossible: accordingly issue should not be diverted.

Acland Hood, Devonshire (?) and Midleton (?) seemed to dislike the scheme. Chaplin raised certain objections. Londonderry, Akers-Douglas, did not speak, nor Halsbury [member of the committee].

Carson said Asquith had a conversation with him prior to the announcement of govt amendments—Asquith seems to think there will be grave disorder in South and West, if H.R. [Home Rule] is defeated. Carson was impressed by Asquith's anxiety on the subject and likewise by his desire to avoid anything like civil war.

Decision: provisionally to agree to amendment of army act, but to leave details and decision as to moment of acting to Lansdowne and B.L. (*This I fancy was against the general desire of those present*) [italics added].

Referendum. Discussion about Salisbury's bill [for this purpose]. B.L. said it was a point of strategy—he attached little importance to it, though the peers might settle for themselves. Decision apparently that Lord Lansdowne should write a letter signifying his agreement with B. Law's pronouncement in favour of a referendum.[29]

The leadership, then, was out of step with the rest of the shadow cabinet.

What is more, the tone of the meeting of 12 March was strikingly different from that suggested by Bonar Law's letter of 30 January in which he recounted his conversations with the other Unionist leaders. At the meeting of 12 March two members of the Finlay committee so favorable to amending the Army Act had little to say; and Long alone had pledged support for the leaders' recommendations. Three powerful members of the House of Lords, where the amendment would be made—Curzon, Selborne, and Derby—had "indicated dissent"; and the shadow cabinet as a whole was hostile, agreeing only "provisionally" and leaving the details and timing to Bonar Law and Lansdowne. It was Crawford's belief that the final decision was contrary to "the general desire of those present"—a strong statement. The scene is far removed from the one painted by Dangerfield, who writes of a party using the Ulster weapon to pummel parliamentary government or that depicted by Fanning in describing the "new style." That Bonar Law read the situation on the same lines as Crawford appears from a letter of 16 March in which he wrote that he could not recommend amending the Army Act if the action threatened party unity. He and Lansdowne found "the difficulties so great that neither had been able to decide what ought to be done." [30]

Yet as late as 15 March Bonar Law, after arranging for Major General Henry Wilson, a leading opponent in the army of home rule, to visit him at Pembroke Lodge, urged the acceptance of his plan to amend the Army Act. [31] This is Wilson's account of the meeting:

We had an hour's talk and he entirely persuaded me to his side. *The proposal is for the lords to bring in an amendment to the effect that the army shall not be used against Ulster without the will of the people expressed at a general election* [italics added]. This gets over my difficulty. . . . We discussed it all backwards and forwards, the handle it will give against the lords, the possibility of no army remaining after April 30th, the effect abroad; and I am convinced Bonar Law is right. *Desperate measures are required to save a desperate situation* [italics added]. [32]

It is little wonder that Selborne recorded as his opinion that Bonar Law had thoroughly bad judgment. [33]

Clearly, with the notable exception of Bonar Law, the tide against tampering with the Army Act was running strongly at the very top of the Unionist leadership by 12 March—about a week before the news of the Curragh incident reached London. Another sign of the direction that opinion was taking can be discerned from a conversation on 17 March between Curzon and John St. Loe Strachey, the Unionist editor of *The Spectator*. The latter was fearful that his party was going to take up the idea. Curzon was reassuring: thanks to his personal representations the danger had passed. [34]

On the following day there were two other developments. An anonymous letter in the Milner MSS, written on that day, reported that Ian Malcolm, secretary of Walter Long's Unionist Defence League, had stated an intention of leaving the party if it were to take up such a policy; and he claimed that private members of the party shared his views. He had added, it was rumored, that a party meeting would decide the strength of feeling.[35] On 18 March Selborne advised Bonar Law to continue negotiations with Asquith. He considered the government to be "in the tightest possible place and . . . hoping to be able to haul themselves off the rocks by the aid of some cable involuntarily tossed to them from our ship." He would toss them such a cable: he hoped that Bonar Law would respond to Asquith by saying

that so far as we are concerned the door is not shut to negotiations, that we accept the principle of the exclusion of Ulster by referendum [which Selborne considered that Asquith had hinted at], and are willing to discuss the details such as the particular method of taking the referendum, the area over which it should be taken, the period for which the exclusion should last, and what should be the course to be pursued when that period has expired.

If negotiations continued, Selborne believed they would have to stand firm for the rights of the Ulster people to decide for themselves at the end of six years, just as at present, but he would leave this point unstated at this time.[36] On 19 March, as mentioned earlier, Bonar Law offered to submit the Liberal plan to a referendum.

On that day Strachey met with Bonar Law, and afterward he described the conversation to Curzon. Bonar Law had assured him that there was no need to be anxious about the plan to amend the Army Act; there was plenty of time and nothing would be decided at present. Moreover, the tenor of his remarks suggested that it was unlikely the policy would be adopted. Strachey wrote:

Further, he told me that *though he was evidently disappointed* [italics added] he could not honestly say he thought there was much chance of the Bill being amended because it would obviously be impossible to do so unless there was a completely united party, and as at present advised, he did not think it at all likely or possible that there could be an undivided party.

Strachey added that he had asked Bonar Law for a pledge not to proceed without a united party behind him, and in return had promised not to alert the people in the party who agreed with him and get them to make their voices heard. Bonar Law had given the pledge; and his action, along with what Strachey knew of Curzon's position, provided the assurance that Strachey required. Gollin, who published this letter in a biography of Milner, considers that Bonar Law's mind was made up as the result of what Curzon had said to him.[37]

Yet clearly Curzon's was not the only influential voice raised against amending the Army Act. Crawford's account reveals a broad-based opposition in the shadow cabinet on 12 March, a full week before Strachey met with Bonar Law. And Selborne had advised Bonar Law on 18 March to continue negotiations with Asquith. Any lingering doubt that the plan had to be abandoned was erased when the parliamentary party, asked for an opinion, gave its verdict on 19 March. Robert Sanders, Unionist Whip, left this account of what transpired:

The idea of the lords amending the Army Annual Act is now being seriously considered. Edmund [Talbot, the Chief Whip] has told us to find out the views of our own people about it. Edmund himself rather favours it. Most of the whips are against it, and on the whole the feeling in the party is against it. The Scotchmen say it would be fatal to Unionist prospects in Scotland. Curiously enough Ronald McNiel says it would be most unpopular with the Orangemen who say they have no quarrel with the army. The one strong point is that it must force an election, and it is rather hard to see how to enforce one otherwise.[38]

Although the time sequence here is uncertain, it really does not matter whether the conversation between Bonar Law and Strachey took place before or after the parliamentary party gave its opinion. If earlier, the Unionist leader surely had an inkling of what to expect; if later, the verdict was already in and it was negative. Only at this juncture did Bonar Law finally abandon a plan which he had contemplated as early as 1911.

The renunciation was in his letter on 20 March to J. P. Croal, editor of the *Scotsman*, when he wrote:

As regards the Army Annual, I think there is a great deal to be said for and against the idea of having an amendment forbidding the use of the troops in Ulster until after an election; but it would be quite fatal to do it if there were any serious opposition to it in our ranks, and I think there is a sufficient amount of that feeling at present to make it impossible to do it.[39]

The reports of the knowledgeable Crawford and Sanders reveal that a formidable opposition to this policy was rising in Unionist circles well before the Curragh incident. Moreover, close examination of the period of decision-making leaves the impression that Bonar Law was the only member of the shadow cabinet who really wanted to move ahead on this front, only to discover that he had no troops. He wrote to Croal on 20 March, and by a striking coincidence word of the Curragh incident reached London that evening. As Asquith recognized and Blake writes, "the Curragh incident transformed the entire situation. It was now no longer necessary to amend the Army Act. As a means of coercing Ulster the army had become useless."[40] By the same token, to amend the act would have been the height of folly for the Unionists. They would have seemed to the electorate the source of the mutiny, which had deprived the Liberals of their major weapon in dealing with Ulster.

If the test of Unionist extremism before 1914 was a willingness to consider amending the Army Act, the shadow cabinet was guilty as charged. Yet its members had acted in accordance with accepted parliamentary practice and in the end rejected the idea despite not having secured the much-desired compromise over Ulster. Since they had no way of knowing as they did so that Asquith would soon be disarmed by the Curragh mutiny, they had divested themselves of the resources to avert what they perceived as an oncoming catastrophe, its dimensions the greater because of Asquith's unconscionable tardiness in coming to grips with the situation. According to Brock, not until July 1914 did Asquith's Irish policy become realistic.[41] Running through Unionist ruminations was the awareness that amending the Army Act by means of the Lords—an action that the leaders deemed within the letter of the constitution—was neither wise nor politically acceptable as a tactic for forcing a general election. The idea had aroused conflicting emotions in Balfour, Curzon, and Lansdowne, and even Bonar Law, more comfortable with it throughout than the others, expressed reservations as late as 16 March four days before the Curragh. By that time his reservations probably reflected not his personal qualms about the policy but rather the pragmatic recognition that he could not proceed without the shadow cabinet's support.

Moreover, in the months before Asquith broached his plan for Ulster's exclusion, the atmosphere in the Unionist camp was anything but extremist. Foreseeing a general election, Selborne and Robert Cecil, working with Curzon, produced a memorandum (January 1914), which displays all the marks of conventional thinking. The memorandum pointed out that the only constitutional project to which the party was definitely committed was reform of the Lords. Beyond the unanimous conviction that the present House would not serve, there was no agreement in the party. In the circumstances the memorandum proposed amending the Parliament Act to provide for the referendum. A new second chamber was still the desideratum; and if attained, it might be possible to do without the referendum—clearly a bow here to Curzon, who disliked it. But in the interim, before such a chamber could be set up, there was a provisional need for the referendum. The course being recommended "would be exactly consistent with the amendments moved to the Parliament Act in the House of Lords and with the principle for which the Unionist party contended."[42] The memorandum circulated to the shadow cabinet.[43] Responding to the group's pressure—and a letter as well from Milner—Bonar Law made the referendum, despite his own lack of interest in it,[44] the centerpiece of a counteroffer to Asquith on 19 March. Nor did the matter end there. On 1 May Cecil and Selborne sent a fully drawn referendum bill to Bonar Law to carry out their referendum proposal.[45]

In summary, an examination of the first six months of 1914, at a time when agitation over the third Home Rule Bill was at its height, reveals that in the outlook of the Unionist leaders there is little to indicate that their party was recklessly endangering the constitution, their goal one of destroying parliamentary government and the Liberal party as Dangerfield charged. If they discussed amending the Army Act, they also conducted a parallel dialogue in which resort to the referendum or a general election invariably figured. To be sure, to make use of the referendum did not of itself exclude the project of amending the Army Act. In his 1913 memorandum Hugh Cecil included both tactics as part of the Unionist strategy that he favored. Amending the Army Act would be the prelude to forcing a reference to the people. Nevertheless, the practice of thinking consistently in these terms was to stay within the constitution as the Unionists interpreted it; and in the end, of course, it was the portion of their tactics involving the Army Act that they discarded.

The interpretation offered here does not appear in historical accounts of this episode, and in fact Blake in his authoritative biography expresses puzzlement that Bonar Law reversed his course. Noting that there is no material to illuminate the subject in the Unionist leader's papers, he suggests that the reversal was probably due to opposition from the party's rank and file, many of them retired officers from the services who may have been alarmed at the implications of his policy. And Blake adds that had it not been for an unexpected development (i.e. the Curragh mutiny) that made the plan unnecessary, Bonar Law might have subsequently revived it.[46] But no such turnabout was possible since the revolt against Bonar Law's authority was at the very top of the party. There was a Tory revolt in 1914, to be sure, but it was not the Dangerfield and Fanning model but rather an in-house revolt in which Selborne better represented the sentiments of the shadow cabinet than Bonar Law. Not for the first time the shadow cabinet imposed its will on the party leader, and when this occurred there was no going back.[47]

Reference Matter

Abbreviations

AECA	Archives du Ministère des Affaires Étrangères
AHR	*American Historical Review*
BIHR	*Bulletin of the Institute of Historical Research*
BL	British Library
BLJ	*British Library Journal*
Bod.L	Bodleian Library
BLP	Bonar Law Papers
Cobbett	William Cobbett, *Parliamentary History of England* . . . *to 1803*, 36 vols. (London 1806–20)
CUL	Cambridge University Library
EHR	*English Historical Journal*
HJ	*Historical Journal*
HLRO	House of Lords Record Office
HMC	Historical Manuscripts Commission
KAO	Kent Archives Offices
JBS	*Journal of British Studies*
JMH	*Journal of Modern History*
LJ	*Lords Journals*
MP	Melbourne Papers
PD	*Parliamentary Debates*
PH	*Parliamentary History*
PRO	Public Record Office
RA	Royal Archives, Windsor Castle
RL	Royal Library
RO	Record Office
SP	State Papers
UL	University Library
WDCM	*Wellington, Despatches, Correspondence, and Memoranda*
WCRO	Warwickshire County Record Office
WP	Wellington Papers
WPC	Wellington, *Political Correspondence*

Notes

Introduction

1. See Valerie Cromwell, "Peers and Personal Networks," in H. W. Blom, W. P. Blockmans, and H. de Schepper, eds., *Bicameralisme* (The Hague, 1992), 383–93.

2. Corinne C. Weston, *The House of Lords and Ideological Politics: Lord Salisbury's Referendal Theory and the Conservative Party, 1846–1922* (American Philosophical Society, Philadelphia, forthcoming.)

3. For an excellent new study of the Lords in the three decades before World War I, see Andrew Adonis, *Making Aristocracy Work: The Peerage and the Political System in Britain, 1884–1914* (Oxford, 1993). For Curzon's role see Derek Blakeley, "Lord Curzon and the Conservative Party, 1905–1925" (Ph.D. diss., Washington University, St. Louis, 1994).

Chapter 1

I wish to acknowledge the gracious permission of Her Majesty The Queen to consult the Stuart Papers. I would like to thank Clyve Jones and John Walsh for their comments on an earlier draft of this essay.

1. By 10 and 11 Vict. c. 108 the archbishops of Canterbury and York and the bishops of London, Durham, and Winchester always have seats in the Lords, together with 21 of the other bishops, according to seniority of consecration.

2. The figures for 1601 and 1719 are taken from Clyve Jones, "'Venice Preserv'd; or A Plot Discovered': The Political and Social Context of the Peerage Bill of 1719," in C. Jones, ed., *A Pillar of the Constitution: The House of Lords in British Politics, 1640–1784* (London, 1989), 90. The figures for 1800 and 1900 (to which have been added 16 Scottish representative peers and, for 1900, 28 Irish) come from J. V. Beckett, *The Aristocracy in England, 1660–1914* (Oxford, 1986), 486–87. No attempt has been made to calculate the number of peers who did not sit because they were Roman Catholics, minors, etc.

3. Roy Porter, *English Society in the Eighteenth Century* (Harmondsworth, 1982), 77. See also, for example, Norman Sykes, *Church and State in England in the Eighteenth Century* (Cambridge, 1934), 63–65.

4. See Mark Goldie, "Danby, the Bishops and the Whigs," in Tim Harris, Paul Seaward and Mark Goldie, eds., *The Politics of Religion in Restoration England* (Oxford, 1990), 75–105.

5. For a more detailed discussion of the following points see Stephen Taylor, "The Bishops at Westminster in the Mid-Eighteenth Century," in Jones, *Pillar of the Constitution*, 137–63.

6. For 1736 see Stephen Taylor, "Sir Robert Walpole, the Church of England and the Quakers Tithe Bill of 1736," *HJ* 28 (1985): 51–77. For 1743 and 1748 see Taylor, "Bishops at Westminster," 151–56.

7. Twice in 1734, on a bill to prevent stockjobbing and on a proposal to meet on Easter eve, and again in 1736, on the proposal to exempt Queen Anne's Bounty from the Mortmain Bill, most bishops voted against the ministry. RA, Stuart Papers, 169/186, 170/26, Nathaniel Mist to James Edgar, 24 [Apr.], 1 May 1734; John, Lord Hervey, *Some Materials towards Memoirs of the Reign of King George II*, ed. Romney Sedgwick, 3 vols. (London, 1931), 2:536.

8. Geoffrey Holmes, *British Politics in the Age of Anne* (London, 1967); G. V. Bennett, *The Tory Crisis in Church and State, 1688–1730: The Career of Francis Atterbury, Bishop of Rochester* (Oxford, 1975); Tim Harris, *Politics under the Later Stuarts: Party Conflict in a Divided Society, 1660–1715* (Harlow, 1993), chap. 6.

9. Bennett, *Tory Crisis*, 22.

10. Linda Colley, *In Defiance of Oligarchy: The Tory Party, 1714–60* (Cambridge, 1982), esp. chap. 4.

11. See J. E. Thorold Rogers, *A Complete Collection of the Protests of the House of Lords*, 3 vols. (Oxford, 1875), 1:225–357 passim.

12. The best account of the religious policy of the Walpole era and of Gibson's role in it remains Norman Sykes, *Edmund Gibson, Bishop of London, 1669–1748: A Study in Politics and Religion in the Eighteenth Century* (London, 1926), esp. chaps. 4 and 5.

13. Hervey, *Memoirs* 1:91. The description of Gibson as "*our* Pope" was coined by Walpole in a letter to Newcastle on 6 Sept. 1723. BL, Add. MS. 32686, fols. 326–27. The phrase clearly passed quickly into common usage. Hervey, *Memoirs* 1:90; 2:546; *The Yale Edition of Horace Walpole's Correspondence*, ed., W. S. Lewis, 48 vols. (New Haven, 1937–83), 17:278.

14. E.g., "First Oars to Lambeth Or Who Strives for Preferment," in Milton Percival, ed., *Political Ballads Illustrating the Administration of Sir Robert Walpole* (Oxford, 1916), 53–56.

15. [William Arnall], *A Letter to the Reverend Dr. Codex* (London, 1734), 15. See also, *An Apology for Dr. Codex: Humbly Addressed to the Doctor* (London, 1734); [Sir Michael Foster], *An Examination of the Scheme of Church-Power, laid down in the Codex Juris Ecclesiastici Anglicani, &c.* (London, 1735).

16. Christ Church, Oxford, Arch.W.Epist. 8, no. 87, Heads of Wake's Speech on the Bill for Strengthening the Protestant Interest. The best account of the repeal

of the Occasional Conformity and Schism Acts is G. M. Townend, "Religious Radicalism and Conservatism in the Whig Party under George I: The Repeal of the Occasional Conformity and Schism Acts," *PH* 7 (1988): 24–44.

17. St. Andrews UL, Gibson Papers, MS. 5303, "The Case of the Bishop of London's retiring from publick Business."

18. All comments on attendance in the House are derived from the lists of peers and bishops present each day in *LJ*.

19. Clyve Jones, "'That Busy Sensless Place': An Analysis of Government and Opposition Lords in Walpole's House of Lords, 1721–42," forthcoming. The one possible exception is the division on 16 May 1721 in the case of the Westminster School dormitory. That division, however, produced complex cross-party voting among the bishops. See Jones, "Jacobites under the Beds: Bishop Francis Atterbury, the Earl of Sunderland and the Case of the Westminster School Dormitory," *BLJ*, forthcoming.

20. Brampton Bryan MSS, Bundle 117; HMC, *Diary of Viscount Percival afterwards First Earl of Egmont* 2:271; HMC, 15th Report, appendix, pt. 6, 168 (Sir Thomas Robinson to Lord Carlisle, 24 Apr. 1736); St. Andrews UL, MS. 5397, Gibson's speech on the Quakers' Tithe Bill. For further details of the Mortmain and Quakers' Tithe Bills, see below.

21. BL, Lansdowne MS. 1037, fol. 77. This speech is dated 1721. Kennett is another bishop who is only recorded in Cobbett as speaking once, like Gibson on the Bill for Strengthening the Protestant Interest. BL, Lansdowne MSS 1037 and 1038, however, contain 24 of his speeches.

22. CUL, Cholmondeley (Houghton) Papers, 78/1C, "Proposals" submitted to the ministry by Bishop Gibson, n.d. [1723].

23. Bod.L, MS. Add. A. 269, pp. 52, 77–78, Gibson to Bishop Nicolson, 20 Dec. 1715, 29 July 1718; Christ Church, Arch.W.Epist. 20, fol. 480, Gibson to Wake, 22 Nov. 1717. For Wake's loss of political influence, see Norman Sykes, "Archbishop Wake and the Whig Party: 1716–23," *Cambridge Historical Journal* 8 (1945): 93–112, and below, 21–22.

24. Bod.L, MS. Add. A. 269, p. 43, Gibson to Nicolson, 20 Oct. 1715.

25. HMC, *Portland MSS* 7:264; BL, Add. MS. 32686, fols. 206–7, Carteret to Newcastle, 28 Sept. 1721.

26. BL, Add. MS. 32686, fols. 312–13, Walpole to Newcastle, 22 Aug. 1723; CUL, CH(H) Papers, 78/1C.

27. St. Andrews UL, MS. 5182, Townshend to Gibson, 2 Oct. 1723 N.S.; BL, Add. MS. 32686, fols. 312–13, 316–19, Walpole to Newcastle, 22 Aug. 1723, Newcastle to Walpole, 25 Aug. 1723

28. BL, Lansdowne MS. 1017, fols. 16–17, Gibson to Kennett, 16 Sept. 1727; Sykes, *Gibson*, 130–43.

29. Though it is a phrase I have used elsewhere. "Walpole and the Church," 73.

30. BL, Lansdowne MS. 1018, fols. 9–10, Reynolds to Kennett, 29 Oct. 1724.

31. Ibid., fol. 7, Reynolds to Kennett, 24 Sept. 1723; Sykes, *Gibson*, chaps. 4 and 5.

32. E.g., Christ Church, Arch.W.Epist. 20, fols. 348–49, Potter to Wake, 19 Mar. 1717. For Gibson's role in Tenison's "whipping system" at the end of Anne's reign,

see *The London Diaries of William Nicolson, Bishop of Carlisle, 1702–18*, ed. Clyve Jones and Geoffrey Holmes (Oxford, 1985), 50, 604–5.

33. Cobbett 9:115–16; HMC, 15th Report, appendix, pt. 6, 118, 119 (Robinson to Carlisle, 26 May, 2 June 1733). Robinson's oft-quoted statement that 25 bishops voted in these divisions appears to be wrong. Neither Wake of Canterbury nor Hough of Worcester were in the House on these days, and neither had deposited his proxy with another bishop. Robinson noted Wake's absence, but said nothing about Hough. Hough, now 82, appears to have been a semi-invalid at Hartlebury Castle and is not recorded as having attended the Lords at any time in this Parliament. Not having taken the oaths, he was, therefore, unable to deposit a proxy. It is possible that only 23 bishops voted on 1 June. We do not possess a complete division list for this vote and Bishop Wilcocks of Rochester, who had voted in person on 24 May, is not listed in the *Journals* as being present on 1 June and he did not leave a proxy. The 6 bishops who voted by proxy on 24 May were Blackburne, Egerton, Peploe, Clavering, Waugh, and Sydall. Hare, who was present on 24 May, also voted by proxy on 1 June. *LJ* 24:277, 291; HLRO, Proxy Books.

34. "The Knight and the Prelate," in *Political Ballads*, ed. Percival, 92.

35. Taylor, "Walpole and the Church," 67.

36. St. Andrews UL, MSS 5297, 5314, Gibson to Walpole, n.d., Hare to Gibson, 7 Aug. 1736.

37. St. Andrews UL, MS. 5218, "The Bishop of Londons Complaints of ill usage."

38. Sykes, *Gibson*, 123–27.

39. Christ Church, Arch.W.Epist. 8, no. 307, Potter to Wake, 23 Oct. 1720; HLRO, Proxy Books (1719/20-1722/3); Robert Anderson, *Memoir of the Life and Writings of John Potter* (Edinburgh, 1824), ix; Hervey, *Memoirs* 2:398, 547–48; St. Andrews UL, MS. 5285, Gibson to Walpole, n.d. [18 Dec. 1733].

40. St. Andrews UL, MSS 5200, 5201, Gibson to Newcastle, n.d. [1727], Gibson to Walpole, n.d. [1727].

41. Hervey, *Memoirs* 2:532–33.

42. HMC, 15th Report, appendix, pt. 6, 118. For his reluctance to put his proxy at the disposal of the ministry in 1734 see BL, Add. MS. 32689, fols. 142–43, John Lynch to Newcastle, 15 Jan. 1734.

43. CUL, CH(H) Papers, 78/1c; BL, Add. MS. 32686, fols. 312–13, Walpole to Newcastle, 22 Aug. 1723; St. Andrews UL, MS. 5209, Gibson to [Townshend], n.d. [1728].

44. In 1736 Hoadly conspicuously failed to join the episcopal opposition to the Quakers' Tithe Bill. He explained that "If I have at any Time differed from Wise and Worthy Men, about the Most effectual Methods of shewing this Regard [for the rights of the clergy], it has been honestly." Benjamin Hoadly, "A Charge Delivered to the Clergy . . . in the Year 1736," in *The Works of Benjamin Hoadly, D.D.*, ed. J. Hoadly, 3 vols. (London, 1773), 3:492.

45. Jones, "'That Busy Sensless Place,'" appendix; BL, Add. MS. 6043, fols. 31, 35, 42, 50, "Reports of the debates in the House of Lords from 1735 to 1745 by Dr. Secker, whilst Bishop of Oxford."

46. William Coxe, *Memoirs of the Life and Administration of Sir Robert Walpole*, 3 vols. (London, 1798), 2:351; *The Diaries of Thomas Wilson, D.D., 1731–7 and 1750*, ed. C. L. S. Linnell (London, 1964), 158.

47. HLRO, Proxy Books. For most of these bishops other evidence also exists to suggest that they were personally close to Gibson. Smalbroke, for example, wrote a laudatory memoir. Richard Smalbroke, *Some Account of the Right Reverend Dr. Edmund Gibson, Late Lord Bishop of London* (London, 1749).

48. HMC, *Egmont Diary* 1:444.

49. Bod.L, MS. Add. A. 269, pp. 73–74, Gibson to Nicolson, 10 Dec. 1717; St. Andrews UL, MS. 5308.

50. 5 Geo. I, c. 4. The Act repeals the whole of the Schism Act of 1714 and part of the Occasional Conformity Act of 1711. Two amendments were made in the House of Lords to the bill introduced on 13 Dec. 1718. A clause was deleted which would have removed the threat of prosecution from clergymen refusing to admit individuals to the sacrament and would have made the offering to receive the sacrament an acceptable qualification for office under the Test and Corporation Acts. Another clause was inserted making it illegal for any mayor or magistrate to attend a meeting house with the insignia of his office. Christ Church, Arch.W.Epist. 8, no. 85; HLRO, Main Papers, 13 Dec. 1718.

51. *A List of the Lords Spiritual and Temporal, who Voted For or Against the Repeal of the Several Acts made for the Security of the Church of England* (London, [1718]).

52. Rogers, *Protests* 1:218–21.

53. Holmes, *British Politics*, 113; Christ Church, Arch.W.Epist. 20, fol. 347, Cowper to Wake, 14 Mar. 1717; Edmund Calamy, *An Historical Account of My Own Life*, 2 vols. (London, 1829), 2:246.

54. Townend, "Repeal of the Occasional Conformity and Schism Acts," 28–31, 37–39.

55. Christ Church, Arch.W.Epist. 21, fols. 75, 81–82, Potter to Wake, 23 Dec. 1718, Nicolson to Wake, 1 Jan. 1719.

56. He had told Gibson that he would support the repeal of the Schism Act. Bod.L, MS. Add. A. 269, pp. 80–81, Gibson to Nicolson, 13 Sept. 1718.

57. *Nicolson's Diaries*, 651.

58. Christ Church, Arch.W.Epist. 8, no. 87, "The Heads of my Speech in the H. of Lords agt Repealing the Occasional Conformity Bill."

59. It might be noted, however, that Nicolson, in his correspondence with Wake on this issue, seems to assume that they shared similar opinions. Nicolson had been a consistent supporter of legislation against occasional conformity throughout Anne's reign. *Nicolson's Diaries*, 25.

60. Brampton Bryan MSS, Bundle X, Edward Prideaux Gwyn to Edward Harley, 8 Jan. 1719.

61. Christ Church, Arch.W.Epist. 8, no. 87.

62. A rumor was circulating in Dec. 1718 and Jan. 1719 that Gibson's support for repeal was to be explained by the fact that his uncle, a rich Dissenter, had told him that he could expect nothing unless he voted in favor of relief for the Dissenters. HMC, *Portland MSS* 7:247; Christ Church, Arch.W.Epist. 21, fols. 81–2, Nicolson

to Wake, 1 Jan. 1719. Such a motive cannot be discounted. However, it is not, in itself, a sufficient explanation, and it should be emphasized that Gibson did act in concert with Blackburne and Hough. See below.

63. Christ Church, Arch.W.Epist. 7, fols. 115–16, Gibson to Wake, 4 May 1716.

64. "Here I was both deserted, & betray'd by my Brethren, some of whom had encouraged me in my Opposition. I pray God forgive them." Christ Church, Arch.W.Epist. 8, no. 87.

65. *Nicolson's Diaries*, 652.

66. BL, Stowe MS. 354, fol. 195, Notes on debates in the House of Lords, 18–19 Dec. 1718; BL, Add. MS. 47028, fol. 262, Viscount Percival to Charles Dering, Dec. 1718; BL, Lansdowne MS. 1039, fol. 196, Bishop Kennett's speech on the repeal of the Occasional Conformity and Schism Acts, 18 Dec. 1718.

67. BL, Stowe MS. 354, fol. 194; BL, Add. MS. 47028, fols. 261–62.

68. *Nicolson's Diaries*, 649.

69. Bod.L, MS. Add. A. 269, pp. 71–72, Gibson to Nicolson, 28 Nov. 1717.

70. Hertfordshire RO, Panshanger MSS, D/EP/F131, fol. 11, Lord Chancellor Cowper's notes on his meeting with the bishops on 23 Mar. 1717, printed in *Nicolson's Diaries*, 704–5.

71. Townend, "Repeal of the Occasional Conformity and Schism Acts," 30; *Nicolson's Diaries*, 651–52.

72. Bod.L, MS. Add. A. 269, pp. 73–74, 75–76, Gibson to Nicolson, 10, 24 Dec. 1717.

73. Ibid., 70–71, Gibson to Nicolson, 23 Nov. 1717.

74. Ibid., 71–72, Gibson to Nicolson, 28 Nov. 1717.

75. Ibid., 73–74, Gibson to Nicolson, 10 Dec. 1717.

76. Christ Church, Arch.W.Epist. 21, fols. 59–60, Nicolson to Wake, 10 Nov. 1718.

77. Hough, Willis, Gibson, Chandler, and Talbot met at Bishop Trimnell's.

78. Christ Church, Arch.W.Epist. 20, fol. 480, Gibson to Wake, 22 Nov. 1717; Bod.L, MS. Add. A 269, pp. 75–76, Gibson to Nicolson, 24 Dec. 1717. It is probably the detailed recommendations from this meeting which are contained in a paper given to Lord Chancellor Cowper by Bishop Willis. Hertfordshire RO, Panshanger MSS, D/EP/F138, fols. 18–21.

79. BL, Add. MS. 47028, fols. 220–21, Percival to Dering, Jan. 1718.

80. Ibid., fol. 264, Percival to Dering, Dec. 1718; HLRO, Main Papers, 13 Dec. 1718.

81. Brampton Bryan MSS, Bundle X, Gwyn to Harley, 23 Dec. 1718.

82. See Christ Church, Arch.W.Epist. 20, fol. 67, anon to Wake, n.d., for a complaint about the clergy being "oblig'd to Administer it [the sacrament] promiscuously to all Officers Civill, & Military, under a very great Penalty." In Jan. 1718 Percival reported, apparently with reference to the meeting of the bishops on 22 Nov., that some regarded the Test as "a prostitution of the most Sacred ordinance of our Religion to political purposes." BL, Add. MS. 47028, fols. 220–21.

83. Bod.L, MS Add. A. 269, pp. 72–73, Gibson to Nicolson, 3 Dec. 1717.

84. Ibid., 40–42, 42–44, Gibson to Nicolson, 6, 20 Oct. 1715.

85. St. Andrews UL, MS. 5219, "My Case in Relation to the *Ministry* and the *Whigs*," n.d.

86. Christ Church, Arch.W.Epist. 21, fols. 63–64, Nicolson to Wake, 29 Nov. 1718.

87. G. V. Bennett, "An Unpublished Diary of Archbishop William Wake," *Studies in Church History* 3 (1966): 258–66.

88. Bod.L, MS Add. A. 269, pp. 71–72, Gibson to Nicolson, 28 Nov. 1717.

89. Ibid., 78–79, Gibson to Nicolson, 23 Aug. 1718. Gibson often referred to himself and those like him as "Church Whigs." See, e.g., St. Andrews UL, MS. 5219; Henry E. Huntington Library, San Marino, Gibson Papers, bound vol., no. 13.

90. Christ Church, Arch.W.Epist. 20, fols. 437, 414–16, Gibson to Wake, 24 Aug., 25 July 1717; *Nicolson Diaries*, 655.

91. Bod.L, MS Eng. d. 2405, fols. 60–61, Gibson to Hough, n.d. [1735].

92. [Edmund Gibson], *The Dispute Adjusted, about the Proper Time of Applying for a Repeal of the Corporation and Test Acts: By Shewing, That No Time is Proper* (London, 1732), 6.

93. Bod.L, MS Eng. d. 2405, fols. 60–61.

94. Huntington Library, Gibson Papers, bound vol., no. 14, "A Letter to Sr Robert Walpole, prepar'd during Archbp Wake's indisposition, in case ye Archbishopric should be offer'd to me."

95. With the exception of Bishop Hoadly. See n. 44 above.

96. For a more detailed account of the arguments against the Tithe Bill see Taylor, "Walpole and the Church," 64–67.

97. There are three sources for Gibson's arguments against the bill: his speech on the second reading in the Lords (St. Andrews UL, MS. 5397), his annotated copy of the bill (St. Andrews UL, MS. 5330), and a short pamphlet entitled "Remarks upon a Bill now Depending in Parliament . . . ," in *Papers Relating to the Quakers Tythe Bill* (London, 1736), 17–21. His speech, however, is very short and is primarily concerned with defending the number of clerical petitions against the bill.

98. St. Andrews UL, MS. 5330; Thomas Sherlock, "The Country Parson's Plea Against the Quakers Tythe-Bill," in *Papers Relating to the Quakers Tythe Bill*, 30; Gibson, "Remarks Upon a Bill," 19.

99. Edmund Gibson, *Codex Juris Ecclesiastici Anglicani* (London, 1713), intro. 17–19. This issue was important for Gibson. He wrote a long memorandum refuting the arguments of Lord Chief Justice Hardwicke, in his judgment in the case of *Middleton v. Crofts*, that convocation lacked the power to make canons which could bind the laity. St. Andrews UL, MS. 5424.

100. Hervey, *Memoirs* 2:530.

101. *The Journals of the House of Commons* 22:567; Taylor, "Walpole and the Church," 55.

102. Northamptonshire RO, MS L(c) 1733, Parliamentary Journal of William

Hay; Hervey, *Memoirs* 2:530–31; N. C. Hunt, *Two Early Political Associations. The Quakers and the Dissenting Deputies in the Age of Sir Robert Walpole* (Oxford, 1961), 146–50.

103. See Taylor, "Walpole and the Church," 53–63, for a discussion of Walpole's policy in the 1736 session.

104. Huntington Library, Gibson Papers, bound vol., no. 14.

105. St. Andrews UL, MSS 5208, 5210, Gibson to Walpole, n.d., Gibson to Townshend, n.d.

106. Ibid., MS. 5209, Gibson to [Townshend], n.d. [1728].

107. CUL, CH(H) Papers, 78/54, "Memoranda" by Bishop Gibson, n.d. [1728].

108. St. Andrews UL, MSS 5208, 5209, Gibson to Walpole, n.d., Gibson to [Townshend], n.d.

109. Ibid., MS. 5209.

110. Bod.L, MS Eng. d. 2405, fols. 31–32, "Queries relating to the Bishops and Clergy."

111. Ibid., fols. 85–86, "Complaints usually made by the Bps and Clergy."

112. Huntington Library, Gibson Papers, bound vol., no. 14.

113. See, e.g., St. Andrews UL, MSS 5201, 5203, Gibson to Walpole, n.d. [1727], Gibson to Walpole, n.d. [Dec. 1727/Jan. 1728]. Queen Caroline's circle of clergymen was remarkably diverse, including the heterodox like Samuel Clarke, Tories like Thomas Sherlock, and Whig high churchmen like John Potter and William Wake. Norman Sykes, in correcting the exaggerations of Mark Pattison, diminishes too much Caroline's influence over church patronage. Norman Sykes, "Queen Caroline and the Church," *History* 9 (1927): 333–39.

114. See Sykes, *Gibson*, 144, and n. 13 above.

115. Lewis Walpole Library, Farmington, CT, Weston Papers, vol. 2, Gibson to Townshend, 8 July 1729, printed in Coxe, *Walpole* 2:646–47; St. Andrews UL, MSS 5312, 5210, Gibson to Hare, 4 Aug. 1736, Gibson to Townshend, n.d. [1728]. See also, e.g., Beinecke Rare Book and Manuscript Library, Osborn Files, 14.84, Gibson to Townshend, 18 Sept. 1724.

116. For one example of contemporary doubts about the depth of Walpole's religious belief see *The Works of the Rev. John Wesley*, 14 vols., 3d ed. (London, 1829), 7:341.

117. CUL, CH(H) Correspondence, 2161, Gibson to Walpole, 27 Apr. 1734; [Arnall], *Letter to Dr. Codex*. For the Rundle affair, see Sykes, *Gibson*, 264–75.

118. St. Andrews UL, MS. 5285A, Gibson to Walpole, n.d.

119. Cf. Hunt, *Two Early Political Associations*, 92.

120. St. Andrews UL, MS. 5315, Gibson to Hare, 10 Aug. 1736.

121. Ibid., MSS 5304–5; Bod.L, MS Add. A. 269, fol. xi, "Queries sent to the Ministry on Occasion of their Resentment against the Bench of Bishops; for their unanimous opposition agst the Quakers Bill," by Gibson; Hervey, *Memoirs* 2:531–32.

122. BL, Add. MS. 32686, fols. 316–19, Newcastle to Walpole, 25 Aug. 1723.

123. Bod.L, MS Add. A. 269, fols. 73–74, Gibson to Nicolson, 10 Dec. 1717.

124. With Nicholas Claggett between 1737 and 1745–46; with John Gilbert in the

sessions of 1746–47 and 1747–48; and with Richard Smalbroke in the last weeks of the 1748 session. HLRO, Proxy Books.

125. BL, Add. MS. 32691, fol. 141, Gibson to Newcastle, 19 May 1738; St. Andrews UL, MS. 5299, "My last letter to Sr. R. W[alpol]e."

126. Cobbett 12:1300–1, 1426; 14:272. Gibson was absent for the second reading of the Spirituous Liquors Bill on 22 Feb. 1743, but was present for the vote on the third reading on 25 Feb. He also signed the protest against the Bill. LJ 26:218.

127. BL, Add. MS. 32716, fol. 277, Newcastle to Pelham, 17 Sept. 1748.

Chapter 2

The quotations from the Stuart Papers in the Royal Archives, Windsor Castle, are by the gracious permission of Her Majesty the Queen, while those from the Panshanger Papers at the Hertfordshire Record Office are by permission of the late Lady Ravensdale. I would like to thank David Hayton, David Lemmings and Stephen Taylor who read an early draft of this essay and made many useful comments, and Eveline Cruickshanks who obtained material from the Archives du Ministère des Affairs Étrangères for me.

1. HMC, *Portland MSS* 7:310. See also HMC, *Carlisle MSS*, 37.

2. C. B. Realey, *The Early Opposition to Sir Robert Walpole, 1720–1727* (Lawrence, KS, 1931), 78. He labeled the group "Cowper's cabal" after the name given it by the French ambassador (ibid., 81), but the group was neither secret nor tightly knit, being more a loose confederation of factions from both main parties whose aims sometimes differed but who were prepared to work together for several common ends.

3. See, e.g., G. V. Bennett, *The Tory Crisis in Church and State, 1688–1730* (Oxford, 1975), 231–32; Linda Colley, *In Defiance of Oligarchy: The Tory Party, 1714–60* (Cambridge, 1982), 63–64.

4. Realey, *Early Opposition*, 82.

5. For a full discussion of the origins of Cowper's group see Clyve Jones, "The New Opposition in the House of Lords, 1720–1723," *HJ* 36 (1993): 309–29.

6. HMC, *Polwarth MSS* 3:30, Secretary of State Carteret to Polwarth, 13 Jan. 1721.

7. B. W. Hill, *The Growth of Parliamentary Parties, 1689–1742* (London, 1976), 181–82.

8. For Sunderland see Bennett, *Tory Crisis*, 225–31; G. M. Townend, "The Political Career of Charles Spencer, Third Earl of Sunderland, 1695–1722" (Edinburgh Ph.D. diss., 1985), 274, 282–87; and Clyve Jones, "Whigs, Jacobites and Charles Spencer, Third Earl of Sunderland," *EHR*, 109 (1994); 52–73. For Cowper see Clyve Jones, "Jacobitism and the Historian: the Case of William, 1st Earl Cowper," *Albion*, 23 (1992): 681–96.

9. See Bennett, *Tory Crisis*, 225–27; and Clyve Jones, "Jacobites under the Beds: Bishop Atterbury, the Earl of Sunderland and the Case of the New Dormitory for Westminster School in 1721," *BLJ* (forthcoming, 1995).

10. E.g., Colley (*In Defiance of Oligarchy*, 49, 313) labels Cowper a "Whig Jaco-

bite," to circumvent the apparent problem of a former Whig minister working with Jacobites in the new opposition. For other historians who have tarred Cowper with the Jacobite brush and a full refutation of this libel see Jones, "Jacobitism and the Historian."

11. *The Private Diary of William, Earl Cowper, Lord Chancellor of England* (Roxburghe Club, Eton, 1833), 42–44; *The Diary of Sir David Hamilton, 1709–1714*, ed. P. Roberts (Oxford, 1975), 34.

12. J. G. A. Pocock, *Virtue, Commerce and History* (Cambridge, 1985), 221–22, 234.

13. In 1699, see David Hayton, "The 'Country' Interest and the Party System, 1689–c.1720," in Clyve Jones, ed., *Party and Management in Parliament, 1660–1784* (Leicester, 1984), 76, 79 n. 5; David Hayton, ed., "Debates in the House of Commons, 1697–1699," *Camden Miscellany vol. 29*, Camden 4th ser. 39 (London, 1987): 347.

14. Hertfordshire RO, D/EP F36 (Panshanger Papers), Commonplace book of Sarah, Lady Cowper (Cowper's mother), 19 Nov. 1701 (unpaginated). I owe this reference to David Hayton.

15. See Daniel Szechi, *Jacobitism and Tory Politics, 1710–1714* (Edinburgh, 1984), 78.

16. See Pocock, *Virtue, Commerce, and History*, 37–50, 236–37.

17. Christ Church, Oxford, Wake MS. 21, fol. 163, 15 Oct. 1719. See also Hertfordshire RO, D/EP F193, fol. 86, Cowper to his wife, 8 June [1721].

18. "Unbypassed Integrity" was the quality first noted in a report of his death: BL, Add. MS. 27980, fol. 174, newsletter, 12 Oct. 1723.

19. *Hamilton Diary*, 53.

20. Ibid., 55–56.

21. Ibid., 51.

22. John, Lord Campbell, *The Lives of the Lord Chancellors and Keepers of the Great Seal of England*, 2d ser., 8 vols. (London, 1846–69), 4:421, 427–29.

23. In 1701 after his own electoral interest had collapsed at Hertford, Cowper was brought into the Commons for Bere Alston by the influence of the Whig Junto, who acknowledged his "known Integrity & Great Abilitys for the service of this Government [i.e. the fallen Whig ministers]." See David Lemmings, *Gentlemen and Barristers: The Inns of Court and the English Bar, 1680–1730* (Oxford, 1990), 209–10.

24. See BL, Add. MS. 47028, fols. 5–8, Sir John Perceval to ?, 26 Jan. 1715.

25. See David Lemmings, "Lord Chancellor Cowper and the Whigs, 1714–16," *PH* 9 (1990): 166.

26. See Clyve Jones, "'Venice Preserv'd; or A Plot Discovered': The Political and Social Context of the Peerage Bill of 1719" in Clyve Jones, ed., *A Pillar of the Constitution: The House of Lords in British Politics, 1640–1784* (London, 1989), 95. The only other opponent of the bill was Lord Oxford, with whom Cowper shared a "Country" background in the 1690s and a dislike of excessive party government.

27. Lemmings, "Cowper and the Whigs," 166; Bod.L, Oxford, MS. Add. A. 269, p. 49, Edmund Gibson to William Nicolson, 10 Dec. 1715. I owe this reference to Stephen Taylor.

28. See below, 37, and n. 52. For a report on the animosity between Cowper and Sunderland in late 1718 see HMC, *Portland MSS* 5:575: "Very high words passed between this Lord [Sunderland] and the late Chancellor in the last Debate, Accusing one another of Dishonesty and betraying their country," (Edward Harely, Jr. to Abigail Harley, 4 Jan. 1719). This exchange presumably occurred during the debates over the Bill to Strengthen the Protestant Interest (i.e. to repeal the Occasional Conformity and Schism Acts), when Cowper opposed the section of the bill which repealed part of the Test and Corporation Acts, with relation to Dissenters: see Cobbett, 7:569, 581.

29. Walpole's latest biographer seems to suggest that Walpole did not want "authoritarian power" (see Jeremy Black, *Robert Walpole and the Nature of Politics in Early Eighteenth Century England* [London, 1990], 19–22). Walpole's opposition to the Peerage Bill was entirely partisan and not based on principle (unlike Cowper's), and is no evidence of moderation. He was probably more realistic than either Sunderland or Stanhope as to what could be achieved.

30. Lemmings, "Cowper and the Whigs," 164.

31. For a full discussion of the origins of the new opposition see Jones, "New Opposition in the House of Lords."

32. PRO, SP 35/23/170, 30 Nov. 1720. Though there is no addressee on this letter, the following one (SP 35/23/171, Coningsby to Delafaye, 30 Nov. 1720) makes it clear that it was sent to Stanhope.

33. Hertfordshire RO, D/EP F55, fol. 51, 20 Apr. 1722. Hutcheson is referring to a preface he wrote to a collection of papers published on the Westminster election which he had asked Cowper to peruse and correct.

34. See the comments of Lord Strafford, one of the quintessential Court peers of Anne's reign and one of Cowper's most active supporters in opposition: ibid., D/EP F57, fols. 49–50, Strafford to [Cowper], 29 June [1721].

35. For Cowper's initial unwillingness to work with the Tories even in opposition see Jones, "New Opposition in the House of Lords," 314.

36. See Lemmings, *Gentlemen and Barristers*, 148.

37. For Cowper and moral reform in the 1690s see David Hayton, "Moral Reform and Country Politics in the Late Seventeenth-Century House of Commons," *Past and Present*, no. 128 (1990): 69, 73, 81.

38. *Private Diary of Cowper*, 50.

39. See Lemmings, "Cowper and the Whigs," 166, quoting Lady Cowper's diary.

40. Hayton, "Moral Reform and Country Politics," 69. For a convenient summary of the immoral charges against Cowper see Edward Foss, *The Judges of England*, 9 vols. (London, 1848–64), 8:26–27. In the 1690s Cowper did have a mistress, one Elizabeth Culling, who bore him two illegitimate children whom he and his second wife acknowledged. See Hertfordshire RO, D/EP F84–86 (Culling papers). I owe this information to David Lemmings. It is an open question how far duplicity (the deception of his first wife concerning his mistress) in his private life spilled over into his public one.

41. *Private Diary of Cowper*, 2.

42. W. A. Speck, "Whigs and Tories Dim Their Glories: English Political Parties

Under the First Two Georges," in John Cannon, ed., *The Whig Ascendancy: Colloquies on Hanoverian England* (London, 1981), 51–70.

43. See, e.g., Geoffrey Holmes, "Colloquy [on Speck]," ibid., 71–75; Hayton, "'Country' Interest and the Party System," 37–85; J. C. D. Clark, *Revolution and Rebellion: State and Society in England in the Seventeenth and Eighteenth Centuries* (Cambridge, 1986), 142–44.

44. The term "the Country party" was again in circulation in the early 1720s, see, e.g., HMC, *Portland MSS* 5:556, newsletter, [6 Dec. 1721], misdated 19 Feb. 1718.

45. The eighteenth-century usage of the term "party" was much looser than today, and thus it is sometimes difficult to draw the line between a "group" and a "party." However, I think that the new opposition, despite their impressive organizational abilities, were not a "party" in the sense that the Whigs or Tories were. Nevertheless contemporaries sometimes called them a party.

46. RA, Stuart Papers 57/163, also printed in *House of Lords Sessional Papers*, ed. F. W. Torrington, 61 vols. (Dobbs Ferry, NY, 1972–78), vol. 1718–19 to 1724–25: 155; for the identification of the author as Atterbury see Bennett, *Tory Crisis*, 239–40.

47. For example Orrery was excluded from the group of five (Atterbury, Strafford, North and Grey, Arran, and Sir Henry Goring) who were the chief plotters in 1722. I owe this information to David Hayton.

48. See *Diary of Mary Countess Cowper, 1714–1720*, [ed. C. C. S. Cowper], (London, 1864), 165.

49. He failed to sign 11 out of the 64 protests entered by the new opposition, and he was present in the Lords on 10 of the 11 occasions.

50. HMC, *Portland MSS* 5:556.

51. Based on figures in J. C. Sainty and D. Dewar, comps., *Divisions in the House of Lords: An Analytical List, 1685–1857*, HLRO, Occasional Publication no. 2 (London, 1976).

52. Report of Destouches from AECA, 338, fols. 233–35, translated and quoted in Realey, *Early Opposition*, 82 (16 Dec. 1721). The information on Cowper's views was given to Destouches by Carteret.

53. AECA, 340, fols. 184–85 (9 March 1722) in ibid., 85.

54. Hertfordshire RO, D/EP F53, fol. 18, Bathurst to [Cowper], [20 June 1721].

55. Ibid., F55, fol. 75 (Wharton), fol. 77 (Bathurst); F59, fol. 57 (Lady Cowper).

56. This analysis is based on a tabulation of protests from the *LJ* from 1685 to 1800 kindly provided by Dr. G. M. Ditchfield of the Univ. of Kent at Canterbury.

57. J. E. Thorold Rogers, ed., *A Complete Collection of the Protests of the Lords*, 3 vols. (Oxford, 1875), 1:209–12. The following protest (7 June 1712) on the peace terms was also published and later expunged from the Journals. It had also been signed by Cowper (ibid., 213–17).

58. See W. C. Lowe, "The House of Lords, Party and Public Opinion: Opposition Use of the Protest, 1760–82," *Albion* 11 (1979): 143–56. Lowe is incorrect, however, in claiming that the early years of George III's reign saw the instigation of mass protesting as part of a propaganda campaign.

59. A complete collection of newsletters covering 1721–23, sent to Lord Perceval,

can be found in BL, Add. MSS 27980, 47076–77. For a detailed discussion see Clyve Jones, "Opposition in the House of Lords, Public Opinion, Newspapers and Periodicals, 1720–23: Lord Cowper's Campaign of Protests," *Journal of Newspaper and Periodical History* 8, no. 1 (1992): 51–55.

60. See Clyve Jones, "The House of Lords and the Growth of Parliamentary Stability, 1701–1742," in Clyve Jones, ed., *Britain in the First Age of Party, 1680–1750: Essays Presented to Geoffrey Holmes* (London, 1987), 96–101.

61. PRO, SP 35/40/423, a list of "Lords to be sent to before the Session [early Oct. 1721]" in Atterbury's hand (printed in Jones, "New Opposition in the House of Lords," 328–29). See also BL, Stowe MS. 750, fols. 386, 388, Abingdon to [Orrery], 11 Nov. 1721, Wharton to Abingdon, 11 Nov. 1721. The Tories had previously organized attendance at Parliament while in opposition, though not on such a scale as in 1721, see, e.g., Bod.L, MS. Add. A. 269, pp. 47–48, Gibson to Nicolson, 29 Nov. 1715. I owe this last reference to Stephen Taylor.

62. AECA, 338, fols. 333–35 (16 Dec. 1721), in Realey, *Early Opposition*, 86; HMC, *Portland MSS* 5:555, newsletter [6 Dec. 1721].

63. See HMC, *Lords MSS*, new ser. 10:11.

64. *LJ* 21:700, 704, 709.

65. Cobbett 7:969; J. D. Alsop, "Manuscript Evidence on the Quakers Bill of 1722," *Journal of the Friends' Historical Society* 54, no. 3 (1980): 255–57.

66. The Election Bill protest of 13 Feb. 1722 had been expunged on 19 Feb., and had also produced a further protest on that day.

67. Only ten protests had been expunged, or partially expunged, before 1722 (Rogers, *Complete Collection of Protests* 1:110–11, 150–51, 156–58, 161–62, 172–73, 204–5, 209–17).

68. Cobbett 7:969, 13 Feb. 1722.

69. See Jones, "Jacobitism and the Historian," 688–92.

70. There was sufficient evidence to convict only Layer by the normal legal process. Plunkett, Kelly, and Atterbury were disposed of by parliamentary bills of pains and penalties where the ministry had only to persuade enough of its supporters to vote in favor to secure a conviction. It was said that Cowper's strong condemnation of this method led to its never being used again. Cowper's attitude in 1723 contrasts with his support of the attainder of Sir John Fenwick in 1696 (see Lemmings, *Gentlemen and Barristers*, 209 n. 82). If at first sight this seems hypocritical, 27 years had elapsed and Cowper may simply have changed his mind as to the justice of such parliamentary proceedings. Also the evidence against Atterbury may have been weaker than that against Fenwick.

71. Jeremy Black, "Giving Life to the Honest Part of the City: The Opposition Woo the City in 1721," *Historical Research* 60 (1987): 116–17.

72. See above n. 61. For an analysis of the membership of the opposition see Jones, "New Opposition in the House of Lords," 314–17.

73. HMC, *Carlisle MSS*, 37, Vanbrugh to Carlisle, 16 Nov. 1721.

74. RA, Stuart Papers 56/78, [Robert Freebairne] to [John Hay], 20 Dec. 1721:

Wharton has left his party in a manner worthy of Himself besides promises he has they say reward 8000 lib. ready money and has settled on him a pension of 3000 per an. On his first appearance in the Court of Requests Lord Bathurst took an opportunity to repeat the two following lines when there was a great crowd about Him complimenting Him on a fine Suit of Velvet he had putt on that day

> Villains change partys to betray the State
> To Shine in Velvet and to eat on plate.

But he took it as calmly as he did a box on the ear next day from my Lord Scarsdale.

75. See above, n. 9.

76. Hertfordshire RO, D/EP F53, fol. 18, Bathurst to [Cowper], [20 June 1721].

77. See above n. 2.

78. In chronological order they are Hertfordshire RO D/EP F182, fols. 26–27, 71–72, 91–92, 93, 89–90; F185, fol. 9; F182, fols. 73–74, 75–76, 65, 113; F186, fols. 15–16; F182, fols. 120–21, 109–10, 122–23; F186, fol. 27.

79. This evidence was given to the privy council committee investigating the Jacobite plot by Philip Neynoe, who claimed to have been told it by another plotter, Kelly: *House of Commons Sessional Papers of the Eighteenth Century*, ed. Sheila Lambert, 147 vols. (Wilmington, DE, 1975), 3:284. For the unreliability of much Jacobite evidence on Cowper and the opposition see Jones, "Jacobitism and the Historian."

80. CUL, Cholmondeley (Houghton) MSS, correspondence 1292, [Semple] to H. Walpole, 27–30 Mar. 1726.

81. This is almost certainly the protest that was entered into the Journals on 6 Dec. 1721 concerning the petition of the City of London over the Quarantine Act (though a second protest on the Quarantine Act was entered on 13 Dec.). Drafts of neither of these protests are to be found in Cowper's papers (see above, n. 78, though a printed version of the second of these two protests is at Hertfordshire RO, D/EP F182, fols. 38–39), so it is possible that Atterbury was the author of this one.

82. BL, Add. MS. 34713, fol. 56 (Lord Chancellor Macclesfield's notes on Atterbury's trial).

83. It should be remembered, however, that because of the Jacobite plot few papers survive for this period for Tory politicians. However, Cowper's own papers were supposed also to have been "weeded" by Lady Cowper.

84. BL, Stowe MS. 251, fol. 14, copy of Walpole to Townshend, 23 July 1723. The three Tories had approached Walpole through Bolingbroke.

85. Ibid.; for Lechmere's approach to Newcastle see ibid., fols. 5–7, Townshend to Walpole, 28 July 1723 N.S.; and for Newcastle's hope still to regain Lechmere several months later after Cowper's death, see BL, Add. MS. 32686, fol. 353, Newcastle to Townshend, 18 Oct. 1723. I owe this last reference to Stephen Taylor.

86. RA, Stuart Papers, 70/46, [Orrery] to [the Pretender], 26 Nov., 31 Dec. 1723.

87. Ibid., 74/58, [Orrery] to [the Pretender], 10 May 1724; 82/18, [same] to [same], 7 May 1725.

88. For an example of such a protest in a newsletter see BL, Add. MS. 27980,

fol. 305. 1725 saw 16 protests and at the end of the session two versions (one of 18 pages and one of 24 pages) of a pamphlet collection of the protests appeared, each containing 6 of the protests.

89. RA, Stuart Papers 125/115, [Hamilton] to [Edgar], 5 Mar. 1729.

90. Lowe, "Opposition Use of the Protest."

Chapter 3

I wish to thank the English Speaking Union and the National Endowment for the Humanities for grants that enabled me to do the research in England, Dr. Grayson Ditchfield for his helpful comments on an earlier draft and the earl of Denbigh for permission to quote from the Denbigh Papers.

1. *The Memoirs and Speeches of James, 2nd Earl Waldegrave, 1742–1763*, ed. Jonathan C. D. Clark (Cambridge, 1988), 6–19.

2. Eveline Cruickshanks, *Political Untouchables: The Tories and the '45* (New York, 1979), 115.

3. Horace Walpole, *Memoirs of the Reign of King George the Third*, ed. G. F. Russell Barker (London and New York, 1894), 1:35; Cobbett 21:223; *The Last Journals of Horace Walpole during the Reign of George III from 1771 to 1783*, ed. A. Francis Steuart (London and New York, 1910), 1:175; *The Yale Edition of Horace Walpole's Correspondence*, ed. Wilmarth Sheldon Lewis et al., 48 vols. (New Haven, 1937–83), 33:411–12.

4. HMC, *Denbigh MSS*, 289–91, 294–95.

5. Keith Grahame Feiling, *The Second Tory Party, 1714–1832* (London, 1938), 85; Marian Balderston and David Syrett, eds., *The Lost War: Letters from British Officers during the American Revolution* (New York, 1975), 2–3; Betty Kemp, *Sir Francis Dashwood: An Eighteenth-Century Independent* (New York, 1976), 53; *The Diary and Letters of His Excellency Thomas Hutchinson, Esq.*, ed. Paul Orlando Hutchinson (New York, 1884–86, repr. New York, 1971), 1:367.

6. *Gentleman's Magazine* 70, pt. 2 (1800): 181; *Walpole's Correspondence* 9:189; 33:411–12 n. 14; WCRO, Denbigh Letterbooks, C2017 C243, fol. 249; *The Noels and the Milbankes: Their Letters for Twenty-five Years, 1767–1792*, ed. Malcolm Elwin (London, 1967), 144, 146, 148; Paul Langford, *Public Life and Propertied Englishmen, 1689–1798* (Oxford, 1991), 307, 560.

7. WCRO, Denbigh Letterbooks, C2017, C244, fol. 454; C2017 C243, fol. 45.

8. BL, Add. MS. 32899, fols. 194, 202; *The Lost War*, 5. Denbigh paid £6,300 to secure his son command of Lord Sheffield's corps six weeks before it was disbanded. WCRO, Denbigh Letterbooks, C2017 C244, fols. 288, 419. The Harriers brought Denbigh £2,300 in 1781, £1,725 in 1780.

9. BL, Add. MS. 32900, fols. 252, 300–1; PRO, A.O., 1/1936/82. Walpole claimed that Temple secured the Harriers for Denbigh, but Temple's undated letter in the earl's printed correspondence suggests that Denbigh owed the post to Bute. *Walpole's Correspondence* 9:334; HMC, *Denbigh MSS*, 291; WCRO, Denbigh Letterbooks, C2017 C243, fol. 16.

10. Ibid., C2017 C243, fols. 15, 45; C2017 C244, fols. 316–17; *Additional Grenville*

Papers, 1763–1765, ed. John R. G. Tomlinson (Manchester, 1962), 195; HMC, *Denbigh MSS*, 293–94.

11. PRO, 30/8/229, fol. 74. *Noels and Milbankes*, 91, 144, 186. Wentworth had to wait seven years before becoming a lord of the bedchamber.

12. Ibid., 208–9; BL, Althorp MSS, F104, Jersey to Lady Spencer, 16 Mar. 1773; J. Wake, *The Brudenells of Deene* (London, 1953), 288, 343.

13. BL, Add. MS. 48403, Uxbridge to A. Paget, 20 Mar. 1804 (provisional classification); *The Farington Diary*, ed. J. Greig (New York, 1923), 1:41.

14. *Noels and Milbankes*, 169–70, 122, 251.

15. *Letters from George III to Lord Bute, 1756–1766*, ed. Romney Sedgwick (London, 1938; repr. Westport, CT, 1981), 199; *The Correspondence of King George Third from 1760 to December, 1783*, ed. Sir John Fortescue (London, 1927–28), 282–83; WCRO, Denbigh Letterbooks, C2017 C244, fols. 463, 294–95.

16. *The Grenville Papers: Being the Correspondence of Richard Grenville, Earl Temple, K.G., and the Right Honourable George Grenville, Their Friends and Contemporaries*, ed. William James Smith (London, 1852–53), 1:316–17; HMC, *Denbigh MSS*, 287; John R. Western, *The English Militia in the Eighteenth Century* (London, 1965), 199.

17. Norma Landau, *The Justices of the Peace, 1679–1760* (Berkeley and Los Angeles, 1984), 322; WCRO, Denbigh Letterbooks, C2017 C243, fols. 226, 245; C2017 C244, fol. 13.

18. BL, Add. MS. 38457, fol. 294; *Additional Grenville Papers*, 209, 213; HMC, *Denbigh MSS*, 294; *The Lost War*, 4–5, 7–8.

19. James Thompson, *The History of Leicester in the Eighteenth Century* (Leicester and London, 1871), 123, 132, 137, 142, 145, 155, 181; WCRO, Denbigh Letterbooks, C2017 C243, fol. 191.

20. David Large, "The Decline of 'the Party of the Crown' and the Rise of Parties in the House of Lords, 1783–1837," *EHR* 68 (1963): 672–74; William Curtis Lowe, "Politics in the House of Lords, 1760–1775" (Ph.D. diss. Emory University, 1975), 225–27.

21. 5th Lord Berkeley of Stratton, 1st Lord Boston, 2d Viscount Falmouth, 4th earl of Lichfield, 4th earl of Oxford, 14th Lord Willoughby de Broke.

22. WCRO, Denbigh Letterbooks, C2017 C243, fols. 350, 87–88, 37, 262, 269; C2017 C244, fols. 492–93; William Clements Library, Sydney Papers, Box 12, Denbigh to Sydney, 10 Jan. 1785.

23. Paul Langford argues that many peers took up in the House of Lords the legislative interests of those who lived in the vicinity of their own estates. See "Property and 'Virtual Representation' in eighteenth-century England," *HJ* 31 (1988): 83–106; *Propertied Englishmen*, 197–206. His work substantially expands on my own earlier study of peers' support of legislative projects of industrial pioneers; however, we agree that such activities enlarged the competence of the unreformed parliament. See "Peers, Patronage and the Industrial Revolution," *JBS* 16 (1976): 84–107.

24. WCRO, Denbigh Letterbooks, C2017 C243, fols. 97, 108–9, 367, 201.

25. Sir John Sainty, "The Origin of the Office of Chairman of Committees in the

House of Lords," HLRO, Memorandum no. 52 (London, 1974): 5–6; WCRO, Denbigh Letterbooks, C2017 C243, fols. 245, 316–17, 327, 392.

26. BL, Add. MS. 32936, fol. 234 (copy).

27. Sir John Sainty and D. Dewar, *Divisions in the House of Lords: An Analytical List, 1685–1857*, HLRO, occasional publications, no. 2 (London, 1976): 13; BL, Althorp MSS, F106, Jersey to Lady Spencer, 14 Nov. 1776.

28. Ibid., Add. MS. 33090, fols. 21–22; WCRO, Denbigh Letterbooks, C2017 C243, fol. 469; C2017 C244, fols. 35, 129, 192, 196–97, 206.

29. Following Wentworth's death Denbigh urged the appointment of Lord Bruce, another bedchamber peer, rather than Lord Sandys whom he dismissed as "stupid as a block." Ibid., C2017 C243, fols. 245, 420.

30. Ibid., C2017 C243, fol. 196, 473; C2017 C244, fol. 287; PRO, 30/8/61, fol. 183.

31. Rochford served as ambassador to Spain (1763–66) and France (1766–68). He became secretary of state for the Northern Department on 21 Oct. 1768, and took over the leadership of the Lords in Dec. 1770.

32. WCRO, Denbigh Letterbooks, C2017 C243, 318–21, 324, 392, 402–3, 470–71; HMC, *Denbigh MSS*, 298.

33. *The Correspondence of John, Fourth Duke of Bedford*, ed. Lord John Russell (London, 1842–46), 3:222. Lord Villiers confirmed Rigby's assessment, reporting that Denbigh spoke "with great Spirit & certainly some Wit, like himself." BL, Althorp MSS, F 82, Villiers to Lady Spencer, 30 Mar. 1763; ibid., Add. MS. 36797, fols. 42–43.

34. WCRO, Denbigh Letterbooks, C2017 C243, fols. 334, 265; *Walpole's Correspondence* 9:334.

35. WCRO, Denbigh Letterbooks, C2017 C243, fol. 409.

36. Cobbett 16:1310–11; John Almon, *The Parliamentary Register; or History of the Proceedings and Debates of the House of Commons [and Lords] during the Fourteenth Parliament of Great Britain* (London, 1775–80), 10:100.

37. Walpole, *Memoirs of George III* 2:153; 3:47; Cobbett, 22:656–57.

38. WCRO, Denbigh Letterbooks, C2017 C243, fol. 28; Cobbett 21:223; 18:1078–81. For other confrontations between the two, see Almon, *Parl. Reg.* 14:323–24; 21:223–24.

39. Arthur Stanley Turberville, *The House of Lords in the XVIIIth Century* (Oxford, 1927), 302; H. Walpole, *Memoirs of the Reign of George II*, ed. Lord Holland (London, 1846), 3:106.

40. Cobbett 18:408–9; Almon, *Parl. Reg.* 2:169–71; John Debrett, *The Parliamentary Register: or the History of the Proceedings and Debates of the House of Commons [and Lords], 1780–96* (London, 1781–96), 4:227.

41. WCRO, Denbigh Letterbooks, C2017 C243, fols. 35–36; C2017 C244, fols. 285, 308.

42. Ibid., C2017 C243, fols. 33, 58–59, 184–85.

43. Ibid., C2017 C243, fols. 141–42, 217, 237; BL, Add. MS. 35609, fols. 165–66.

44. Cobbett 16:978; WCRO, Denbigh Letterbooks, C2017 C243, fols. 395, 426; Lord Fitzmaurice, *Life of William Earl of Shelburne* (London, 1912), 2:212.

45. Cobbett 18 : 813–14.

46. *The Lost War*, 158–59; WCRO, Denbigh Letterbooks, C2017 C243, fols. 174, 156.

47. Cobbett, 18 : 268; WCRO, Denbigh Letterbooks, C2017 C243, fol. 435.

48. Ibid., C2017 C244, fols. 127, 131, 211, 174.

49. Ibid., C2017 C244, fols. 313–14, 336, 460, 417, 456.

50. *The Later Correspondence of George III, 1783–1810*, ed. Arthur Aspinall (Cambridge, 1963–69), 3 : 228; WCRO, Denbigh Letterbooks, C2017 C244, fols. 323, 585, 587.

51. Ibid., C2017 C243, fols. 35–36, 245; John Brewer, *Party Ideology and Popular Politics at the Accession of George III* (Cambridge, 1981), 58.

52. Western, *The English Militia*, 168, 191; *Correspondence of George III* 2 : 514.

53. *Grenville Papers* 4 : 224; WCRO, Denbigh Letterbooks, C2017 C243, fols. 263, 269, 308–9; C2017 C244, fols. 127, 278.

54. HMC, *Denbigh MSS*, 286–87, 289, 291; BL, Add. MS. 38203, fols. 20–21.

55. Ibid., Add. MS. 38202, fol. 358; HMC, *Denbigh MSS*, 295–96; WCRO, Denbigh Letterbooks, C2017 C243, fol. 207; C2017 C244, fol. 323.

56. Paul Langford, *The First Rockingham Administration, 1765–66* (London, 1973), 53–54; *Grenville Papers* 3 : 115; *Walpole's Correspondence* 38 : 528–29.

57. Walpole, *Memoirs of George III* 2 : 153; M. Bateson, ed., "A Narrative of the Changes in the Ministry, 1765–67," *Camden Miscellany*, n.s., 59 (London, 1898): 50; Frank O'Gorman, *The Rise of Party in England: the Rockingham Whigs, 1760–1782* (London, 1975), 165–66; *Grenville Papers* 3 : 368.

58. WCRO, Denbigh Letterbooks, C2017 C243, fols. 217, 237, 396; C2017 C244, fol. 308.

59. Ibid., C2017 C244, fols. 386, 398, 410–11; BL, Add. MS. 59362, fols. 124, 143, 145.

60. M. McCahill, "The House of Lords in the 1760s," in Clyve Jones, ed., *A Pillar of the Constitution: The House of Lords in British Politics, 1640–1784* (London, 1989), 189–90; Grayson Ditchfield, "The House of Lords in the Age of the American Revolution," ibid., 211.

61. *Letters from George III to Lord Bute*, 198; WCRO, Denbigh Letterbooks, C2017 C243, fols. 332–33.

62. *Hutchinson's Diary* 1 : 187; WCRO, Denbigh Letterbooks, C2017 C244, fol. 235.

63. *The Journal of Elizabeth, Lady Holland (1791–1801)*, ed. earl of Ilchester (London, 1908), 2 : 108; Stephen Taylor, "The Bishops at Westminster in the Mid-Eighteenth Century," in *Pillar of the Constitution*, 149.

64. Kemp, *Francis Dashwood*, 1–4. Prof. John B. Owen described this as a "Country" rather than an Independent outlook. "The Survival of Country Attitudes in the Eighteenth-Century House of Commons," in John S. Bromley and E. H. Kossman, eds., *Britain and the Netherlands: IV, Metropolis, Dominion and Province* (The Hague, 1971), 42–43, 45–46.

65. WCRO, Denbigh Letterbooks, C2017 C244, fols. 197, 285.

66. Cf. Grayson Ditchfield who argues not only that offices were granted to

reward pre-existing loyalty and did not invariably bind their occupants, but that there were ideological factors—adherence to the Crown and opposition to the Americans' rebelliousness—which bound ministerial supporters together. "The House of Lords in the Age of the American Revolution," *Pillar of the Constitution,* 211, 217; see also Taylor, "The Bishops at Westminster," ibid., 147.

67. Almon, *Parl. Reg.* 15:216–17; ibid. 4:69–70.

68. *Noels and Milbankes,* 184, 194; Bod.L, Lovelace Byron Dep., 1, fols. 110–11; 2, fols. 3–4; WCRO, Denbigh Letterbooks, C2017 C244, fols. 405–6.

69. See, for example, Frank O'Gorman, "The Myth of Lord Bute's Secret Influence" in Karl Schweizer, ed., *Lord Bute: Essays in Re-interpretation* (Leicester, 1988), 57–81.

70. BL, Add. MS. 51379, fols. 204–5.

71. For the court and Catholic emancipation, see R. E. Willis, "William Pitt's Resignation in 1801: Re-examination and Document," *BIHR* 44 (1971): 239–57.

72. Sir John Sainty, "Leaders and Whips in the House of Lords, 1783–1964," HLRO Memorandum, no. 31 (London, 1964): 15.

73. WCRO, Denbigh Papers, C2017 C269, fols. 4–5. Paul Langford claims that, towards the end of the eighteenth century, more peers took an active part in public affairs as a result of a religious revival among at least a portion of the group. In particular, he claims the court peers saw a need to continue to have religious leadership in a period of upheaval. *Propertied Englishmen,* 560–80.

Chapter 4

I wish to thank the earl of Denbigh and Warwickshire Record Office for permission to consult the papers of the sixth earl of Denbigh; Olive, Countess Fitzwilliam's Wentworth Settlement Trustees and the Director, Sheffield City Libraries, for permission to consult the Wentworth Woodhouse Muniments; the Centre for Kentish Studies for permission to consult the North MSS and Stebbing MSS at County Hall, Maidstone; and the Bodleian Library, Oxford, for permission to consult the Wilberforce MSS. I am grateful to Dr. Jeremy Black and Dr. Paul Langford for their valuable comments on a draft of this paper and to Dr. Michael McCahill for providing me with many helpful references. I should like to express my thanks to my colleague Dr. David Shaw who has been immensely helpful in preparing this essay for publication.

1. *Autobiography and Political Correspondence of Augustus Henry, Third Duke of Grafton,* ed. Sir William Anson (London, 1898), 229 and n.

2. John, Lord Campbell, *Lives of the Lord Chancellors,* 8 vols. (London, 1845–69), 5:473–678. Even Campbell (p. 633) conceded that Thurlow was "entirely free from personal corruption."

3. T. B. Macaulay, *Critical and Historical Essays,* Everyman ed., 2 vols. (London, 1907), 1:641.

4. For Burke's description, made at the height of the Regency Crisis, see Cobbett 27:822, 1117.

5. C. Ryskamp, *William Cowper of the Inner Temple, Esq.* (Cambridge, 1959), 79–83, 119–20; James Boswell, *The Life of Samuel Johnson, LL.D*, ed. George Birkbeck Hill, rev. by L. F. Powell, 6 vols. (Oxford 1934–50), 4:336, 348–49; *The Letters of Edward Gibbon*, ed. J. E. Norton, 3 vols. (London, 1956), 3:200.

6. See *Sunday Telegraph*, 7 Apr. 1991, for the furore over the proposed sale of 86 items of Thurlow papers to a purchaser in the United States.

7. R. Gore-Browne, *Chancellor Thurlow: The Life and Times of an XVIIIth Century Lawyer* (London, 1953). This work deploys a good deal of primary material but—infuriatingly—does not give references to it.

8. HMC, *Abergavenny MSS*, 36; PRO, 30/8/183, fol. 184 (Chatham Papers).

9. BL, Egerton MS. 3498, fols. 243–44. Worontzov was in the process of bearding as many cabinet ministers as he could find to complain about George III's role as elector of Hanover, in the *Fürstenbund*.

10. KAO, Stebbing Bequest (Hibgame Papers), U924 C3/3.

11. Paul Langford, *Public Life and the Propertied Englishman, 1689–1798* (Oxford, 1991), 541, 546–47.

12. Cf. Richard Savage, *The Bastard*:

He lives to build, not boast, a gen'rous race;
No tenth transmitter of a foolish face.

The usual source for Thurlow's famous remark is Charles Butler, *Reminiscences*, 4th ed., 2 vols. (London, 1828), 1:188, but there is also a manuscript account in BL, Egerton MS. 2232, fol. 14. Almon, *Parliamentary Register* 14:188 (24 Mar 1779) gives Grafton's attack but quotes Thurlow's reply only as "The Lord Chancellor said, such a language would not be permitted over a table among gentlemen."

13. John Debrett, *Parliamentary Register* 54:532–33. Bishop Horsley, whose preferment owed much to Thurlow, delivered a similar rebuke to Lansdowne, in a Lords' debate on the impeachment of Warren Hastings in March 1795. To Lansdowne's sneer at Cheyt Singh's alleged lack of an honorable lineage, Horsley retorted that it was of no consequence whether or not Cheyt Singh could boast a long line of ancestry. "Be he of ever so obscure origin, he was entitled to justice as an individual, much as any other man"; F. C. Mather, *High Church Prophet: Bishop Samuel Horsley (1733–1806) and the Caroline Tradition in the Later Georgian Church* (Oxford, 1992), 247. As the author observes, "Doubtless he [Horsley] recalled that he was not himself a nobleman bishop."

14. As solicitor-general, 1770–71 and attorney-general, 1771–78.

15. For Thurlow's opinion on the Gaspée incident, see HMC, 14th Report, appendix, pt. 10, *Dartmouth MSS*, 91.

16. HMC, *Fortescue MSS* 1:504.

17. See especially Thurlow's speeches of 2 Feb. and 20 Nov. 1775; Cobbett 18:225–26, 998–99.

18. See P. D. G. Thomas, *Tea Party to Independence: The Third Phase of the American Revolution, 1773–1776* (Oxford, 1991), 333: "On the point of parliamentary sovereignty over America, British politicians were at one."

19. For a report that North's father, the first earl of Guilford, "has prayers read every morning at Waldershare by a clergyman," see *A Kentish Parson: Selections from the Private Papers of the Revd. Joseph Price, Vicar of Brabourne, 1767–1786*, ed. G. M. Ditchfield and Bryan Keith-Lucas (Kent County Council, 1991), 153.

20. See J. C. D. Clark, *English Society 1688–1832: Ideology, Social Structure and Political Practice During the Ancien Regime* (Cambridge, 1985), esp. pt. 4.

21. The familiar anecdote about Thurlow's witty but unyielding response to "a body of Presbyterians" is in Campbell, *Lives of the Lord Chancellors* 5 : 662. In 1780 Thurlow did not support the anti-Catholic bill for the security of the protestant religion but urged that Catholics "be not suffered to keep boarding schools, or any such seminary as give them the exclusive government of the children under their direction"; Cobbett 21 : 759–62 (3 July 1780).

22. See N. Havard, *Narrative . . . of the Prosecution against the Rev. Edward Evanson*, 30ff.

23. For examples, see Gore-Browne, *Chancellor Thurlow*, 126ff. and *Correspondence of Charles, First Marquis Cornwallis*, ed. C. Ross, 3 vols. (London, 1859), 1 : 259.

24. Quoted in W. Weber, "The 1784 Handel Commemoration as Political Ritual," *JBS* 28 (1989): 56.

25. Mather, *High Church Prophet*, 63.

26. HMC, 14th report, appendix, pt. 1; *Rutland MSS* 3 : 362.

27. *The Correspondence of George III*, ed. Sir John Fortescue, 6 vols. (London 1927–28), 4:nos. 2272, 2284.

28. Ibid. 4 : 2844; 6 : 3779.

29. HMC, 12th report, *Abergavenny MSS*, 34.

30. BL, Add. MS. 38192, fols. 139–40 (Liverpool Papers). The circular, dated 21 Nov. 1788, is not in Thurlow's handwriting but is signed by him.

31. HLRO, Proxy Books, sessions 1778–79 to 1792. The peers whose proxies he most frequently held were Bridgewater, Oxford and Mortimer, Denbigh and Darlington.

32. National Maritime Museum, Sandwich Papers F43a/20, Portland to Sandwich, 8 Dec. 1783. Thurlow duly cast Wentworth's proxy against the India Bill on 15 and 17 Dec; *Political Magazine* 6 (1783): 404–5.

33. Thurlow did not serve as a chairman of Lords' committees and was only once a teller in a division.

34. Michael W. McCahill, *Order and Equipoise: The Peerage and the House of Lords, 1783–1806* (London, 1978), 113ff.

35. See, for example, *The Historical and Posthumous Memoirs of Sir Nathaniel William Wraxall, 1772–1784*, ed. H. B. Wheatley, 5 vols. (London 1884), 1 : 408–12; *The Diary and Correspondence of Charles Abbot, Lord Colchester*, 3 vols. (London, 1861), 1 : 21.

36. *The Journal and Correspondence of William, Lord Auckland*, 2 vols. (London, 1861), 2 : 414–15.

37. Debrett, *Parliamentary Register*, vol. 42, passim.

38. Campbell, *Lives of Lord Chancellors* 5 : 476.

39. *Letters from the Late Lord Chedworth to the Rev. Thomas Crompton; written in the period from Jan. 1780 to May 1795* (London, 1828), 243.

40. See *The Letter-Journal of George Canning, 1793–1795*, ed. P. Jupp, 4th ser. (Camden Society) 41:279–80.

41. H. Butterfield, *George III, Lord North and the People, 1779–1780* (London, 1949), esp. 126–28, 133, 137ff; *Correspondence of George III* 4:nos. 2797, 2855, 2897.

42. Butterfield, *George III, Lord North and the People*, 126–27.

43. WCRO, CR2017 C244, fol. 271; Denbigh to Sandwich, 7 July 1781.

44. Abergavenny MSS, 29, 32, 35.

45. WCRO, CR2017 C244, fol. 267.

46. WCRO, CR2017 C244, fol. 270 (Denbigh MSS). The Powder Bill was designed to reward an entrepreneur for destroying vermin in the Navy. Thurlow's rather factious objections to it may be found in Cobbett, 22:588. The bill was thwarted by repeated postponements in the House of Lords in 1781.

47. For evidence as to the non-party nature of North's ministry, see William C. Lowe, "Politics in the House of Lords, 1760–1775" (Emory Univ. Ph.D diss., 1975), 936–37; I. R. Christie, "Party in Politics in the Age of Lord North's Administration," *PH* 6 (London, 1987): 47–68; G. M. Ditchfield, "The House of Lords in the Age of the American Revolution," in Clyve Jones, ed., *A Pillar of the Constitution: The House of Lords in British Politics, 1640–1784* (London, 1989), 199–239.

48. Denbigh MSS, CR2017, C244 fol. 210; Wentworth to Lord Denbigh, 8 July 1779; HMC, Carlisle MSS, 538.

49. *The Diary of Joseph Farrington*, eds. K. Garlick and A. MacIntyre, 10 vols. (New Haven and London, 1978–82), 3:712; *Correspondence of Auckland*, 4 vols. (London, 1861–62), 2:378.

50. See *The Political Memoranda of Francis, Fifth Duke of Leeds*, ed. Oscar Browning (Camden Society, n.s., 1884) 34:157–63.

51. BL, Add. MSS 29194, fol. 149 (Hastings Papers); Thurlow to Hastings, n.d.

52. *Correspondence of George III* 4:no. 2855.

53. See John Cannon, *The Fox-North Coalition: Crisis of the Constitution, 1782–84* (Cambridge, 1969), chap. 1. Some of the correspondence between Thurlow and Rockingham is printed, though not without error, in earl of Albemarle, *Memoirs of the Marquis of Rockingham and his Contemporaries* 2 vols. (London, 1852), 2:453ff. It is best to study the correspondence itself in Sheffield City Library, Wentworth Woodhouse Muniments, Rockingham Papers, R1–1989 to R1–1998. It covers the period 12 to 18 Mar. 1782 and crucial to it all is Rockingham's minute of his interviews with Thurlow (R1–1992) which outlines the possible terms on which the Rockingham group might take office.

54. K. A. O. North (Waldershare) MSS U471/C23/3; document (?in the hand of North's father, the first earl of Guilford) headed "What I said to the K. from Ld. N. upon Ld. S'n's [i.e. Shelburne's] going out."

55. Cobbett 23:430–35.

56. Cannon, *Fox-North Coalition*, 126ff; Cobbett 24:125. This was the occasion (9 Dec. 1783) when Thurlow declared that should George III give the royal assent

to the India Bill, he would "take the diadem from his own head, and place it on the head of Mr Fox."

57. See, for instance, Thurlow to Sackville, 29 Dec. 1783, HMC, *Stopford-Sackville MSS* 1:80.

58. Debrett, *Parliamentary Register* 14:135.

59. HMC, 14th report, appendix pt. 1 *Rutland MSS* 3:152.

60. HMC, 14th report, appendix pt. 9, *Buckinghamshire MSS, etc.*, 187.

61. HMC, *Rutland MSS* 3:231.

62. BL, Add. MS. 38307, fol. 162; Add. MS. 38308, fols. 76, 157, 159.

63. HMC, *Rutland MSS* 3:298.

64. Lieut.-Gen. James Grant to Lord Cornwallis, 16 Apr. 1787; *Correspondence of Charles, First Marquis Cornwallis*, ed. C. Ross, 3 vols. (London, 1859), 1:287.

65. BL, Add. MS. 39882, fols. 64, 97, 104, 123.

66. *Auckland Correspondence*, 2:217–8.

67. See, for example, *Political Memoranda of the Duke of Leeds*, 124, 130–31, 133, 139; *Life and Letters of Sir Gilbert Elliot, First Earl of Minto, from 1751 to 1806*, 3 vols. (London, 1854), 1:249–50, 275–76.

68. *The Correspondence of George, Prince of Wales, 1770–1812*, ed., A. Aspinall, 8 vols. (London 1963–68), 1:418–19.

69. Gore-Browne, *Chancellor Thurlow*, 336ff., 351.

70. Campbell, *Lives of Lord Chancellors* 5:584ff.

71. *Letters from Lord Chedworth*, 115–16.

72. *Life and Letters of Elliot* 1:250; Campbell, *Lives of Lord Chancellors* 5:585.

73. Bod.L, MSS Wilberforce d. 56, fol. 11. See also R. I. and S. Wilberforce, *The Life of William Wilberforce*, 5 vols. (London 1838), 1:385–87. For a rather unconvincing defense of Thurlow's conduct during the Regency Crisis, based on the claim that he met Fox only in order to be able the more effectively to brief Pitt, see G. T. Kenyon, *The Life of Lloyd, First Lord Kenyon, Lord Chief Justice of England* (London, 1873), 180ff.

74. WCRO, CR2017 C244, fol. 396, Denbigh to archbishop of York, 15 Nov. 1790. Denbigh's loyalty to Thurlow is demonstrated in Michael McCahill's essay in the present volume; I am grateful to Dr. McCahill for permission to consult his essay before publication.

75. *The Later Correspondence of George III*, ed., A. Aspinall, 5 vols. (London, 1966–70), 1:501–2.

76. See, for instance, HMC, *Fortescue MSS* 1:611, 2:89, and BL, Add. MSS 58938, fol. 102.

77. HMC, *Fortescue MSS* 1:572, 2:198–203, 234–35; Gore-Browne, *Chancellor Thurlow*, 293ff.

78. BL, Add. MSS 58938 (Dropmore Papers), the volume which contains Grenville's correspondence with Thurlow, includes no items from 1792.

79. Jeremy Black, *British Foreign Policy in an Age of Revolutions, 1783–1793* (Cambridge, forthcoming, 1994). I am grateful to Dr Black for allowing me to consult this work in draft.

80. Cobbett 26:585–87.

81. This is the interpretation of Gore-Browne, *Chancellor Thurlow*, 241–42.

82. See John Ehrman, *The Younger Pitt: The Years of Acclaim* (London, 1969), 526–27 and I. R. Christie, "The Cabinet in the Reign of George III, to 1790" in Christie, *Myth and Reality in the Late Eighteenth Century British Politics* (London, 1970), 103–4.

83. Black, *British Foreign Policy, 1783–1793*.

84. PRO, 30/8/183 fols. 174–75 (Chatham Papers), Thurlow to Pitt, Sept. 1787. The day of the month is missing from this letter.

85. *Political Memoranda of the Duke of Leeds*, 118–19.

86. Cobbett 29:45–46, 82–83, 95–96.

87. *Political Memoranda of the Duke of Leeds*, 157ff.

88. See Earl Stanhope, *Life of the Right Honourable William Pitt*, 2d ed., 4 vols. (London, 1862), 2:149.

89. Gore-Browne, *Chancellor Thurlow*, 294.

90. See, for instance, *Caledonian Mercury*, 26 May 1792, for a comment on divisions within the "party of the Crown" caused by Thurlow's criticisms of the ministry of which he was still a senior member.

91. See, for instance, J. Holland Rose, *William Pitt and the Great War* (London, 1911), 34.

92. *Later Correspondence of George III* 1:595.

93. See *Auckland Correspondence* 2:406–7, James Bland Burges to Auckland, 18 May 1792.

94. *Correspondence of Cornwallis* 2:183–84, Charles Grant to Lord Cornwallis.

95. *The Oracle*, 30 May 1792; A Aspinall, *Politics and the Press, 1780–1850* (London, 1949), 74. For other rumors of Thurlow's survival see *Auckland Correspondence* 2:407 and Denbigh MSS CR2017, C244, fol. 408.

96. For example in the *Maidstone Journal*, 28 Feb. 1792.

97. *Political Memoranda of the Duke of Leeds*, 179.

98. *Auckland Correspondence* 2:415–17.

99. Northamptonshire RO, Fitzwilliam Correspondence, Drawer 44, Carlisle to Fitzwilliam, 19 Oct. 1792. I am grateful to the trustees of the estate of the late Earl Fitzwilliam for permission to consult this correspondence.

100. HMC, 14th report, appendix pt. 4, *Kenyon MSS*, 540.

101. On 7 May 1793 he voted against the Commercial Credit Bill; on 9 and 14 Dec. 1795 he voted against the second and third readings of the Seditious Meetings Bill; on 27 June 1798 he voted for Bessborough's Irish resolutions; *Evening Mail*, 8–10 May 1793; Debrett, *Parliamentary Register* 45:164, 206; 51:487. Of course Thurlow also opposed abolition of the slave trade, but on that issue the division was not one between government and opposition.

102. BL, Add. MS. 28067, fols. 67, 69–70.

103. North Yorkshire County RO, Wyvill of Burton Constable MSS, ZFW 7/2/95/27; Lindsey to Wyvill, 7 Dec. 1795.

104. Sir Gurney Benham, *Benham's Book of Quotations, Proverbs and Household Words*, new ed. (London, 1948), 400a.

105. *Diary and Correspondence of Lord Colchester* 1:477–78.

106. *LJ* 39:483.

107. P. J. Marshall, *The Impeachment of Warren Hastings* (Oxford, 1965), esp. 28, 71, 84.

108. Cobbett 22:1387.

109. Robert Stevens, *Law and Politics: the House of Lords as a Judicial Body, 1800–1976* (London, 1979), chap. 1.

Chapter 5

1. Two biographies of Lord Grey have recently appeared, my own *Lord Grey, 1764–1845* (Oxford, 1990) and one by John Derry, *Charles Earl Grey, Aristocratic Reformer* (Oxford, 1992). Both stress the aristocratic nature of Grey's character and principles. G. M. Trevelyan's *Lord Grey of the Reform Bill* (London, 1920) is less critical of Grey but it remains a literary classic.

2. *Letters of Dorothea, Princess Lieven, During Her Residence in London, 1812–34,* ed. L. G. Robinson (London, 1902), 278–79, Grey to Princess Lieven, 10 Nov. 1830.

3. University of Durham, Grey MSS, Grey to Lady Grey, Jan. 1808; Lord Edmond Fitzmaurice, *Life of . . . Second Earl Granville* (London, 1905), 1:239.

4. *The Creevey Papers*, ed. Sir H. Maxwell (London, 1903), 1:287.

5. BL, Add. MS 51545, fols. 30–34, Holland to Grey, 17 Nov. 1815.

6. University of Durham, Grey MSS, Rosslyn to Grey, 25 Dec. 1815.

7. J. Grant, *Random Recollections of the House of Lords from 1830 to 1836*, 2d ed. (London, 1836), 259–81.

8. *The Holland House Diaries, 1831–40*, ed. A. D. Kriegel (London, 1977), 156; *The Private Letters of Princess Lieven to Prince Metternich, 1820–1826*, ed. P. Quennell (London, 1937), 47.

9. *Hansard*, n.s. 3:1573–74.

10. Smith, *Lord Grey*, 232.

11. *Hansard*, n.s. 17:720–33.

12. Smith, *Lord Grey*, 245.

13. *Hansard*, n.s. 21:308–48; Grey MSS, Adair to Grey, 5 Feb. 1829.

14. *Mirror of Parliament* (London, 1831–32), 2:1812–16; *Holland House Diaries*, 169–70.

15. *Hansard* 3d ser. 16:1313–15; J. C. Hobhouse (Lord Broughton), *Recollections of a Long Life*, ed. Lady Dorchester (London, 1909–11), 4:353; *Creevey Papers* 2:282–83.

16. *The Grey Festival: Being a Narrative of the Proceedings Connected with the Dinner given to Earl Grey at Edinburgh, on Monday 15 September 1834* (Edinburgh, 1834).

17. For the House of Lords in this period see E. A. Smith, *The House of Lords in British Politics and Society, 1815–1911* (London, 1992), esp. pt. 2:50–146.

18. A. Goodwin, *The Friends of Liberty* (London, 1979) provides the best general account of the later-eighteenth century parliamentary reform movement in Britain.

19. I. R. Christie, *Wilkes, Wyvill and Reform* (London, 1962), passim.

20. *English Historical Documents* 11 (1783–1832), ed. A. Aspinall and E. A. Smith (London, 1959): 216–39; T. H. B. Oldfield, *Representative History of Great Britain and Ireland* (London, 1816); *A Key to Both Houses of Parliament* (London, 1832).

21. *Parliamentary Debates* 17:560–73.

22. *The Times*, 3 Oct. 1831.

23. E. A. Smith, *Reform or Revolution?* (London, 1992), 90–109.

24. Grey to Althorp, 11 Mar. 1832: Sir D. Le Marchant, *Memoir of John Charles Viscount Althorp, Third Earl Spencer* (London, 1876), 407–13; *The Correspondence of the Late Earl Grey with H. M. King William IV and with Sir Herbert Taylor*, ed. 3d Earl Grey (London, 1867), 2:68–73; *Mirror of Parliament* (London, 1831–32), 2:1812–16.

25. *The Times*, 10 Oct. 1831; O'Connell to R. Barrett, 5 and 8 Oct. 1831: *The Correspondence of Daniel O'Connell*, ed. M. R. O'Connell (Dublin, 1977), 4:354, 356; [J. Wade], *Appendix to the Black Book* (London, 1834).

26. Smith, *House of Lords*, 136–37.

27. N. Gash, *Reaction and Reconstruction in English Politics, 1832–52* (Oxford, 1965), 30–31; *A Political Diary, 1828–30, by Edward Law, Lord Ellenborough*, ed. Lord Silchester (London, 1881), 1:358, 2:6.

28. C. C. F. Greville, *Journal of the Reign of Queen Victoria, 1837–52*, ed. H. Reeve (London, 1885), 1:129.

29. Ibid.

30. D. C. Large, "The Decline of the 'Party of the Crown' and the Rise of Parties in the House of Lords, 1783–1837," *EHR* (1963), 77:669–95.

31. Smith, *House of Lords*, 96–105.

Chapter 6

Some of the research represented in this essay was done in connection with earlier projects on the politics of the 1820s and 1830s. The most recent and most important research was in the Wellington Papers at the University of Southampton Library. I am grateful to the Controller of Her Majesty's Stationery Office for permission to include Crown Copyright material from the Wellington Papers. And I should like to thank Dr. C. M. Woolgar and his staff for some of the kindest and most efficient assistance I have ever received. The Goodwood Papers are used by courtesy of the Trustees of the Goodwood Collections and with acknowledgements to the West Sussex Record Office and the County Archivist. I should also like to thank Professor Corinne Weston for her careful critical reading of the manuscript, and for suggestions that have made the essay a better one.

1. Walter L. Arnstein, *Britain Yesterday and Today: 1830 to the Present*, 6th ed. (Lexington, MA, 1992), 16–17. Contemporaries, including Wellington, thought so as well; see Corinne Comstock Weston, *English Constitutional Theory and the House of Lords, 1556–1832* (New York and London, 1965), 243.

2. Norman Gash, *Aristocracy and People: Britain, 1815–1865* (Cambridge, MA, 1979), 172–73.

3. J. C. D. Clark, *English Society, 1688–1832: Ideology, Social Structure and Political Practice during the Ancien Regime* (Cambridge, 1985), 409–10.

4. University of Southampton, WP 1/930/39, draft Wellington to the duke of Montrose, 29 and 30 Apr. 1828; printed in *WDCM* 4:411–12.

5. University College, London, Brougham Papers 39289, Durham to Brougham, 1 Jan. 1829.

6. BL, Add. MS. 38757, fols. 190–93, Goderich to William Huskisson, 12 Jan. 1829.

7. BL, Add. MS. 40398, fols. 192–95, Peel to the bishop of Limerick, 8 Feb. 1829; *WDCM*, 5: 439, Peel's memorandum to the king, n.d. Jan. 1829. Though the government did not invoke public opinion, as such, in favor of Catholic Emancipation, the Whigs, who had worked hard to bring about demonstrations of such opinion, did. Durham, for example, argued that "the force of public opinion" was a factor that ought to induce Wellington to take the right course; Brougham Papers 39288, Durham to Brougham, 27 Dec. 1828. Everyone would now agree that the most widespread opinion was that expressed in the anti-Catholic meetings organized by the Brunswick Clubs and other Ultra Tories. But neither the government nor the Whigs would dignify such views as "public opinion." Those who attended the meetings, whom Lord Holland dismissed as "Clodpoles and bigots," were not, for the most part, people of sufficient substance and standing to qualify as "the public"; Public Record Office, PRO 30/22/1A/201–02, Holland to Russell, 15 Oct. 1828. On what constituted "public opinion," see R. W. Davis, "The Whigs and the Idea of Electoral Deference," *Durham University Journal* (Dec. 1974), 82–83.

8. In fact, the motion in the House of Commons elected in 1818 failed by two votes, 243 to 241. For the embarrassment caused by the parliamentary course of the Catholic question, see Gash, *Aristocracy and People*, 125–28.

9. WP 1/1197/8, draft Wellington to the marquis of Bath, 22 Sep. 1831, printed in *WDCM*, 6: 531–32. For others, including Peel, who accepted the convention enunciated by Wellington on the relations between the two Houses, see Weston, 254–57.

10. WP 1/1197/5, Wellington to W. J. Bankes, 15 Sep. 1831.

11. *The Correspondence of Charles Arbuthnot*, ed. by A. Aspinall (London, 1941), 149–50.

12. *The Holland House Diaries, 1831–1840*, ed. by A. D. Kriegel (London, 1977), 85.

13. *WPC*, vol. 1, 1833–1834; vol. 2, 1834–35, *Prime Ministers Papers Series* (London, 1975, 1986), 1: 639.

14. Ibid., 121. For the fullest development of Wellington's notions, see WP 2/33/78–79, his draft of a memorandum to Lord Lyndhurst, 8 May 1835.

15. *WPC* 1: 121.

16. WP 2/38/85, Wellington to the earl of Winchilsea, 2 Mar. 1836.

17. George Kitson Clark, *Peel and the Conservative Party: A Study in Party Politics, 1832–1841* (London, 1964), 187.

18. *WPC* 1: 678–79, 693.

19. WP 2/45/50, Wellington to Peel, 23 Mar. 1837.

20. Kriegel, 381.

21. Ibid., 321–22.

22. Arbuthnot, *Correspondence*, 171.

23. Ibid., 277, Graham to Arbuthnot, 24 Mar. 1841.

24. Norman Gash, *Reaction and Reconstruction in English Politics, 1832–1852* (Oxford, 1965), 41. For the Radical attacks on the Lords, see Weston, chap. 4.

25. A. Aspinall, ed., *Three Early Nineteenth Century Diaries* (London, 1952), 334–37, 340.

26. *WPC* 1:652, 664.

27. Kitson Clark, 261–65.

28. WP 2/34/14–17; 63–64.

29. Kitson Clark, 269; West Sussex RO, Goodwood MS. 1590, Stanley to the duke of Richmond, 5 Aug. 1835.

30. Benjamin Disraeli, *Letters*, 2, ltr. 216.

31. BL, Add. MS. 40323, fols. 292–99, Lord Fitzgerald to Peel, (10 Aug. 1835).

32. *WPC* 1:235, Wellington to Lyndhurst, 15 Jun. 1835; and see examples given later in the text.

33. BL, Add. MS. 40323, fols. 278–81, Fitzgerald to Peel, 13 Aug. (1835).

34. Carola Oman, *The Gascoyne Heiress: The Life and Diaries of Frances Mary Gascoyne-Cecil* (London, 1968), 177; WP 2/34/122, Lord Eldon to Wellington, docketed 25 Jul. 1835.

35. Ibid. 35/38, Wellington to the duke of Northumberland, 22 Aug. 1835.

36. Ibid., 59, Wellington to Sir Henry Hardinge, 26 Aug. 1835.

37. BL, Add. MS. 40323, fols. 253–57, Fitzgerald to Peel, (29 Aug. 1835); WP 2/35/79, Wellington to Alderman Heygate, 5 Sep. 1835.

38. Ibid. 43/10, Wellington to Lyndhurst, 15 Oct. 1836.

39. Kitson Clark, 347.

40. WP 2/45/112, Wellington to Peel, 15 Apr. 1837.

41. Disraeli, *Letters*, 3, ltr. 709, Disraeli to Sarah Disraeli, 20 Jan. 1838.

42. WP 2/60/24, Wellington to Peel, 7 Jul. 1839; ibid. 28, same to same, 8 Jul. 1839.

43. Ibid. 63/154–55, Peel to Wellington, 15 Dec. 1839; ibid., 156–58, Wellington to Peel, 18 Dec. 1839; ibid. 64/12–14, same to same, 23 Dec. 1839.

44. Ibid. 69/102, Peel to Wellington, docketed 3 Jul. 1840; ibid., 116, Wellington to Sir James Graham, 4 Jul. 1840.

45. BL, Add. MS. 40312, fols. 322–23, Aberdeen to Peel, 5 Jul. 1840.

46. Arbuthnot, *Correspondence*, 221.

47. Kitson Clark, 458–59.

48. BL, Add. MS. 40312, fol. 23, Aberdeen to Peel, 5 Jul. 1840; WP 2/69/102, Wellington to Graham, 4 Jul. 1840. For an interesting account by Wellington himself of his leadership in the 1830s, see Walter Bagehot, *The English Constitution* (Garden City, NY, n.d.), 146–50. Though the duke's lack of partisanship was genuinely remarkable, he rather overemphasizes it in this account, especially with regard to the Canada Act of 1840.

49. WP 2/69/131, Melbourne to Wellington, 9 Jul. 1840.

50. Ibid. 35/97, the duke of Newcastle to Wellington, 5 Sep. 1835.

51. For an excellent collection of essays on Wellington, see Norman Gash, ed., *Wellington: Studies in the Military and Political Career of the First Duke of Wellington* (Manchester and New York, 1990). Of particular relevance to this essay is Professor F. C. Mather's "Achilles or Nestor? The Duke of Wellington in British Politics, 1832–46," 170–95. Though we do not agree in every respect, Professor Mather's is a wise and stimulating essay.

Chapter 7

1. I. Newbould, *Whiggery and Reform, 1830–41* (London, 1990), 54.
2. P. J. Jupp, "The Landed Elite and Political Authority in Britain, ca. 1760–1850," *JBS* 29 (1990): 74, 78–79.
3. P. Mandler, *Aristocratic Government in the Age of Reform: Whigs and Liberals, 1830–1852* (Oxford, 1990), 35; Newbould, *Whiggery and Reform*, 317.
4. For the duke's life see D. Spring, *The English Landed Estate in the Nineteenth Century* (Baltimore, 1963), 14, 20–26; R. G. Thorne, *The House of Commons 1790–1820* (London, 1986), 5:61–63.
5. G. Blakiston, *Lord William Russell and His Wife 1815–1846* (London, 1972), 82, 97, 106, 189; C. Arbuthnot, *Correspondence*, ed. A. Aspinall (London, 1941), 150–51; *Northampton Mercury*, 12 Nov. 1825.
6. Earl of Ilchester, *Chronicles of Holland House 1820–1900* (London, 1937), 341.
7. University of Durham, Grey MSS, Bedford to Earl Grey, 19 and 21 Jan. 1812.
8. *PD* 20:220–21, 10 Feb. 1829.
9. Blakiston, *Lord William Russell*, 505. G. Blakiston, *Woburn and the Russells* (London, 1980), 179; A. Adonis, "Aristocracy, Agriculture and Liberalism," *HJ* 31 (1988): 79.
10. He was already spoken of as "the chief of the House of Russell" as early as 1817; earl of Dudley, *Letters to the Bishop of Llandaff* (London, 1840), 167.
11. C. Greville, *Memoirs, 1814–1860*, L. Strachey and R. Fulford, eds. (London, 1938), 6:15, 20 Feb. 1848.
12. For the earl's life see D. Spring, "Earl Fitzwilliam and the Corn Laws," *AHR* 59 (1954): 287–304; Thorne, *House of Commons* 3:769–74.
13. Duke of Argyll, *Autobiography and Memoirs* (London, 1906), 1:152.
14. *PD* 63:204, 6 May and 63:455ff, 12 May 1842. He had had a history of being unmanageable and protested quite reasonable rules of debate in the Commons—24:119–20, 1 Dec. 1812.
15. Ibid. 58:684, 24 May 1841; 28:357, 2 June 1835.
16. G. Mee, *Aristocratic Enterprise, the Fitzwilliam Industrial Undertakings 1795–1857* (Glasgow, 1975), 6.
17. For the earl's life see E. A. Wasson, *Whig Renaissance: Lord Althorp and the Whig Party, 1782–1845* (New York, 1987); Sir D. Le Marchant, *Memoir of John Charles, Viscount Althorp* (London, 1876).
18. Wasson, *Whig Renaissance*, 239; E. A. Smith, *Lord Grey, 1764–1845* (Oxford, 1990), 306; this was a time-honored custom, see M. McCahill, *Order and Equipoise, the Peerage and the House of Lords, 1783–1806* (London, 1978), 142.
19. Wasson, *Whig Renaissance*, 346; E. Meyers, *Lord Althorp* (London, 1890), 192; Northampton RO, Fitzwilliam MSS, Spencer to Fitzwilliam, 18 Dec. 1834; Lord Hatherton, *Memoir and Correspondence, 1834*, ed. H. Reeve (London, 1872), 88; Greville, *Memoirs* 3:56–58.
20. BL, Add. MSS, Spencer to Lady Holland 6 July 1842; Royal Library, RA MP 15/118, Spencer to Viscount Melbourne, 3 Feb. 1839.

21. J. Brooke and M. Sorensen, eds., *W. E. Gladstone III: Autobiographical Memoranda, 1845–1866* (London, 1978), 19.

22. Smith, *Lord Grey*, 83; Greville, *Memoirs* 7:163.

23. Le Marchant, *Memoir*, 549.

24. Greville, *Memoirs* 1:199; Sir R. Cooke, *The Palace of Westminster* (New York, 1987), 153.

25. E. A. Wasson, "The Third Earl Spencer and Agriculture, 1818–1845," *Agricultural History Review* 26 (1978): 89–99; Jupp, "English Landed Elite," 68–69.

26. Sir N. Pevsner, *Northamptonshire* (London, 1973), 78; *Recollections of a Long Life by Lord Broughton*, ed., Lady Dorchester (London, 1911), 5:30 and 6:86; Blakiston, *Woburn*, 197–98; Sir. H. Maxwell, *The Life and Letters of the Fourth Earl of Clarendon* (London, 1913), 2:296.

27. Greville, *Memoirs* 5:358; Spring, *English Landed Estate*, 35ff.

28. Mee, *Aristocratic Enterprise*, 38, 90, 203.

29. Wasson, *Whig Renaissance*, 326–30; E. A. Wasson, "A Progressive Landlord: the Third Earl Spencer, 1782–1845," in C. W. Chalkin and J. R. Wordie, eds., *Town and Countryside: the English Landowner in the National Economy, 1660–1860* (London, 1989), 85–98.

30. *The Later Correspondence of Lord John Russell*, ed. G. P. Gooch (London, 1925), 1:89; *The Letters of Queen Victoria, 1837–1861*, ed. A. C. Benson and Viscount Esher (New York, 1907), 2:154–55; Greville, *Memoirs* 5:309.

31. RA MP 15/III, Spencer to Melbourne 16 Nov. 1834; Viscount Althorp to 2d Earl Spencer, 12 July 1834, consulted at Althorp but now kept at the British Library, Althorp MSS; N. Gash, *Sir Robert Peel* (Totowa, NJ, 1972), 78–79; Greville, *Memoirs* 5:216; Wasson, *Whig Renaissance*, 346; Devon RO, Fortescue MSS 1262M FC91, Spencer to Viscount Ebrington, 21 Feb. 1835; *The Holland House Diaries, 1831–1840*, ed. A. D. Kriegel (London, 1977), 389; Le Marchant, *Memoir*, 550–53.

32. Greville's close link with Bedford may, perhaps, have made the diarist exaggerate the extent of the duke's influence; Greville, *Memoirs* 6:409 and passim; Maxwell, *Clarendon* 1:320–21; Blakiston, *Lord William Russell*, 422.

33. Greville, *Memoirs* 4:417; *Cambridge Illustrated Encyclopedia of British History* (Cambridge, 1987), 431; Ilchester, *Holland House*, 165.

34. Greville, *Memoirs* 4:230; 6:443–44; 7:52; F. A. Dreyer, "The Whigs and the Political Crisis of 1845," *EHR* 80 (1965): 529; M. Chamberlain, *Lord Aberdeen* (London, 1983), 443; F. D. Munsell, *The Unfortunate Duke* (Columbia, MO, 1985), 139.

35. John Prest has painted a dark picture of Bedford's parsimony in dealing with Lord John, *Lord John Russell* (London, 1972), 6–7, 219–20, 222. This suggests a lack of understanding about how property was regarded in great families. Bedford was generous to his brother and left him Irish estates not in settlement; Greville, *Memoirs* 4:400; 5:430; 7:27; Blakiston, *Lord William Russell*, 468–69; BL, Add. MS. 51679 fol. 57., Lord John Russell to Lady Holland [Nov. 24, 1823]; S. Walpole, *The Life of Lord John Russell* (London, 1889), 1:208, 290, 371, 375; 2:69–70.

36. Mandler, *Aristocratic Government*, 161; Gooch, *Later Correspondence* 2:116–17; Greville, *Memoirs* 4:399; 6:72; 7:420.

37. Southampton UL, Broadlands MSS GC/F1/13, Viscount Palmerston to Fitz-

william, 24 Sept. 1852; PRO, Russell MSS 30/22/6E and 9E, Fitzwilliam to Lord J. Russell, 20 and 27 Aug. 1847 and 4 Aug. 1851; RA, MP 67/41, 25/59 and 25/23, Fitzwilliam to Melbourne 11 May 1836 and 22 Mar. 1837 and Melbourne to Fitzwilliam, 6 Apr. 1840; Gooch, *Later Correspondence* 1:40.

38. *PD* 73:1167, 18 Mar. 1844; 89:936, 8 Feb. 1847; 96:983, 21 Feb. 1848; 99:1057, 23 June 1848; 118:1295, 22 July 1851; Mee, *Aristocratic Enterprise*, 12. Fitzwilliam was a good landlord on his Irish estates; National Library of Ireland, Fitzwilliam MSS 3987, Robert Chaloner letter book 1846–47; K. T. Hoppen, *Elections, Politics, and Society in Ireland, 1832–1885* (Oxford, 1984), 130; PRO, Russell MSS 30/22/7D, Fitzwilliam to Lord J. Russell, 31 Oct. and 2 Nov. 1848.

39. Devon RO, Fortescue MSS 1262M/LI 98 copy, Ebrington to Fitzwilliam, 15 Sept. 1839.

40. BL, Althorp MSS. Melbourne to Lord Holland, 6 May 1839; BL, Add. MS. 51559 fols. 27–28, Melbourne to Spencer, 2 Mar. 1836; Kriegel, *Holland House*, 400; Dorchester, *Recollections* 5:103–4; Greville, *Memoirs* 7:11; Gooch, *Later Correspondence* 1:14; Staffordshire RO, Hatherton MSS 26/9/55–57, Littleton Diary, 5 Mar. 1835; PRO, Russell MSS 30/22/1E fol. 23, Grey to Melbourne, 1 Feb. 1835.

41. Prest, *Russell*, 167.

42. See Althorp/Russell correspondence PRO 1835–45 and Russell letters in Althorp MSS, BL; also see Shaw Lefevre MSS in HLRO.

43. PRO, Russell MSS 30/22/4B fol. 9, Spencer to Bedford, 4 July 1841; Northampton RO, Gotch MSS GK 488, Spencer to Gotch, 26 and 29 Nov. 1835; Nottingham UL, Ossington MSS 172, Spencer to Denison, 30 May 1841; RA, MP 15/113, 117, and 120, Spencer to Melbourne, 13 Apr. 1835, 28 Jan. 1839 and 28 July 1841; RL, Queen Victoria's journal, 28 Aug. 1841.

44. Fitzwilliam MSS EX, Spencer to Fitzwilliam Jan. 1844; Sir Francis Baring, *Journals and Correspondence, 1808–1852*, ed. earl of Northbrook (Winchester, 1905), 1:182; RL, RA Y55/66, G. E. Anson notes 19 Dec. 1843; Greville, *Memoirs* 5:216; Le Marchant, *Memoir*, 559; PRO, Russell MSS 30/22/4C fol.1, Spencer to Russell, 1 Aug. 1842; Fitzwilliam MSS CV, Spencer to Fitzwilliam, 18 Jan. 1842.

45. Greville, *Memoirs* 4:322; Dorchester, *Recollections* 6:81.

46. Mandler shows convincingly that Russell's statement has been misunderstood: *Aristocratic Government*, 169 and n. 52; D. Southgate, *The Passing of the Whigs, 1832–1886* (London, 1962), 71.

47. E. A. Wasson, "The Great Whigs and Parliamentary Reform, 1809–1830," *JBS* 24 (1985): 434–64; RA, MP 25/66, Fitzwilliam to Melbourne, 18 May 1838. (I am grateful to David Spring for this and subsequent references.) *PD* 112:773–74, 1 July 1850; Broadlands MSS GC/Fi/11/1, Fitzwilliam to Palmerston, 26 Sept. 1852.

48. Wasson, *Whig Renaissance*, 205–7, 246, 402.

49. K. Bourne, *The Foreign Policy of Victorian Britain, 1830–1902* (Oxford, 1970), 249–50.

50. Ibid., 251; Dorchester, *Recollections* 6:81; Broadlands MSS, Spencer to Palmerston, 4 Oct. 1840; K. Bourne, *Palmerston, the Early Years, 1784–1841* (New York, 1982), 607; Gooch, *Later Correspondence* 1:25–26.

51. R. Bullen, *Palmerston, Guizot and the Collapse of the Entente Cordiale* (Lon-

don, 1974), 33; PRO, Russell MSS 30/22/4C fol. 35, Fitzwilliam to Bedford, 3 Nov. 1842.

52. *Northampton Mercury*, 2 June 1827; Southgate, *Passing of the Whigs*, 109; Dreyer, "Crisis of 1845," 516.

53. *PD* 59:60, 24 Aug. 1841; see Spring, "Earl Fitzwilliam and the Corn Laws" and Wasson, "The Third Earl Spencer and Agriculture" cited above.

54. McCahill, *Order and Equipoise*, 189; A. S. Turberville, *The House of Lords in the Age of Reform, 1784–1837* (London, 1958), 21; Wasson, "The Progressive Landlord," 90; Althorp MSS, Spencer to Sir Francis Baring, 15 Jan. 1835.

55. *PD* 17:1179, 1189, 14 May 1833; 57:1476, 6 May 1841.

56. A. Aspinall, ed., "Extracts from Lord Hatherton's Diary," *Parliamentary Affairs* 17 (1964): 255; Maxwell, *Clarendon* 1:260; J. Hogan, "Party Management in the House of Lords, 1846–1865," *PH* 10 (1991): 139.

57. W. Dyott, *Dyott's Diary, 1781–1845*, ed. R. W. Jeffrey (London, 1907), 2:117.

58. *PD* 43:350–52, 28 May 1838.

59. Althorp MSS, Spencer to Brougham, 8 June and 5 Oct. 1836; *Northampton Mercury*, 28 May 1831, Althorp speech; *PD* 87:564, 16 June 1846; 111:513–14, 31 May 1850; Kriegel, *Holland House*, xviii.

60. Fortescue MSS 1262M/FC 87, Fitzwilliam to Ebrington, 7 Oct. 1831; RA, MP 57/42, Fitzwilliam to Melbourne, 19 April 1835; *PD* 86:107–08, 5 May 1846.

61. J. W. Burrow, *A Liberal Descent: Victorian Institutions and the English Past* (Cambridge, 1981), 24; Corinne Comstock Weston, *English Constitutional Theory and the House of Lords, 1556–1832* (London, 1965), 222–23.

62. Althorp MSS, Althorp to Spencer, 12 July 1833; BL, Add. MS. 47223, Marquis of Tavistock to J. C. Hobhouse, 18 Mar. 1834; *PD* 112:773, 1 July 1850. Viscount Milton to Ebrington 6 and 7 Oct. 1831, Fortescue MSS 1262 M/FC 87.

63. Weston, *Constitutional Theory*, 238–40; N. Gash, *Reaction and Reconstruction in English Politics, 1832–1852* (Oxford, 1965), 34–43; Turberville, *House of Lords*, 320ff.

64. Southgate, *Passing of the Whigs*, xvi; W. Thomas, "Lord Holland," in H. Lloyd Jones et. al., eds., *History and Imagination* (London, 1981), 297; J. Hamburger, "The Whig Conscience," in P. Marsh, ed., *The Conscience of the Victorian State* (Syracuse, 1979), 20–21; G. Watson, *The English Ideology* (London, 1973), 16.

65. Smith, *Lord Grey*, 321; Argyll, *Autobiography* 1:363.

66. I. Newbould, "Whiggery and the Dilemma of Reform," *BIHR* 53 (1980): 231–34.

67. D. Beales, "Peel, Russell and Reform," *HJ* 17 (1974): 874–81; Newbould, *Whiggery and Reform*, 7–11, 316–19; Gash, *Reaction and Reconstruction*, 184, 199–200.

68. H. W. Carless Davis, *The Age of Grey and Peel* (Oxford, 1929), 279; Mandler, *Aristocratic Government*, 1–8, 41–42, 119–20, 157, 160, 200–1.

69. R. Brent, *Liberal Anglican Politics, Whiggery, Religion, and Reform, 1830–1841* (Oxford, 1987), 16, 92, 102, 125–26; B. Hilton, *The Age of Atonement, 1795–1865* (Oxford, 1988), 240ff; J. P. Parry, *Democracy and Religion, Gladstone and the Liberal Party, 1867–1875* (Cambridge, 1986), 16ff.

70. Gotch MSS GK 394, Milton to J. C. Gotch 23 Dec. 1832; West Sussex RO,

Bessborough MSS, Fitzwilliam to Viscount Duncannon, 18 Nov. 1834; Bourne, *Palmerston*, 545; Althorp MSS, Spencer to Baring, 15 Jan. 1835; Le Marchant, *Memoir*, 532, 552.

71. Hilton, *Age of Atonement*, 13; *PD* 15 : 353, 18 Apr. 1826; Dorchester, *Recollections* 6 : 27–28.

72. J. T. Ward, *Sir James Graham* (New York, 1967), 335 n. 15; Maxwell, *Clarendon* 2 : 296. The Spencers were the junior line of the dukes of Marlborough. The Wentworths held the Jacobite dukedom of Strafford 1722–91 and Earl Fitzwilliam felt entitled to the higher rank; RA, MP 25/65, Fitzwilliam to Melbourne, 10 Sept. 1838.

73. S. Collini, D. Winch, J. Burrow, *That Noble Science of Politics* (Cambridge, 1983), 34; O. F. Christie, *The Transition from Aristocracy, 1832–1862* (New York, 1928), 185; J. G. A. Pocock, *Virtue, Commerce, and History* (Cambridge, 1985), 231. My Old Whigs are not to be confused with the Old Whigs Pocock discusses; Brent, *Liberal Anglican Politics*, 43 and 63.

74. Beales, "Peel, Russell and Reform," 881; Althorp MSS, Fitzwilliam to Althorp, 16 July 1834, and Spencer to Brougham, 30 Aug. 1837; Lord William Russell, *Letters from Various Writers, 1817–1845* (London, 1915–17), 1 : 45; *PD* 112 : 773, 1 July 1850.

75. PRO, Russell MSS 30/22/5A, Fitzwilliam to Bedford, 30 June 1846; *PD* 84 : 1407, 23 Mar. 1846; Parry, *Democracy and Religion*, 47.

76. RA, MP 25/70, Fitzwilliam to Melbourne 6 Dec. 1839. *PD* 102 : 67, 1 Feb. 1849; *Leeds Mercury*, 21 Oct. 1843. I am grateful to Prof. David Spring for this reference.

77. Bedford RO, Whitbread MSS W1/2455, 6th duke of Bedford to S. Whitbread, 3 Feb. 1809; McCahill, *Order and Equipoise*, 45; E. A. Smith, *Whig Principles and Party Politics, Earl Fitzwilliam and the Whig Party, 1748–1833* (Manchester, 1975), 309.

78. Elie Halévy, *Victorian Years, 1841–1895* (London, 1951), 56.

Chapter 8

1. Two short biographies of Derby appeared in 1892. T. E. Kebbel, in *The Life of Lord Derby* (London) placed Derby in the Beaconsfield tradition, while George Saintsbury's *The Earl of Derby* (London) puts a Tory perspective on Derby's career. The only modern biographical study is W. D. Jones's *Lord Derby and Victorian Conservatism* (Oxford) published in 1956. None of these studies, however, had the advantage of access to Derby's correspondence. There is, therefore, a heavy reliance on Disraeli's papers. For an attempt to correct this bias see Angus Hawkins, "Lord Derby and Victorian Conservatism: A Reappraisal," *PH* 6 (1987): 280–301. Robert Stewart, *The Politics of Protection: Lord Derby and the Protectionist Party, 1841–1852* (Cambridge, 1971), uses some of Derby's papers for this eleven-year period.

2. For a useful recent survey of the Victorian House of Lords see E. A. Smith, *The House of Lords in British Politics and Society, 1815–1911* (London, 1992).

3. J. J. Bagley, *The Earls of Derby, 1485–1985* (London, 1985), narrates a 500-year span of the Stanley family history.

4. See G. E. Cockayne, *The Complete Peerage* (1916), 4 : 218.

5. See ibid., 219.

6. In his childhood Derby remembered hearing "a sort of political catechism, beginning thus, 'What does A stand for? An Axe. What is an axe for? To chop off kings' heads. . . . I remember it as if it were yesterday,' he said, 'hearing of Perceval's death: I was a boy at school, and my comment upon it was, that it was too good news to be true. Such was the feeling of the Whig opposition of that day.'" John Vincent, ed., *Disraeli, Derby and the Conservative Party: Journals and Memoirs of Edward Henry, Lord Stanley, 1849–1869* (Brighton, 1978), 184.

7. See Peter Mandler, *Aristocratic Government in the Age of Reform: Whigs and Liberals, 1830–1852* (Oxford, 1990), 96–104.

8. Derby MSS 920 DER(14) 115/1, Lansdowne to Stanley, 12 Sept. 1822; and ibid., Stanley to Lansdowne. n.d. (?1822). See also A. D. Kriegel, "Liberty and Whiggery in Early Nineteenth-Century England," *JMH* 52 (1980): 253–78.

9. Ibid.

10. It was this constitutional view that the legal jurist John James Park described in his published lectures of 1832, *Dogmas of the Constitution* (London). What Park called "parliamentary government" (to my knowledge the first public use of the term in this precise way) was replacing "prerogative government." The government was formed from the leadership of the majority party in Parliament. As the executive had to manage and control the legislative process, executive and legislative functions were fused. Loss of the management of the legislature by the executive required resignation from office. Constitutional sovereignty resided in Westminster. See Angus Hawkins, "'Parliamentary Government' and Victorian Political Parties, c.1830–c.1880," *EHR* 104 (1989): 638–69.

11. Derby MSS 920 DER(14) 177/2, Stanley to Bentinck, 27 Oct. 1847, cited in Robert Stewart, *The Politics of Protection*, 222.

12. Vincent, *Disraeli, Derby and the Conservative Party*, 104.

13. W. F. Monypenny and G. E. Buckle, *The Life of Benjamin Disraeli, Earl of Beaconsfield*, 6 vols. (London, 1910–20), 4:236.

14. Derby to Malmesbury, 15 Dec. 1856 cited in Lord Malmesbury, *Memoirs of an Ex-Minister*, 2 vols. (London, 1884), 2:54. Palmerston's biographer described Derby as "reckless in his language, aristocratic in his tendencies . . . above all haughty and domineering in his tendencies, though gay and playful in manner . . . But what was worst of all was the eternal habit of quizzing, or, to use the modern word, 'chaffing,' which the inconsiderate noble Lord indulged in, and which the somewhat prim and stately commoner could not endure." Lord Dalling, *The Life of Henry John Temple, Viscount Palmerston*, ed. E. Ashley, 3 vols. (London, 1874), 3:183–84.

15. Malmesbury, *Memoirs* 1:42.

16. Vincent, *Disraeli, Derby and the Conservative Party*, 72.

17. Lytton MSS C13, fol. 21, Bulwer Lytton memo, n.d. (?1869).

18. M. S. Hardcastle, *Life of John, Lord Campbell*, 2 vols. (London, 1881), 2:324.

19. Jones, *Derby and Victorian Conservatism*, 6.

20. Creevey to Miss Ord, 1 Nov. 1829, H. Maxwell, *The Creevey Papers*, 2 vols. (London, 1904), 2:203.

21. *Hansard* n.s. 11:559–65, Stanley, 6 May 1824.

22. Derby MSS 920 DER(14) 14/1, Stanley to Spring Rice, 15 June 1825.

23. *Hansard* n.s. 18:517, Stanley, 18 Feb. 1828.

24. Ibid.

25. Ibid. 19:23–26, Stanley, 22 Apr. 1828; and ibid. 711–12, Stanley, 13 May 1828.

26. Graham to Stanley, 15 July 1828 cited in C. S. Parker, *Life and Letters of Sir James Graham*, 2 vols. (London, 1901), 1:71.

27. Spencer MSS, Althorp to Grey, 26 Aug. 1832, cited in A. D. Kriegel, "The Irish Policy of Lord Grey's Government," *EHR* 86 (1971): 24.

28. *Hansard* 3d ser., 1:55, Grey, 22 Dec. 1830.

29. Derby MSS 920 DER(14) 169, Stanley to Grey, 1 Aug. 1832, and ibid., 167/2, Stanley to Anglesey, 19 Jan. 1833.

30. Ibid., 168, Stanley to Anglesey, 18 Feb. 1832.

31. The Marquess of Anglesey, *One-Leg: The Life and Letters of Henry William Paget, First Marquess of Anglesey, 1768–1854* (London, 1961), 264.

32. A statement by Lord Skelmersdale (Stanley's father-in-law) quoted by Croker in Croker to Peel, 8 Jan. 1835, cited in C. S. Parker, *Sir Robert Peel from his Private Papers*, 3 vols. (London, 1899), 2:277.

33. Stanley at Glasgow University cited in *The Times*, 22 Dec. 1834, 3.

34. Derby MSS 920 DER(14) 167/2, Stanley to Ripon, 27 Nov. 1834.

35. Stanley to Peel, 11 Dec. 1834 cited in Parker, *Peel* 2:257.

36. *The Times*, 22 Dec. 1834, 3.

37. Ibid., 18 Dec. 1834, 2.

38. Graham to Hornby, 23 Dec. 1834, cited in Parker, *Graham* 1:222.

39. Derby MSS 920 DER(14) 171, Stanley to Denison, 20 Jan. 1835.

40. Lord Broughton, *Recollections of a Long Life*, ed. Lady Dorchester, 6 vols. (London, 1909–11), 6:229.

41. Monypenny and Buckle, *Disraeli* 3:317.

42. See John Hogan, "Party Management in the House of Lords, 1846–1865," *PH* 10:1 (1991), 124–50.

43. Broadlands MSS GC/GR 1863, Granville to Palmerston, 18 June 1859.

44. Stanley to Croker, 7 June 1847, cited in L. J. Jennings, *The Correspondence and Diaries of John Wilson Croker*, 3 vols. (London, 1885), 3:107.

45. See Hogan, "Party Management in the House of Lords."

46. Derby MSS 920 DER(14) 178/2, Stanley to Disraeli, 13 Nov. 1849.

47. Robert Stewart, *The Foundation of the Conservative Party, 1830–1867* (London, 1978), 234.

48. Derby MSS 920 DER(14) 179/1, Stanley to Malmesbury, 15 Feb. 1851.

49. Monypenny and Buckle, *Disraeli*, 3:343.

50. Ibid., 331–32.

51. Derby MSS 920 DER(14) 179/1, Derby to Croker, 22 Sept. 1851.

52. Ibid., Derby to Hope, 15 Dec. 1851.

53. Ibid., 177/1, Stanley to Croker, 19 Aug. 1846.

54. Malmesbury, *Memoirs* 1:198.

55. Derby MSS 920 DER(14) 179/1, Stanley to Beresford, 1 Dec. 1850.

56. Ibid., 182/1, Derby to Liddell, 4 Jan. 1853. Derby prefaced this remark with the comment that "the great difficulty will be to keep the Conservative party together without the excitement of a systematic opposition which we must avoid as far as possible."

57. Ibid.

58. Vincent, *Disraeli, Derby and the Conservative Party*, 92. Derby also described this strategy as "armed neutrality." Derby MSS 920 DER(14) 182/1, Derby to Walpole, 30 Jan. 1853.

59. Monypenny and Buckle, *Disraeli* 3:483.

60. Derby MSS 920 DER(14) 144/1, Malmesbury to Derby, 8 Sept. 1853.

61. Ibid., Malmesbury to Derby, n.d. (?Dec. 1853). See also D. Krein, "War and Reform: Russell, Palmerston and the Struggle for Power in the Aberdeen Cabinet, 1853–54," *Maryland Historian* 7 (1976): 67–84.

62. Derby MSS 920 DER(14) 145/3, Disraeli to Derby, 7 Nov. 1855.

63. Hughenden MSS B/XX/S/148, Derby to Disraeli, 24 Apr. 1857.

64. See Angus Hawkins, "British Parliamentary Party Alignment and the Indian Issue, 1857–1858," *JBS* 23 (1983): 79–105.

65. Derby MSS 920 DER(14) 144/2A, Malmesbury to Derby, 1 Jan. 1860. See P. M. Gurowich "The Continuation of War by Other Means: Party and Politics, 1855–1865," *HJ* 27 (1984): 603–31.

66. Derby MSS 920 DER(14) 188/2, Derby to Pakington, 28 May 1860.

67. Monypenny and Buckle, *Disraeli* 4:273.

68. Derby MSS 920 DER(14) 188/2, Derby to Malmesbury, 25 Dec. 1860.

69. Broadlands MSS GC/MA 196, Malmesbury to Palmerston, 20 Jan. 1861.

70. Hughenden MSS B/XX/S/280, Derby to Disraeli, 27 Jan. 1861.

71. Derby MSS 920 DER(14) 188/2, Derby to Malmesbury, 27 Jan. 1861.

72. Jones, *Derby and Victorian Conservatism*, 267.

73. Malmesbury, *Memoirs* 2:215.

74. Monypenny and Buckle, *Disraeli* 4:344–45.

75. Jones, *Derby and Victorian Conservatism*, 281.

76. Hughenden MSS B/XX/S/334, Derby to Disraeli, 24 July 1864.

77. Derby MSS 920 DER(14) 190/1, Derby to Carnarvon, 17 Nov. 1865.

78. *Hansard* 3d ser. 149:22–44, Derby, 1 Mar. 1858.

79. See D. E. McCracken, "The Conservatives in 'Power': The Minority Governments of 1852, 1858–9 and 1866–8," an unpublished Univ. of VA Ph.D. diss., 1981.

80. G. I. T. Machin, *Politics and the Churches in Great Britain, 1832–1868* (Oxford, 1977), 292.

81. See Angus Hawkins, *Parliament, Party and the Art of Politics in Britain, 1855–1859* (London, 1987), 177–240.

82. See Maurice Cowling, *1867: Disraeli, Gladstone and Revolution* (Cambridge, 1967), 306–9.

83. Jones, *Derby and Victorian Conservatism*, 318.

84. Monypenny and Buckle, *Disraeli* 3:328.

85. C. Greville, *The Greville Memoirs*, ed. H. Reeve, 8 vols. (London, 1888), 8:182. In his biography Saintsbury declared that Derby had "not merely no coherent or

complete Tory theory of politics, but had no coherent or complete theory of politics at all." Saintsbury, *Derby*, 179.

86. J. B. Conacher, "Party Politics in the Age of Palmerston," *1859: Entering an Age of Crisis* (Bloomington, 1959), 166. The letter of Lennox to Disraeli, 7 Jan. 1857, is often quoted in support of this view, see R. Blake, *Disraeli* (1966), 369.

87. See Angus Hawkins, "'Parliamentary Government' and Victorian Political Parties," *EHR*, 638–69.

88. Derby MSS 920 DER(14) 182/2, Derby to Blandford, 26 Jan. 1854. This paragraph also draws on some of the analysis in P. M. Gurowich "Party and Independence in the Early and Mid-Victorian House of Commons," an unpubl. Univ. of Cambridge Ph.D. diss., 1986.

89. James FitzJames Stephen, *Horae Sabbaticae*, 2 vols. (London, 1892), 2:201.

90. Leslie Stephen, "The Value of Political Machinery," *Fortnightly Review* 24 (1875): 849.

91. J. A. Froude, "Party Politics" in *Short Studies on Great Subjects*, 3 vols. (London, 1894), 3:437.

Chapter 9

1. Selborne MS. 80, fol. 287. The Selborne MSS are used in this essay with the present earl of Selborne's permission.

2. Jenkins, *Asquith* (London, 1964), 278, 282; Trevor Lloyd, *Empire to Welfare State: English History, 1906–1967* (London, 1970), 46.

3. *The Political Diaries of C. P. Scott, 1911–1928*, ed. Trevor Wilson (New York, 1970), 403; Robert Blake, *Unrepentant Tory: The Life and Times of Andrew Bonar Law, 1858–1923, Prime Minister of the United Kingdom* (New York, 1956), 97.

4. *The Strange Death of Liberal England* (New York, 1961), 81, 96; see also Dangerfield, *The Damnable Question: A Study in Anglo-Irish Relations* (Boston, 1976); for Dangerfield's continuing influence since the initial publication of *Strange Death*, see *Albion*, 17, no. 4 (winter 1985).

5. "'Rats' versus 'Ditchers': The Diehard Revolt and the Parliament Bill of 1911," *Parliament & Community, Historical Studies*, 14, ed. Art Cosgrave and J. I. McGuire (Belfast, 1983), 206.

6. See *PD*, Lords, 5th ser., 9:929, Lord St. Aldwyn's speech on the night of 9 Aug. 1911. And also *The Crawford Papers: The Journals of David Lindsay Twenty-seventh Earl of Crawford and Tenth Earl of Balcarres, 1871–1940, During the Years 1892–1940*, ed. John Vincent (Manchester, 1984), 208, 217.

7. Jalland, *The Liberals and Ireland: The Ulster Question in British Politics to 1914* (Brighton, Sussex, 1980), 65–77.

8. *Albion* (winter, 1985), 420.

9. Blake, *Unrepentant Tory*, 96, 130–31; see also A. T. Q. Stewart, *The Ulster Crisis: Resistance to Home Rule, 1912–14* (London, 1979), passim. Bonar Law later stated that before making the speech he had read the statements made by leaders of his party (Salisbury, Balfour, etc) in 1886 and 1893; but unlike them he had to contend with the Parliament Act, which had crippled the House of Lords. BLP,

33/6/11. These papers are in the HLRO and are used with the permission of the clerk of the records.

10. Blake, *Unrepentant Tory*, 130.

11. Blake, *The Conservative Party from Peel to Churchill* (Fontana ed., 1972), 190, 192; R. C. K. Ensor, *England 1870–1914* (Oxford, 1936), 455–56.

12. Blake, *Unrepentant Tory*, 70.

13. Fanning, "'Rats' versus 'Ditchers'," 120, n. 76.

14. Blake, *Unrepentant Tory*, 174–75; A. M. Gollin, *Proconsul in Politics: a Study of Lord Milner in Opposition and in Power* (London, 1964), 101, 121, 177–80, and 204. Hugh Cecil's memorandum is dated 4 June in the Bonar Law Papers; 5 June in Selborne's, BLP, 32/3/1; Selborne MS. 77, fols. 21–22. The memorandum is printed in *The Crisis of British Unionism: The Domestic Political Papers of the Second Earl of Selborne, 1885–1922*, ed. George Boyce (London, 1987), 94–99. Boyce, uncertain about its authorship, assigns it to Lord Willoughby de Broke, but Selborne on the back of Selborne MS. 77, fol. 53 wrote "No. 2 Hugh Cecil 1913. Suggestions for defeating home rule bill."

15. Selborne MS. 77, fols. 21–22, Selborne to Mr. Platt, 19 Sept. 1912.

16. Ibid., fol. 44. Selborne's comment is in the margin.

17. Blake, *Unrepentant Tory*, 175.   19. BLP, 34/1/25.

18. Ibid.   20. Ibid. 31/3/1.

21. Ibid. 34/3/26; Blake, *Unrepentant Tory*, 176–77.

22. Ibid., 177.

23. BLP, 34/1/28. Ernest Cassel, a foreign-born financier, moved in high political circles.

24. Blake, *Unrepentant Tory*, 177. BL Add. MS. 49730, fols. 266–266v, Lansdowne to Balfour, 5 Feb. 1914; ibid., fol. 268., Lansdowne to Balfour, 6 Mar. 1914.

25. Ibid., the same to same. BL, Add. MS. 49730, fol. 270, Balfour to Lansdowne, 13 Mar. 1914.

26. *Real Old Tory Politics: The Political Diaries of Sir Robert Sanders, Lord Bayford, 1910–35*, ed. John Ramsden (London, 1984), 73. Hugh Cecil's comment is cited in *H. H. Asquith: Letters to Venetia Stanley*, ed. Michael and Eleanor Brock (Oxford, 1982), 54, n. 4.

27. Jalland, *The Liberals and Ireland*, 206.

28. Ibid., 205, 246–47, 262, 263, 268; Cameron Hazlehurst, "Asquith as Prime Minister," *EHR* (July 1970), 527–28, 531; *Letters to Venetia Stanley*, 59.

29. *Crawford Papers*, 328–29.

30. Blake, *Unrepentant Tory*, 180–81.

31. The date is not given in vol. 1 of Sir Charles Callwell, *Field Marshall Wilson: His Life and Diaries* (New York and London, 1927), 138, where his visit with Bonar Law is described. It is, however, in the original diaries, which can be seen in microfilm in the department of documents of the Imperial War Museum in London. The author of this essay would like to record her thanks to Dr. Peter Thwaites for his kind assistance in this matter.

32. The account comes from the printed diaries and is quoted in Blake, *Unrepentant Tory*, 180. Leading into this account in the original diaries is Wilson's state-

ment that he had gone to Pembroke Lodge dreading the idea of action in the Lords hostile to the Army Act.

33. Selborne MS. 109, fol. 118, Selborne to his son Bobby, 28 Nov. 1915.

34. Gollin, *Proconsul in Politics*, 205.

35. Milner MS. 40, fol. 58; see also Stewart, *The Ulster Crisis*, 136–37. The Milner MSS are used by permission of the Warden and Fellows of New College, Oxford.

36. BLP, 31/4/33.

37. Gollin, *Proconsul in Politics*, 204, 206.

38. Sanders, *Real Old Tory Politics*, 74.

39. BLP, 34/2/44.

40. Blake, *Unrepentant Tory*, 182; see also Sanders, *Real Old Tory Politics*, 75.

41. Brock, "The Strange Death of Liberal England," *Albion* (winter, 1985), 417. He is relying on the *Letters to Venetia Stanley*, 100–1; see also 101 n. 2.

42. BLP, 31/2/50.

43. Selborne MS. 77, fols. 68–69, Lansdowne to Selborne, 20 Jan. 1914; ibid., fols. 70–71, Robert Cecil to Selborne, 29 Jan. 1914; ibid., fols. 72–72v., Austen Chamberlain to Selborne, 25 Jan. 1914.

44. Bonar Law's indifference to restoring the Lords' referendal theory by means of the referendum can be seen in Selborne MS. 77, fols. 70–71, Robert Cecil to Selborne, 29 Jan. 1914; Selborne MS. 6, fols. 198–99, Selborne to Salisbury, 26 Aug. 1916; Milner's letter, dated 17 Mar. 1914, is in BLP, 31/4/30.

45. Ibid. 32/3/1; see also Selborne MS. 77, fols. 106–7, Selborne to Lansdowne, 1 May 1914. The Referendum Bill was to be the first order of business if and when the Unionists came to power. It would set in motion, Selborne believed, a national settlement to which the Liberals would also be a party. He explains his reasoning in a letter to Steel Maitland, 3 July 1914 (Selborne MS. 77, fols. 159–62). The letter also reveals that Selborne's zeal for undoing the Parliament Act and establishing a proper second chamber was undiminished. It is not clear whether the national settlement would encompass the referendum, but he does say that if such a settlement were not obtained—that is, if the Liberals would not cooperate—the Referendum Bill that he and Cecil had prepared would "have secured the greatest amount of safety possible for us under the circumstances." (Ibid., fol. 160). For the fact that Curzon placed a referendum low in his scale of values, see his letter to Selborne, 18 Jan. 1914 (Selborne MS. 10, fols. 165–66v). Unlike Selborne he would not give the highest priority to dealing with the Parliament Act if the Unionists were returned to power.

46. *Unrepentant Tory*, 181–82; Stewart, *Ulster Crisis*, 136–37.

47. For a somewhat different view of Bonar Law from the one expressed here, see Brock, *Albion* (winter, 1985), 420; also Donald Southgate, ed., *The Conservative Leadership, 1832–1932* (London, 1974), 178; Blake, *The Conservative Party*, 194–95; Gollin, *Proconsul in Politics*, 179; Jeremy Smith, "Bluff, Bluster and Brinkmanship: Andrew Bonar Law and the Third Home Rule Bill," *HJ* 36, 1 (Mar. 1993): 161–78.

Index

In this index an "f" after a number indicates a separate reference on the next page, and an "ff" indicates separate references on the next two pages. A continuous discussion over two or more pages is indicated by a span of page numbers, e.g., "57–59." *Passim* is used for a cluster of references in close but not consecutive sequence.

Library of Congress Cataloging-in-Publication Data

Lords of Parliament : studies, 1714–1914 / edited by R. W. Davis
   p.   cm.
Includes bibliographical references and index.
ISBN 0-8047-2476-8
1. Great Britain. Parliament. House of Lords—History.
2. Legislators—Great Britain—History.   I. Davis, Richard W.
JN621.L67   1995
328'.41'071—dc20   94-17743   CIP

⊗ This book is printed on acid-free, recycled paper.